UNTIL I BREATHE THIS LIFE

DR. MARY MEADOWS

UNTIL I BREATHE THIS LIFE ©

Always Will I Fear…

Always Will I Grieve…

Always Will I Suffer…

By Dr. Mary C. Meadows

PUBLISHED BY SACRED SANCTUARY

"Until I Breathe This Life" by Dr. Mary Meadows
Published April, 2016

All rights reserved. No part of this book may be reproduced or transmitted in any form or by any means, electronic or mechanical, including photocopying, recording or by any information, storage, and retrieval system, without the written permission of the Publisher, except where permitted by law. For information, write:
Sacred Sanctuary, 17017 N. 12th St., Ste. 1125, Phoenix, AZ 85022
www.drmarymeadowsLLC.com

Other books published by author

"The Last Breath"   published by Kite Foundation   1993

"Breath of Light"   published by Kite Foundation , 1996

Updated Version of   "Breath of Light"   July 2003
published by Sacred Sanctuary

ISBN -10: 0692674365
ISBN-13: 978-0692674369

TABLE OF CONTENTS

                                                                                                      Page

Dedications and Acknowledgements
Preface to Revised and Updated Book   1.

Introduction   Crossing the Threshold   10.
        Evolutionary Quest ~ A journey from dense material and sensual addictions to true function of spirit, ~ Paradigms crumbling ~ Addicted to suffering ~ Option is death

Chapter 1   From The Eye of the Sun - Initiation   14.
        How I was healed of Multiple Sclerosis, Cancer and Heart Disease ~ The Author's own story of her life ~ Years of suffering leads to disease ~ Twice through the Tunnel to the Light ~ Learning cause of disease ~ Learning how to heal ~ Finally the miracle of instantaneous healing. My treatment philosophy about Multiple Sclerosis, Health Sources and Protocols

Chapter 2   Healing – An Ongoing Journey   76.
        Belief systems ~ Emotional trauma ~ Spiritual immaturity ~ Cellular level ~ Initiation into the Sacred Breath~ Swimming with Dolphins ~ Collective consciousness ~ Unspeakable love, Sedona – Shamanic Training, Rebirthing, Divine Mother, Contreras Hospital Internship, European tour, Building Health Resort and Clinic in Corpus Christi, Producing Breath CD in Holland, Hydrogen Project in Montana, Lessons Learned, Back to Phoenix, Disabled by Cipro Poisoning, Return to Healing and the Breath of Light

Chapter 3   Theta Breathing Into A New Dimension   196.
        Physically detoxifies ~ PH balance from acid to alkaline ~ Oxygen ~ Mental clarity ~ Emotions ~ Wisdom in flesh ~ Communing with God ~ The Great Comforter – The Holy Spirit ~ Theta - Science ~ Dream State ~ Processing emotional trauma in the subconscious ~ Benefits of Theta

Chapter 4   Healing with the Elements –   207.
        Air, Earth, Fire, Water, Community

Chapter 5	Let Me Leave You Breathless Step by step method of Breathing the Light	257.
Chapter 6	Time – How to Use the Concept of Time For Power, Freedom & Happiness	275.
Chapter 7	Beauty – Essential For Healing	279.
Chapter 8	The Last Breath: Marrying Heaven and Earth~ Materialism ~ Values of success, achievement and power ~ Soul virtues rarely chosen over wealth and control ~ Vows of poverty ~ Walk in two worlds – right way to obtain gifts of Spirit ~ Price of Admission	284.
Chapter 9	The Ultimate Invitation Set free of the addiction to suffering ~ Breath is the Gateway	294.

Declaration of Intention	302.
About the Author	305.
Health Protocols	308.
Epilogue & Update from Dr. Mary – Personal Healing	355.
Products Available`	357.
Testimonials	358.
Notes for Reader (Declaration of Intention)	364.
Personal Notes to Myself for Reader	366.

DEDICATIONS AND ACKNOWLEDGMENTS

To My Human Family - My Mother and Father, Al & Bobbie Jean Meadows, and four younger sisters, Charlotte, Paulette, Kathy & Teresa. We came together as all families do to experience all the emotions possible to experience. We played the roles in each other's lives to learn and grow. I am grateful for all the ways you served me and the gifts you gave me through cruelties and abuse. Yes, I was different as you often reminded me, and I learned the art of survival. I made it out of the dark terror of victimhood that was perpetuated by both of you, my mother and father. None of my sisters chose the Light and still carry on your legacy of hatred, rage, terror, victim consciousness and worse. I could not have known about forgiveness and love in any other way -- a melting of my heart into compassionate love.

To Brad, Logan and Susan -- My children who became wonderful people I am proud to know. You endured much in your young years with me as your mother. I can only be grateful at your strength and your willingness to forgive me and love me through it all. I can only hope that the vast love I feel for you can be imparted to you in the blessing of your beings. And, because I have become who I am, you too, will become who you are. And you will know it was worth it all.

To Ama -- You foretold that I would write this book and that my life would touch multitudes. You imparted wisdom, spiritual understanding, and courage to go on living. Most importantly, you gently instructed me in the art of forgiveness and of the heart. Sometimes I was furious with you, because you made me look at myself through eyes of truth and I hated it when I could not lie any longer. I can never go back, and my heart is grateful to you. You would be so pleased. I send you my love wherever you are.

To Dr. Roy Swank, MD, who started me on my path to healing. I thank him for being such an extraordinary person and doctor to so many. His life and courage to be a pioneer will have made a difference in this world.

To John Cundiff – Your mentoring continues to guide me every day of my life. You are exemplary of what you teach. Thank you for encouraging me through the darkness.

To Jan de Roos –my co-creator of the CD, "Breathe the Light". You are a very special and gifted musician who has been able to bring forth the frequency of Light in your music – you have joined me in my "vision" to share the Breath of Light through the music.

To my many friends and supporters who have loved me and encouraged me, and breathed with me. There are too many to list, but I have to thank my team of committed Breatharians: Karen Burke Stewart, Janet McCabe, Maryanne Hastings, Irene LeRoi, Dawn Chorley, Steven Barret, Henny Van der Horst, Helga Macko and Cherie Rife Smylie, who went with me around the world to share the

Breath of Light. Thanks to Mae Malone & Betty Potter in Houston, & Mary Goodman in New Orleans (now in Dallas) for their loving support and promotion. Thanks to Helen Stembridge of *Earth Angel Oils* for knowing that we should co-create the Breath of Light Oils. They are divine.

To Brad and Sherry Steiger, wonderful friends and authors. We were brought together in 1986 by Spirit when I was used by an angelic being with a message to bring Brad and Sherry together. They were destined to be together. We spoke at Whole Life Expos and had sweet times hanging out after the long days for a nice relaxing dinner, and met up often back in Phoenix, home base. They authored "Love Is a Miracle" and many, many, more which you can find on Amazon.

To the Doctors at the Contreras Hospital in Mexico, especially Dr. Francisco Contreras, who invited me on staff and gave me the freedom and support to do the Breath with all their patients. I learned about the miracles of healing with alternative, detoxification protocols. You gave me the foundation and training to become a healer of Body, Mind, and Spirit. Dr. Francisco, you are my Hero and I witnessed your compassionate care which gave many hope, where there had been none. You were kind to all who came to you.

PREFACE TO REVISED AND UPDATED BOOK

I have come to powerful revelations as I started revising and updating this book. When I wrote the first version in 1993 with an updated version in '96, I felt that I needed to write my story in a "soft" way in order that my parents would not be hurt. After all, they were still alive. I thought that those of you who had similar lives could read between the lines. I wrote the story of my history in a lovely, prose-like style, trying not to offend anyone. I held back much of the information and the experiences that have made me who I am as I entered and passed the many Initiations. I thought that people would think that I was weird and it would be too scary for them. But, I am telling it all and holding back nothing. And, what has emerged is a whole new book.

As I have reread the book, it has made me cry. Not from the sadness of the story, for I have healed my heart of the grief and heartbreak with my parents. But the sadness has come in the realization that I was *holding out*, hanging onto the thread of hope that I would someday get their approval and blessing. Lord knows I tried. I gave and gave, and when the abusive explosions of anger came, I dutifully went and made up, thinking I could overlook it one more time. In the interest of keeping the family relationship going, even with all of the dysfunction, I thought we could create some happiness in the midst of the craziness. And with their selective memory, it was as if it never happened – until they needed to remember it again to punish me. It messes with your head when they don't remember it and then they do remember it. There are very important events that had life shattering effects on us girls that they refused to remember. Dad absolutely denied he ever hit Mother, even though he broke her collarbone and I called the police. After the beating I got, I never called them again. And then he denied that he ever hit us. But, we were there and we all remember. I lived in such fear and terror. I lay in bed at night and stared at the doorknob, praying it would not turn. Many times I was pulled out of bed in the midst of one of their fights because they needed to escalate the violence. It had nothing to do with me. I kept thinking, "If I can just be good enough, they won't hurt me." But I could never be good enough.

And where was my mother in all of this? I wondered that too. She never defended us against him. I think she sold out early on in the name of security (material possessions) and accepted the abuse. But, years of it made her sick in her spirit, and sick in her mind. She sacrificed herself and she sacrificed her daughters.

This is what I now know about it. Love brings up everything unlike itself. If a person feels unworthy of love and has the belief they are not good enough, when you show them love and compassion, they can only react out of their belief system and reject the love. They also reject the lover. All those dark, negative patterns are brought up to be healed, but they show up just as they are. When we love miserable, angry people, we expect to get back love – to transform their misery with our love. That is what we are told by all the "Light & Love teachers". I have even been guilty of teaching it myself. I wanted to believe it for my own situation. We do plant seeds that may yield a harvest, but usually not when we want it. And maybe, in the scope of eternity and karma, it does happen, somewhere, in a future life. Some are guilty of trying to save others from their lessons, their pain and suffering. They try to "fix" them. They often take it on themselves and rob the person of their lessons, prolonging their misery. They have to learn the lesson and lift themselves out of "victim consciousness".

I do know that when we change ourselves, everyone around us has to change because the dynamics of our roles and interplay of patterns have shifted. Sometimes, it enrages others when we become happy, and don't play their games anymore. Eric Berne who authored "Games People Play" absolutely nailed it. Miserable, angry people demand that everyone around them be miserable as well. My father who was a bully and a terrorist (before we heard much about that notion), ruined every holiday, celebration, and special event, making sure we all suffered. He could never be happy for our successes or happy events. He hated it when we laughed and put a stop to that nonsense. After being punished and crying, we were told, "I'll give you something to cry about". And we could not laugh or cry.

I was the oldest of five daughters to a father who only valued males. We all tried to be his "boy", but he resented us for assuming that we could even try. We still had no value and in his eyes were failures. He demeaned us at every opportunity when we made ourselves vulnerable to his scrutiny.

Once, after his scathing dressing down of me, I finally lost it. I have prided myself in being kind, calm and in control. My father was the only person who could push me over the edge and I could feel the rage bubbling up. He could access it in a way no one else could. After I exploded and lashed back with tears of anger, I went through the guilt and self-punishment of "Why couldn't I have been calm and just leave or talk it through? I am a spiritual teacher and I should be above this behavior." After doing a breathing meditation, I was shown that from the very beginning he instilled his rage in me. It was never mine. He thought if he could make us act out and get angry, it somehow absolved him and made him more normal. Yes, I took it on. Maybe, I wanted him to be normal and had to equalize the situation. He could access the rage in me because he originated it. I know I have always sought peace – sometimes at any price. I feel sad at giving my peace over to him.

Part of our healing has to do with self-love and it demands that we no longer accept abusive treatment, ever. Our sovereignty has to be restored. We must come into self-empowerment in order to move back onto the grid of our blueprint which is our plan and purpose for being on this earth. We have to get off the roller coaster of emotional lessons which keeps us stuck in a victim consciousness. As long as we are just students learning the lessons, we can justify a life spent in apathy, - no action – no self-responsibility. By stepping onto our grid, we can then do our work. It is time to unsheathe the victim consciousness and step forth as Masters and Messengers of Light.

In my telling of my journey and initiations, I will share the stories of my relationships and interactions with the people who played the roles of tyrants, tormenters, torturers, and terrorists who gave me the great lessons and Initiations which purified me of the human density, cleansed me of my victim consciousness, tested me in the depths of darkness, honed me like a samurai sword and brought me to the full **I AM** awakening into the Light. They were my greatest teachers, but it was a very painful process. I am grateful for every one of them and every experience that led me to the Light.

I will be sharing with you the many Initiations I went through and the ones who played the roles of tormentors, betrayers, and tyrants who threatened my existence, my life, my health, and my joy. They took away my life savings, tried to destroy and kill me. I tell these stories not as a Victim. I did feel victimized and violated at the time. I was not fully conscious and had attachments which is why I went through the Initiations. That is why anyone goes through them. But, I chose Consciousness, and emerged victorious over my attachments, addiction to sense satisfaction and fulfillment, and certainly over the Victim Consciousness.

That brings me to the point of how we perceive our persecutors, and the forgiveness and release we must hold in our hearts for our own freedom. Hatred and resentment toward them just holds us in a locked relationship with them forever. It cannot matter to us what happens to them. Will they be punished or will they prosper? That is none of our business. We all know the Bible verse, "Revenge is Mine, saith the Lord". Oh, I admit that I have wanted to make them pay for what they did to me. In the Silence I heard that I must exalt them. WHAT??? How do I do that! In the Silence, God's voice said, "Thank them for giving you the opportunity to learn a huge lesson and receive a precious gift – the gift of Consciousness. Thank them for assisting you in the blessing of Victory. They may go on in unconsciousness, living out their patterns of destruction, but it matters not to you. They did not get the blessing that you and I did. They only played out the roles that were catalysts for us to be able to see through the "Maya" and illusions that we were living with. They allowed us the opportunity to heal ourselves and to heal those patterns for all humanity.

Being born into our earth family, is for our transformation – for transcending the life as a human and embracing our spiritual self – our true being. It is akin to forgiveness in that we forgive others in order to have our own release. We have been afraid that if we become who we really are, that our families will leave us. The truth is, we leave them, because that segment of our earth life is complete. We can still love our families – and some of you are lucky enough to have families who are embracing love and a spirit-directed life. That is a precious part of our human heart. Others of us have to find our family in other beings of Light as we do need the sharing of our hearts and the great compassionate love.

We are here to raise the human consciousness. First we have to come into consciousness, ourselves. The blessing I was waiting for from my parents would never come. They were not capable of giving me that. They would never give me their approval and acceptance. That has to come from within – through my connection to the Divine which is the source of all Love, Mercy and Understanding.

Writing this new, more truthful and authentic book is a great blessing for me. It has been a catharsis to move on. It has been a catalyst to let go of the myths of a fantasy I held onto. "They" were never going to change. They had several huge wake-up calls and they did not budge. My sister was murdered as a result of her devastated life. She wanted their love and attention so much, she ended up dead. Mother had cancer and went through debilitating treatment and eventually, death. They chose not to deal with any of it. I think there is a point of no return where a person can no longer hear the calling of spirit. The choice has been made. I, too, made my choice – for myself – for my worth. I choose to fill my life with goodness overflowing, with beauty, with service to humanity and the servers of humanity. I have chosen to become a Bringer of the Light.

As I am entering the "Golden Years" of my life, I am contemplating my life here on this planet. Recently, I was exposed to a toxic substance and came face to face with death. The question that was posed to me by my higher self was, "Do I stay or do I go home?" I have done much. I have been faithful to all that has been given to me. I do not want to stay here if I am going to suffer and to sacrifice myself with no joy or happiness. I negotiated with the Higher Beings telling them that if I stayed, I must have some joy and happiness with abundance of good things. I have paid the price of admission. I did get confirmation that my life is now being blessed with all the good things that I desire and with that, I decided to stay. I still have much to offer humanity. I am anointed and all will be given that I need just as I need it. I can give you the same assurance that you are anointed and our Divine Creator made you with all that you need to do your work, live your life, and fulfill your mission. You would not have the dreams and desires otherwise. When God laid out the plan for your life, the Divine deposited in you the skill, the wisdom, the creativity; everything you need to fulfill your destiny.

For some of us, it is our purpose to BE the Presence, BE the Love, BE the Peace and hold the Divine Light for all of humanity. We have learned enough, nothing more to do, or produce. Just Be. We have paid the price of admission and have been faithful to all that we have been given, passed our Initiations, feel Victorious and see clearly all the energies at work in our world. We are not living with illusions anymore or driven by the patterns of survival which produce greed, manipulation and betrayal of others.

I know full well that I can live happily with little or nothing. Material things do not bring happiness. Those things can support us in comfort and ease, but we cannot rely on things or others to fulfill our needs and make us happy.

It is only in a Spirit filled life that we can find a peaceful mind and a peaceful heart. It is communing with God that we find the bliss and ecstasy which we are seeking and do remember in our cells from the beginning of our existence. It is in the Breath of Light that we find the wondrous flow of the Holy Spirit which lifts us up out of the density of this world. Jesus the Christ came to show us how to live and be in Spirit and to awaken the Christ in each of us.

I offer the Ultimate Invitation. Will you go with me? Will you be Spirit filled? Will you transcend all the densities of this earth and embrace the Christed being that you truly are? Will you remember where you came from and why you are here? Choose to be that Love and bring Consciousness of the Divine to the human race for their awakening.

INTRODUCTION - CROSSING THE THRESHOLD

Humankind stands at the Threshold of a most remarkable and exciting time in our evolutionary quest in consciousness. Many are anxious. Many are confused. Many are frightened. All are seekers and all want to know how. This is evidenced by the many workshops, seminars, books, and tapes focused on self-growth and the process of enlightenment.

It is said that the human "Over-Soul" originally fell from the Light into the world of shadows. As time passed, it identified with desires of the senses, with material things, and it became heavier, more dense and opaque. It lost its light, its wisdom and its consciousness. The veils multiplied, but once the soul grows weary of its captivity and becomes conscious of its exile from the world of Light, this longing to return home begins the ascent back to the Light.

That journey back, from the dense material and sensual addictions to that of the true function of the Spirit, is the Evolutionary Quest. Some are calling this ascent the change of consciousness. Moving from the dense 3rd Dimension into the 5th Dimension, almost eclipsing the 4th Dimension altogether has caused many much angst because they have not done their inner work, their purification of body, mind, emotions and spirit. They are still very addicted to the physical and material world.

As consciousness moves upward from sense to spirit it becomes the spiritual heart of pure love. It is this heart that finally unites with the Oneness of All. Duality is the stronghold of the third dimension representing division and control – who has the control has the power.

Many are in resistance to the change. We see paradigms crumbling and falling away as new ones are struggling to be born. Nothing is the same anymore -- Relationships, Business, Success. Many people are still addicted to terrible suffering and are tormented by the changes. Most of these do not want to live and, instead, opt for disease and death. In order for us to positively shift our consciousness, we each must reclaim our divinity. We must lift the veil of lies and ignorance that have imprisoned us in unhappiness with no peace anywhere. We must take responsibility for our purpose in being here and reclaim the throne of power and aliveness that is our birthright.

Yes, the transition is underway. Make no mistake about it. If we close our eyes too long, when we look again, every cell of all living beings and material consciousness will be changed -the old way will be gone with a reorganization of the earth and a new creation. There will be no more memory of suffering, no more conflicts, everything flowing within one and the same rhythm. Things will not be done because you have learned to do them a certain way and have been programmed with self-destructive belief system -- rather you will have a spontaneous response -- a new method of consciousness which knows the right thing at the exact moment of doing it and does all with a profound Celebration of Life.

In order to go into this new realm, we have to prepare ourselves and cleanse out all dense, cellular patterns that would keep us in old limiting prisons of darkness. One of the biggest challenges we face is to let go of our addiction to suffering. We think that we have to prove we are human by suffering, and that it is unthinkable to let go of suffering. We believe it is inhuman to be joyful when others are suffering. However, the only way we can affect anyone else is to be a living truth to the fact that we can be free of suffering. The only trust is in the living proof to any theory.

The reason we are here on this planet earth is to do this very thing. We came here to experience accelerated growth by donning bodies and experiencing emotions. It is the emotional body that is the greatest challenge and mystery for our species. However, we are now being given the way through this seemingly enormous and unconquerable force that runs our lives - with pain, unhappiness and torment being the result.

In our enlightenment process, it is important to regain the gentleness, dignity and vast compassionate love for which we long and from which we came. That is why I am honored to bring a gateway that is being opened for the first time to serve us as we leave this dream and return to Reality.

The Holy Spirit is guiding us and using the Breath as this gateway revealing the presence of Light. It is the portal between the despair, the dark and guilty suffering - and the holy return Home, for which we are truly longing.

I present to you the Ultimate Invitation - the invitation to choose Life - to choose Freedom -- to choose Divinity - to come home to Love.

In the Spirit of the Breath of Light,

Dr. Mary Meadows

CHAPTER 1   FROM THE EYE OF THE SUN:

INITIATION

We are all here by Divine appointment. Each of us has come here to play out our own unique role. We have chosen to accept the Ultimate Invitation -- the invitation to awaken to who we really are and where we came from -- and the purpose we each have to bring about the shift to this planet! We are being given the opportunity to live in a new reality. - A reality totally opposite from the one we have lived and believed in for centuries.

We cannot go back. There really is no choice. We now choose consciousness or unconsciousness. To choose unconsciousness is to choose death and destruction. To choose consciousness is to give expression to God -- to Christ qualities-- to express love -- to choose to contribute to the good, the happiness, the well-being of the world -- to choose to be a Light in the world.

To get to that place of illumination, many of us choose hard, rocky paths . . . crisis, trauma, loneliness, illness, fear, unhappiness, struggle and pain....many forms of Initiations.

I chose to come into this current life from the very beginning with a life script so filled with challenges that I would have to grow and evolve rapidly in order to survive. I chose to accept the ultimate invitation. I chose to take on the human condition and infuse the race with consciousness. I chose to be part of the most exciting time of our human race. I chose a life of Initiations which I now know was necessary to grow and become strong through each testing. We are given more gifts and enlightenment when we pass each Initiation test.

When I came out of the womb, I came calling and longing for God's compassionate presence. I wanted only goodness and peace. I remembered the angelic realms of Divine Love from whence I came and could not accept the cruelty and inhumanity of this world. Nothing except nature resonated with me.

I was born at 6pm on July 30, 1941 making me a Leo with a Capricorn rising and Scorpio moon. The Leo sun gave me a "sunny and full of light" disposition always yearning for joy and happiness. The Capricorn aspect helped me to be practical and grounded me. The Scorpio moon demanded purity and integrity in all things. I knew at an early age that I had to be above reproach and there was karma for every decision. While making some wrong decisions throughout my life, I have quickly made the corrections as I knew the instant repercussions of karma.

Truth and right action has been primary driving forces for me and I do love it when someone can give me the gift of truth. It also allows me to see through the illusions to truth. I see who people really are....not who they project. Sometimes I see the potential in people and grant that to them before they have earned it and realized it for themselves. That can cause a problem because each one has to pay the price of admission for enlightenment. It cannot be given from another person. And, the person is robbed of their own initiation and enlightenment.

As a child, I was lonely - alone. I spent much time with nature in the forests by myself. I read constantly as an escape from the harsh world I saw around me. I looked at the people around me and kept asking, "Who are these people?"

I was born in East Texas and spent my early years in a small town, Gladewater. This was one of those pockets of ignorance and unconsciousness. This was the seat of the Ku Klux Klan and there was much prejudice, redneck ignorance, and hatred. Not only toward black folk, Jews, and Asians, but also women were demeaned and subject to oppression. There was a macho male egotism and it was clear who was in charge.

I grew up in an era where children were often not allowed to express emotions or show anger even when we were subjected to violence and abuse ourselves. At that time, parents were called "strict". Today, we call it abuse and dysfunctional. I lived in constant terror. My father was a bully and a terrorist. I have come to believe he was a member of the KKK as were many of the "upstanding" citizens of that small town and the Baptist Church. Oddly, he became a 33rd degree Mason and Shriner, even though he was quite ignorant of the metaphysical teachings of the Masons. Again, there was a "good ole boy's club" that gave admittance into many privileged groups. But, underneath the prestige, there was often deep evil and sick men masquerading. I learned early on that everything is not as it appears and that many of those around me were wearing masks of deception.

Besides reading every book in the public library, I started taking refuge and finding my inner light through creating art. Drawing and painting allowed me to feel all those deep emotions and express them in beauty. I certainly could not express openly in communication with the family and people I was surrounded by. Being able to be creative has been and still is essential to my being able to stay here on this foreign planet. I find joy and happiness when I am creating and I am sure that it is connecting me to the Divine Creator and the memory of who I truly am.

At age seven, I had an amazing awakening into the full knowledge of who I am and where I came from. I can remember it still just as if it happened today. I was in a four legged cast iron tub in the late afternoon. The light was streaming into the four paned window and was warm upon my skin. All of a sudden, there were angelic beings who spoke to me in all of their golden splendor. They showed me my true family, my people, where I come from – the Second Great Central Sun where there is only the most Divine, Perfect Love that is indescribable. They showed me that I was chosen to come here to be and bring that Divine Love to the Human Race of this Earth planet. I was inserted into this human family which was filled with a history of darkness and ignorance. I was to be the one that awakened the lineage for all time and bring the Light to them. However, I did not know that it was going to be so lonely, cruel and difficult. How I longed to go home and to be surrounded with that love which I was finding none of here on this human planet and in the human family I was in. Even though I had this precious awakening, it did not prevent me from suffering and longing for my people.

My father, Al Meadows, was born to Luther Meadows and Martha Wilder Meadows, who taught him well what their parents had taught them. The violence, the lack of worth and ignorant ideas were beaten into him. It led to him being a mean person with no capacity to love or give. He was so self-absorbed that he did not care about the deep devastation he was causing his family. Indeed, he reveled in it and seemed to thrive on all the misery that he inflicted.

My mother, Bobbie Jean Smith Meadows, was somewhat of a mystery to me as she came from a very different family. Her father, Robert Tune Smith was perceived to be a kind and quiet man who "never said anything bad about anybody". But, after looking at the history of his life with my grandmother, Nora Finney Smith, I have a very different view of him. Most of the family thought my grandmother was a mean, bitchy woman, but the truth was, she always had to shoulder all the responsibility of their family. She was the disciplinarian because "Papa" Smith did not do any discipline, especially with their sons. He was a weak man and it fell on "Mama" Smith to handle everything. They had three sons and three daughters. The three sons, Lawrence, Dreabon, and Buford turned out to be worthless and flawed men. They were spoiled and unappreciative of their good life. Buford was an alcoholic and died young in a car accident when he was drunk. Early in their teens, Lawrence and Dreabon killed the neighbor's son in a dispute. Mama and Papa Smith had to sell their cotton plantation and move in order to defend the boys and to get them away from the neighbor who vowed to kill them. They sold everything at a huge loss and were poor the rest of their lives. In the end of their lives, their sons did not take care of them and were ungrateful until the very end. The daughters, Lorraine, Naomi, and my mother, Bobbie Jean, were more caring of their parents. Naomi was the selfish one and carried a meaness like her brothers all her life. Lorraine and Bobbie Jean both had a victim personality which came from my Mama Smith's sacrificial life. Women's roles in those days were expected to be submissive and victims.

My mother, Bobbie Jean, played the perfect victim and martyr, all the time allowing and even condoning the abuse of her children and herself. She sold her soul for security – the material world that she was devoted to. And through years of subjecting herself to abuse, she paid a very high price. She became ill and diseased, mentally and physically. And she lost the connection as a mother to her children. She never became the person that she could have been. Even until her death, I did not know who she was.

My early years were so very lonely. I did not resonate with almost everyone that I knew. There were two bright lights in my life, Annie, our black maid, who was my beloved caretaker, and my grandmother, Mama Smith. They were two wise and loving women who nurtured and cared for me, always keeping me safe and loved. They gave me the love and lessons that have sustained me through all the tests of my life. I learned wonderful things from them.

Annie was our maid and nanny, but was an angel in disguise to look after me. I knew every moment of every day that she loved me just for me. She came from a different world, literally from across the tracks in "shanty town". One day, my mother needed to get a message to her and we loaded up in the car to go to Annie's house as she did not have a telephone. We went to the poor part of town and stopped in front of a shack that was very run down. There were kids of all ages and for the first time, I realized that Annie was a mom and had nine kids of her own. I always thought of her as "mine". Annie did not have a husband and had to take care of all those kids on the $25.00 a week that we paid her. How did she do it? And, who took care of her kids when she was taking care of us? It broke my heart to know that my beloved Annie had to live as she did. She loved me as my mother should have loved me, and acted in such a kind, sweet way, all the time having to live such a simple and sacrificial way with her own family. She helped me to look beyond a person's skin color and see the true value that comes from their heart and values. I did not understand the prejudice against the black folks in our town. When I went to the $.25 movies on Saturday and saw 28 cartoons, 2 serials, and 2 full length features, I saw that the black folks entered by their own entrance, sitting up in the dark cavern of the balcony. They also had to buy their popcorn at a separate window and who knows what the situation was for their restrooms. I did not like that and, innately, knew it was very wrong.

And Mama Smith took me fishing, pickin' blackberries, and let me help her in her very special garden. We would walk along admiring all the beautiful vegetables, picking a fresh tomato or some green peas eating them right on the spot. Never has food tasted so wonderful as those garden forays. She also loved flowers and had a yard full of them.

Even though life was hard for them and work filled their every waking hour, she always had time to grow flowers and make some beauty there at the farm. I especially remember her lilac trees with those lilting fragrances that captured our every sense and made us pause and pay homage to their beauty. She gave me the gift of appreciation for nature. I have drawn on that connection with nature all of my life. I have always known that when there is no joy, no hope, and confusion, I can go to nature and Divine Mother will cleanse me, nurture me, heal me, and bring clarity. My Mama Smith was a wise and wonderful inspiration for me my whole childhood. She had the most infectious laugh which bubbled up and her whole body shook before she made a sound. She rarely laughed from her mouth, she laughed with her whole body.

Mama and Papa Smith lived in the big house with huge oak trees and towering pines completely isolated in a forest. My cousins and I would go down into those piney trees, make whole rooms complete with furniture by shaping piles of pine needles. Mama Smith indulged our fantasies and let us do just about anything we could dream up.

I especially liked it when I could go up to Mama Smith's alone and have all of her love and attention. She would make a huge blackberry cobbler filled with biscuit dumplings and butter just for me. When my male cousins were there, they made life miserable for me – often stealing my blackberry cobbler and running off to the woods with it. I had three female cousins and we were all born the same year. Joan, Elsie, JoAnne and me. We were inseparable as children, but grew apart as adults. Joan and I have had a lovely connection as adults even though we live in different states. Joan is still in Houston with her husband, Paul.

There was one step-cousin, Raymond Leroy Bearden who always wanted to be a "Meadows" as our family was the most affluent of all the relatives. Raymond coveted the superficial superiority of swagger that Al Meadows flaunted. He wanted to be the son that Al never had. In later years, he would play a pivotal role as he plotted to take my place with my father.

The whole family knew how violent Al was and many times, mother would escape with us up to Mama and Papa Smith's after she had been beaten and the black eyes, bruises, cuts, all spoke clearly of the abuse she was subjected to. Once, Uncle Dreabon chased Al through the fields with a gun and was going to kill him if he caught him. What a scene as everyone was in the chase and screaming for him to stop. So much drama played out in the whole family's ignorance and dysfunctional dynamics. Mother always went back to him after he pleaded for her to come back and everything would be different. Different for about 2 days and then the abuse began once again.

Mama Smith adored me and gave me a foundation that I have been able to draw upon for my whole life. I can only feel so very sad that kids today do not have the opportunity to have this experience with nature. The connection with nature is essential to our foundation of security, trust, gratefulness and simplicity. I see that the kids today are disconnected and do not have an anchor that sustains them. Nature shows us our priorities, values, and helps us connect to Spirit.

I went to Mama and Papa Smith's every chance I could. And when I was back in the house with my family, I would escape to the woods. I would take green plums or lemons with salt to suck on while I read my many books there by the creek. I swung out over the creek on grape vines and dropped into the water to swim to shore and do it all over again. The birds came and sat on my hand and I had complete communion with God through the beauty of nature. I still to this very day worship the nature wherever I am and draw nurturing from it. They had to come find me most of the time, as I never wanted to come back into that house. I kept thinking that if I can just be "good enough" they won't hurt me. I could never be good enough to avoid the unwarranted attacks. There were many beatings, brutal interactions and demeaning experiences that no child should have to endure. I was innocent, but Al Meadows was determined to beat me down to dirt and make me like him so he could be superior. I accepted the deep-seated belief that

"I am not Good Enough!" which shaped the many choices that I made for many years.

Shame, fear and guilt were frequent emotions experienced by children. Children were "seen and not heard." Females of all ages were sheltered, controlled and kept in their place. As a girl, I longed to be a boy. They were more esteemed - declared worth more just because of their gender, and were allowed to do so much more. I learned what many of us learn: that we're not quite capable, not quite lovable. The voices around me dwelt on negative conditions, strife, pain, turmoil, severity and judgment. I felt like a stranger in a foreign land. I could not relate to the cruelty and inhumanity around me. I knew there was a better way to live and be. I found myself longing for another place - perhaps in another universe - a place of unspeakable love and constant, ever sustaining peace. Life was frightening, overwhelming, and painful. I started withdrawing at an early age - searching for a source to sustain me - to set me free of the bondage of this life.

There was a quiet inner voice that whispered, "My dear one, the world seems dark everywhere, but within your heart there is a place of light and joy. I am with you always. Take my hand in yours, my child, and know you are my beloved. I will never forsake you on your journey." As a child, I saw God's face in the clouds, the sunshine, the birds, butterflies, and the fragrant flowers that sustained my fragile heart with the light and fragrance of the Divine.

When I was seven years old, I had an illumined experience which was vividly imprinted in my mind and shaped my destiny. I was in a claw-footed bathtub, with the sunlight bright outside and streaming ribbons of light through the paned window in the bathroom. I had a visitation of angelic beings and masters who gave me the strong memory of my origin and the angelic kingdom where I came from. I was given the vision of why I had been chosen to come to this earth to bring the Love of my real family to the human race. I remembered being one of the many angelic beings that came from the Great, Great, Central Sun to seed this birthing planet, earth, Gaia, Urantia, with consciousness. And, we left to go back to source and allow the evolution to take place for millions of years. We watched the time of gases, water/oceans, soil, mountains, life of plants, animals, dinosaurs, early primitive man, and then early civilized humans. Some of us then came back through the ages of advancing civilizations of Lemuria and Atlantis, inserting ourselves and our advanced consciousness in order to assist the evolution process of conscious human development.

I knew that I had come to serve and Bring the Light. That reawakening gave me purpose and determination to endure what the coming years were to bring. I was no longer just a seven year old child, but already a conscious, wise being. Though that memory faded at times, it never was lost.

However, as years passed, simplicity was set aside, as were other soul qualities of innocence, faith and trust. One incident that made a huge impression on me and showed me that I meant nothing to my father was a summer day when I was about 5 years old. I was going with my father to his jewelry store for the day as there was no one to watch me. I was secretly thrilled at the thought that I might be special since I was joining him for the whole day. We stopped at the post office and Dad told me to go stand over in the corner while he mailed something at the window. As I stood there, I watched my father walk right out the door when he finished. I stood there for a very long time trying to figure out what to do. Was he coming back for me? He had sternly told me to stand there and not move. But finally after a very long time, I realized he was not coming back. I started walking toward downtown and after a few hours I found the store. When I walked in, Dad only laughed and casually commented, "I guess I forgot you". No reassurance or worry for me. I knew then that I did not matter to him.

Material thought, desire of the senses, and emotions (born out of the belief systems and patterns that I had finally bought into and accepted as truth) ruled my life. I finally believed that I was "not good enough" and that I would always have to keep on subjugating my spirit in order to gain the approval and "love" of those around me. I looked for love in physical, emotional selfish places and entered a period of many years of confusion. I was caught in an emotional whirlwind that tossed me, battered me, and exhausted me. These experiences were a huge test and initiation in order to know and eventually become the master of emotions. I have been teaching and helping people to transcend and transmute those false belief systems that we are taught and then believe.

My father moved our family from Gladewater, Texas to Anchorage, Alaska when I was fourteen. Al had been a private pilot, starting to fly when I was 5 years old. It was a very special thing when I was able to go up with him in the plane and I think I loved it as much as he did. The freedom of being high in the sky and floating around in the clouds was heaven. So, one summer, Al and his friend flew up to Alaska and returned with the announcement that we were moving there. My mother had a fit as we had been living in her dream home for a very few years and she did love that house. We packed everything up in a trailer we towed behind a red '53 Cadillac. The year was 1954. In those days, the Alcan Highway between Alaska, Canada and the U.S. was not fully paved leaving about 1500 miles of very rough gravel. There were few facilities along the highway and many times we slept at night on camp-side tables we would find along the way. When we met other people on our travels, it was like a homecoming and we would have a great time visiting with our new found friends.

I have to say that the sense of adventure was one of the best gifts that my father gave me. He was the ultimate adventurer. I am forever grateful that he moved us out of that little East Texas town and opened a new life in a very metropolitan place. That trip over the Alcan Highway was a fantastic experience in raw nature with no distractions of civilization. We were in the car for long hours at a time, but when we stopped, the chance of being in untouched nature full of unknown plants, trees, animals, smells, and foliage was a new adventure every time. We even found some thermal hot springs along the way which I had never experienced before. They were divine and I became a hot springs fanatic which has taken me to many amazing places.

When we arrived in Anchorage, it was still very much a pioneer time and life was very different than Gladewater, Texas. We had lived a life of wealth in Texas, having a big home with servants, new cars, nice clothes and all the comforts that I took for granted.

My parents had a jewelry store which had done very well for many years. However, my father extended credit to people and carried accounts since there were no credit cards in those days. People did not pay their accounts and he ended up going bankrupt, a fact that I did not know for some years. So, when we went to Alaska, we ended up in a very modest house, a shack located in the area of Bootlegger Cove of Anchorage. What a shock! And no servants! No cook. Mother had to go to work as well. So....I had to learn to cook for the family, clean the house and take care of my three younger sisters. I was not prepared for this new role. But, I learned and actually loved doing the cooking. It became a passion through the years.

My younger sisters made my life miserable as they would not help me and were very uncooperative in doing chores. I got punished for their unwillingness to do their part. And, they would just laugh and thought my misery was very funny. My sisters, Charlotte and Paulette were the bane of my existence and continued to make life miserable for me. My youngest sister, Kathy, was 10 years younger and she became my shadow, hoping that I would protect her against the other two. I did a good job, but they found ways to torment her when I was not watching. I worked very hard with both my school and the home chores. But, one thing about living in Bootlegger's Cove, it was in nature and so beautiful. The grass was so verdant green and smelled like pure life. I would lie down in that soft, alive grass and soak in the chlorella nutrients through my skin. I would look up at that beautiful, pure sky with big puffy clouds and see all the divine shapes up there with the sun's rays beaming down its life energy. I needed nothing else when I could immerse myself in that wonderful nature. It saved my life in those days.

We started attending the First Baptist Church which had a large congregation and a wonderful youth program. The church's music directors, Frank Lauter and his wife, Irene were trained classical musicians. They had a great music program with a large choir. I had not had much exposure to music, but found that it was a true talent that I could develop. Frank and Irene took me under their wings and trained my voice, giving me many opportunities to sing solos in church and also on the church's Saturday television show. My confidence grew with their wonderful mentoring. For the first time, I felt my worth.

I had my one true love at an early age, but there is no doubt that he was my soul mate that I met and loved. I was singing a solo one Sunday evening service, and I saw a young man walk in and stand at the back of the church, not moving the whole time I was singing. I felt his energy the minute I saw him and it was both magnetic and inflammatory in my whole being. After church, he came straight away and introduced himself. He was Joseph Tapia, in the military service there. He was from Las Vegas and more worldly than the students I went to high school with. Joe was very handsome, elegant, with strong charisma but always the perfect gentleman. I was only 15 and he was 19. I was very young but the connection was too strong to be denied. I was definitely in awe of him, very innocent, and Joe could have easily taken advantage of me, but he never did. Joe put me on a pedestal the minute he saw me. He told me that when he saw me singing on the stage, he beheld an angel and that is how he treated me always. I finally felt adored and loved.

My father was outraged at the idea of Joe and me dating. But, I think it was more than that. He did not want anyone loving me, making me feel special, and taking his harsh control away. And, Joe by loving me, did set me free and showed me a different life. My father was losing control and I had an ally with Joe. My father took desperate measures and moved the family back to Texas in order to break us up. I wrote Joe every day and gave the letters to my mother to mail. I could not understand why Joe was not answering me. After about 6 months, my parents decided that they had ended the relationship because I no longer had any contact with Joe. We packed up and moved back to Alaska. When packing, I found the letters in my mother's drawer – all the ones I wrote to Joe and all the letters he had written to me. I never trusted my mother again.

The very minute we arrived back in Anchorage, I tracked Joe down and told him what had happened. Joe was devastated by my absence and we were more determined than ever, but we had to see each other in secret. We enjoyed the many church activities that allowed us to be together and I had to sneak out even for those as my parents were alerted that we were seeing each other. Then, suddenly, Joe disappeared. Military police came to see me and said they found my photos and letters in his personal things. I was devastated and puzzled at why he would have disappeared without any communication. I never heard from him again. I was so naïve and did not put it together until many years later.

I have realized that my own father and his low-life buddies killed him. Harsh? Unbelievable? Not when you take in consideration my father's violent nature and activities with other sordid sorts who were totally unconscious. The men that Al hung out with were the dregs of society that loved to drink, hunt and kill. While my father was prosperous, having a lot of material things, he always picked the derelicts for his friends. They made him feel superior and indeed, were loyal hoping that they would benefit from his wealth. I now know that Al and his pals took care of Joe so that he was gone from my life forever. Whenever I have looked for Joe or thought about him, I have known in my heart that he is not alive. And, now in my golden years, I have realized that romantic love was not to be part of my life's journey even though I kept looking for it for many years - looking for that pure, deep soul connection that I had a small glimpse of, but it was not to be. The love that I would finally come to know is only possible by knowing the merging with the heart and mind of Divine Mother/ Father God. That is the real love affair that is also the most exciting and thrilling of all.

In writing about Joe, many emotions have come up for me and I realized that I was feeling a deep sorrow at losing him. Even though I can see the spiritual test in this, I was feeling my heartbreak all over again. A wonderful gift came to me one night in February 2015. Some would call it a dream, but I know it for what it was – a visitation that was a virtual experience. Joe came walking out of a house that I was about to enter. He grabbed me and just held onto me tightly. Then he looked into my eyes and I was able to see every feature of his face...his eyes crinkling with adoration and joyous recognition...eyebrows...hair....every hair to see the color and how it grew....the pores of his skin....his mouth which was slightly open with his breath barely breathing. He was looking at me the same way I was looking at him. But, Joe was still so young – about 20 years old. Did he not realize that, while I still looked youthful and radiant, I was 73 years old? But, I could tell that he only saw and felt the love that flowed between us. He picked me up and carried me inside to a private sanctuary to finally have our sacred union. The love we shared that night was the most intimate, sweet, passionate and a true spiritual union of every part of our beings. I have never experienced that with anyone else. We soon left on a trip with many people all around us, but Joe was oblivious to everyone except me. His every move was about taking care of me with tenderness and such sweetness. I kept thinking about how could this be and how Joe was so young. But every time I looked into his eyes or observed his motions which were ultimately devoted to me, I knew and felt the depth of his love. We were never separated and never will be. After I awoke, I knew that it was not over and that this great love that I was feeling was inside of me and emanating from within me. It was a divine love, coming from my source creation of the divine union of Mother/Father God. I feel whole, reunited, filled up with unspeakable love and it is mine to have – to keep – and to be every moment of my life. I can commune with Joe with every breath as we are crossing dimensions and even parallel universes through the awakening of our Christed creator beings. Mary and Joseph. I have had visitations from Joe since and they are Divinely Blissful.

My high school years were full of studies and singing not only at church but also in the school choir with Cora Horton, the choral director, as an additional coach for my voice, which led to many concerts, solos, and eventually being chosen to represent Alaska at the Northwestern Music Festival. It was such an honor and I was so excited. But, again, my father ruined my chance at having such a wonderful honor. He would not let me go, and I suffered such deep sadness. I am sure he took great delight in taking away my joy. What kind of father had I chosen to have the human experience with?

Another young airman, John Steppert, started coming to the Baptist church and was flirting with me. I was flattered by the flirtations, but was not so sure about him. He was really different than Joe and there was not that same connection. He was quiet, more introverted and was not easy to talk to. I finally agreed to go on a date with him. We went to a movie and then pulled to a popular parking spot – I thought we would talk. John became very aggressive and started forcing himself on me. No romance and no tenderness. I immediately started resisting and saying, No! No! No! But, he just kept on forcing his way and all the time, I was hysterically crying. Today, we call it "date rape". It was a terrible way to lose my virginity and was traumatic. In fact, it was so traumatic that I hemorrhaged. Later that night after I finally got home, I felt that I was in trouble and needed to go to the hospital. I knew that my parents would absolutely kill me dead.

I called John and told him to come get me. I slipped out of the house and we went to a local emergency room. I was so naïve that I did not know to lie about my age and they could not examine me because I was underage. A doctor overheard my hysterical crying and he came in the room to find out what was wrong. His name was Dr. Starr and he became my knight in shining armor. He proposed that I go home and tell my parents that I slipped on the ice and bring my mother with me for an exam. Dr. Starr backed me up and helped me with the physical trauma. My parents were furious with me but did not have any real reason to punish me.

The mental anguish was just starting for me. John and I went to see the pastor of the church for counseling. He told me that since I had "given" myself away to John that I had to marry him – who would want me now? He laid a guilt trip on both of us, but more on me as I was the woman and it was my fault – according to him. This led to me marrying John as soon as I graduated even though I had two music scholarships and one academic scholarship. I never used those scholarships as I had to go to work and put John through college and seminary. John had decided to become a Baptist Minister. I cried out, "Oh My God!!! Really? This troubled and flawed man? A *man of God*"? Was he called of God or trying to work out his salvation? I did not feel that I had a choice nor was I ever asked if I wanted to. It was demanded by my pious husband who I now had to serve.

John enrolled at Belmont Baptist College and I worked at the Baptist headquarters in Nashville, Tennessee. I was quickly disillusioned by the corruption and hypocrisy that I found there in Nashville. I started mentally moving away from the Baptist church and also the South. I was starting to feel stirrings in my spirit that called me to a higher understanding of spirituality and less of rigid religion which called for punishment in hell by a furious God.

I was in Nashville when the first racial sit-ins happened. A favorite person I worked with at the Baptist Sunday School Board was fired because he participated in one. I was furious and had to leave because of the terrible prejudice I saw there. I found another job, but the South was just too painful for me.

In these awakening years, I had my first real Initiation and a powerful awakening experience. For years, I had awakened after a night of deep sleep feeling exhausted, like I had been up all night studying for an exam. There was a filmy barrier that would not allow me to remember something important. I felt very agitated about it. Something was happening to me and I did not know what it was. This was increasingly agitating and I finally declared to the Heavens and to whoever was in charge, "I demand to know what is happening to me". I was serious. But, there were strange memories that troubled me and I knew something was going on in my sleep. So, one night, "they" allowed me to remember and experience the whole thing.

I was greeted and guided up the ramp of a space vehicle by very luminescent tall beings who had human features, but were not dense and they were filled with a light. In walking up the ramp, I kept sinking to my knees and they just walked right up. I asked about it and they said that I was still very dense and had not translated into my Light body yet. I entered a lab with about 20 other students along with about 7 of the Luminous teachers. This particular night they were teaching us about the brain and its brain waves, functions, and neurons. I was mystified and asked why I was learning about the brain. They said that in time I would need to know about the science of the brain and I would remember it all at that time. I asked why I couldn't remember now all that I was being trained in on the ship. They replied very simply that I would ruin my own timing. I would only be allowed to have the knowledge as needed.

Sure enough, when I was initially writing this first book in 1993, and also working with the Breath, I did remember about Beta, Alpha, Theta and Delta. Theta was the most important brainwave and the Breath would carry us into that essential dream state. Theta was little known about and rarely documented in those early years. Recalling what I had been taught was a tremendous gift of knowledge. You will read more about it in the chapter on the Breath. It was a huge relief to know that I could count on knowing all that I needed to know – just when I needed it. We call it "being downloaded" with vast amounts of knowledge from the Divine Intelligence which allows us to move with surety and faith. I continued with my other dimensional training for many years even into my adulthood.

The nighttime when we sleep, is the time when we leave the rejuvenating physical body and go commune with the Divine teachers. We can all connect to the Divine Intelligence and know all that we need to know. The Breath of Light is a great instrument to connect to Divine

Intelligence and the flow of knowledge which quickens our Christhood and Mastery of this human condition.

I told John after he graduated from college that I wanted out of the South and also find a more compatible church. He actually agreed, as he did not want to lose his meal ticket in me. We went to San Francisco where he eventually graduated from the Presbyterian Seminary.

Our first pastoral ministry was in a very small town, Wendell, Idaho, which was very conservative being mostly Mormons.

I was the perfect minister's wife, accepting my role and playing it to perfection. Always dependable, I went to all the church meetings, sat on committees and sang in the choir. I stood behind my husband, always careful to be submissive and not usurp his limelight. There was no love or respect, a mere facade of a marriage. We stayed together for 13 years. The consequences of divorcing a minister were too painful to consider. He was doing that for which he had trained and studied. I had given up the three scholarships for college, and instead went to work to support us and put him through college and seminary. He never asked me to do it, he just told me that I was going to do it. He never did nor has he ever thanked me for what I did for him. And all his behavior supported my belief that I was not good enough. I allowed him to do it. I was a self-imposed victim, conditioned by years of abuse. I felt trapped. I did not realize that I had the power to change me and my life.

I had unfulfilled dreams of a life with love, support and joy. I wanted to be appreciated and acknowledged. I wanted to make a contribution to life. All the while I smiled and nodded politely with deep resentment and resignation.

PHASE 1: THE AWAKENING

The only source of hope for me in those unhappy days of my loveless, demeaning marriage were some new friends I met. They were also interested in spiritual, metaphysical studies. We met in secret, disguising our unacceptable studies. Those conversations that we had kept me alive as well as some new experiences. I started having visitations of several close friends who made their transitions and crossed over, but came to me shortly after their deaths to commune with me. I never felt afraid and it seemed very normal.

The first was John's aunt Frances, who I had been very close with. She would come in the night and her favorite perfume, Arpege, would fill the room so strong that I would awaken to her standing by the bed. She shared about how wonderful it was to be on the other side and told me that she was always with me. She came until my daughter, Susan, was born. It was revealed that Aunt Frances reincarnated as my daughter so that she could be with me. And, Susan remembered who she was when she was young.

Another wonderful friend, Carole, who was married to a womanizing, irresponsible husband, had five children. She was killed in a car accident. She was my best friend and I was so devastated that I could not go to her funeral. But, she came to me in her spirit which was still very much intact, and told me that this was her grand plan and not to be sad. This was her gift to her husband to awaken him. And he did. He became the devoted father to those five children and honored Carole with his honorable life.

I started reading the books that were the awakeners and I have met so many other seekers who read the same ones. Ruth Montgomery's *Strangers Among Us* and *Threshold to Tomorrow, Companions Along the Way*; James Michener's *The Source*; Alice Bailey's, *The Rays and the Initiations, Serving Humanity, A Treatise on White Magic: The Way of the Disciple;* Manley Hall's *Death to Rebirth, The Initiates of the Flame;* Baird T. Spaulding's *Life and Teaching of the Masters of the Far East*, and many others. I have been rereading the Alice Bailey "*I Am*" teachings along with the *Life and Teaching of the Masters of the Far East* which has 6 volumes in all. Another amazing, must read book that I have recently discovered is by Eugene Whitworth, *Nine Faces of Christ, The Quest of the True Initiate*. About 6 years ago I discovered *"The Science of Success: The Science of Getting Rich* by Wally Wattles which he wrote over

100 years ago and it is the original metaphysical book that all the others like *The Secret* have been based on. However, no one gives Wally the credit and he was the real deal. Get his series of books and read them whatever you do – a Must!!! Another series of books which are translated from The Dead Sea Scrolls by Edmond Bordeaux Szekely are the *Essene Gospel of Peace* books with another whole host of titles by this same author. They are life-changing to read these amazing accountings of The Essene Community and Jesus' interaction with them. The book that took me years to read and it recently called to me to reread is *"The Urantia Book"* which has the whole history of all creation, the angelic realms, the history of this universe, the accountings of Jesus and his disciples. I love this book so much and hope you will find it. There are many more, and we are all led to the ones that we need in just the right moment.

We had three children, Brad, Logan, and Susan. I desperately wanted children as I needed to be able to share my pent-up love. Brad was born after seven years of marriage while in California during our seminary years and we were told that we would have no more children.

Brad came in quite aware and still awake as he remembered some of his past lives and told me vivid stories about them. He was special as many of the kids coming in are and called Indigo Children. As he grew older, he seemed to forget, but in his adult years has reawakened. He is a very special man who is a pleasure to have as a friend.

Several years later after moving to our first church (Presbyterian) in Wendell, Idaho, our local doctor asked us if we wanted to adopt a son who was in need of a family. I saw Logan in the hospital when he was 5 days old. He looked at me through the eyes of a little old wise man. We were destined to be together. From the first moment we brought him home, he fit in and was my son.

Only two months later, I was pregnant with Susan. While elated, I felt overwhelmed with having two babies in one year. Susan's birth was extremely difficult as I was very ill, but had not yet been diagnosed. Susan's rough start in life set in place a challenge that she would have to deal with later called Bulimia. She was very underweight at 4 pounds and was put in an "isolette incubator" which prevented me from holding her until she was two weeks old. These developed as patterns of not being nurtured and she felt "alone". But, remember, she was Aunt Frances reincarnated and that would be a big bond always. Susan will be an inspiration to many who will relate to her life.

I had no help from John, and no money to hire babysitters. John was now married to the church. With such deep sorrow in my heart, I felt overwhelmed with the responsibility of caring for everyone and making them happy. I was drained and in emotional turmoil. The stress of my life was setting in and my physical being was beginning to show up in illness. I had extreme colitis and could not seem to get it under control. It was debilitating.

We moved to our second church in Kelso, Washington. John was in his element. I was miserable.

When we were interviewed by the church elders, they asked me my opinion about something and I replied, "I let my husband speak for me". I had lost my confidence and worth, abdicating my throne of self-worth. That is so disgusting and sad to think about now. But, I was a different person back then.

PHASE 2: LEAVING AND EMBRACING ILLNESS

It was in those days that the first signs of illness started - the fatigue, the numbness and pain in my arms and legs, colitis, a strange strain of strep throat that lasted for a year. Every day the bright spots in my life grew dimmer. At last, there was no light anywhere and I knew I could not go on. I was suicidal, emotionally bereft, and in therapy because I could not see any way out. I saw three choices: to kill myself, to have a mental breakdown, or to leave. We went to therapy and John only went for my benefit. Of course, he felt above it because of his position of Minister of a large church. My therapist told me that it was his business to help marriages stay together, but his strong advice to me was to leave my husband. He perceived that John was not going to wake up and become aware. John was prone to throwing temper tantrums which became more violent through the years. He threw a huge jug at me that splintered the door behind me. I then felt there was nothing left. I was afraid of what would come next.

My homework from my therapist was to imagine my life without John – alone – on my own. It was incredibly painful and seemed impossible to do so. I was hardly able to speak anymore and felt I had nothing worth saying. I could only feel darkness inside me. But as I allowed myself to write down what my life could be like, I could finally envision that I was capable of being alone. Even though I was not able to know how I was going to support myself or any details, I could only faintly hear my spirit speaking to me and I knew I had to follow the leading of my heart.

I chose what I now know was the most difficult decision with eternal consequences. I left. To leave a husband, especially a minister, was bad enough. To leave your children was unforgivable. I loved my children deeply, yet I felt I had no choice. My physical and emotional state was deteriorating, and I knew that to care for both boys and my baby daughter would push me over the edge. I had no education, no recent or skilled job experience, and no money to hire baby-sitters. I made the decision as consciously as I was capable of at the time, knowing it was ultimately the only choice available in my very damaged and diseased state. And I have to say that I was not very conscious or awake during those years. Emotionally, I was devastated and reacting to my circumstances - not responding from wisdom and spiritual direction. If I were granted one thing that I could do over, it would be to have had my children with me. Somehow, that pain can never be completely healed – no matter the justification. I have not been able to fully reconcile it. I still feel it in my heart.

I will never forget the devastation as I left my two confused, crying little sons. I could only blindly stumble out of their lives carrying my little infant daughter, Susan, who would endure with me deep grief and separation through the next years. I could not bear the pain and guilt of failing my little children, whom I loved deeply, but could not physically care for. I locked the guilt and grief deep inside me in order to continue on. While I saw them often, I missed so much of their lives. I did take comfort in the fact that their father did have a stable job and I felt he would be a good father to them. I only found out a few years ago, he was not a good father. He did not step up to the plate even when I was gone. He did not take the boys to their ball games or practices. He just dropped them off and they were so very alone. He was not there for them. He continued to have temper tantrums and that was so very confusing for those two little boys to witness.

Brad and Logan, each, finally came to live with me when they turned fourteen years old. Brad came first and I was living in Sedona, Arizona by that time. I had moved to Phoenix when Logan came later. For those last high school years with them, I am so very grateful. And it has only been through the grace of spiritual understanding that I have been able to reconcile the deep grief and guilt. That higher understanding is that my children chose me and their father to come into this world through, and thereby set in motion all of the challenges and growth they needed for their evolution and soul-healing.

We all came in to heal our mother and father within ourselves. How can we hold it against our parents and hate them - because they kept their bargain with us. We forgive them to free ourselves as well as them. As long as we hold our parents in anger and hatred, we are forever tied to them and are still held prisoner. Sometimes our parents do not change or become loving. They also have their own journey and lessons.

What I have realized out of my parent's misery that continued into their aging years even unto their deaths, the lesson is to detach and not be affected by their actions. Easier said than done. It is incredibly difficult. It can be an emotional roller coaster trying to get their approval and blessing, when all the time they are incapable of giving love and acceptance to anyone. Most of what they do had nothing to do with me. When I was loving and kind to them, they were triggered by their own perceptions and patterns of their misery. Love brings up everything unlike itself. They lash out against it and push away the kindness, unable to accept and embrace it. The best thing to do is to fill your own life with lots of good things that make you happy. Most of the things I did were artistic, but, also exploring exotic places in the world fulfilled my adventuring spirit. Being in nature in some way has always been my saving grace and never fails to bring me nurturing and peace.

One thing I decided to do at one point, was raise orchids which had been a dream since I was a child. I loved flowers and used to sit in my mother's flower beds, eating roses, pansies, geraniums, instinctively knowing about herbology and the healing power of plants. I joined the Orchid Club and nurtured myself by building a greenhouse and filling it with orchids. I soaked up the beauty and healing energy of these exquisite beauties. I always have many green plants including orchids all around me. I have painted gourds, did beading, studied Feng Shui, learned how to sprout, and to cook delicious, healthy food. I served on the Council on Aging which supports the programs at the Senior Citizens Center of "Meals on Wheels" and other great projects. I was able to serve other seniors even though my own parents wouldn't accept it. The word *Ecstasy* means to stand apart – to detach. We don't always get the results we want from others, and we have to find other ways to fill those empty wounds.

PHASE 3: A GLAMOUROUS LIFE

In the years that followed my divorce, I thought I had dealt with the guilt and was done with it. But I hadn't, and it wasn't done with me. While I played the new role of single career woman, that guilt - like the resentment of the years before, ate away at my nerves to bring the days of my imprisonment closer. I kept looking for love and acceptance from others. And of course, I had the deep belief system that constantly confirmed that I was "not good enough"! So I looked at glamour and material things as power. I sought after them in my quest to prove that I was worth something and "good enough."

I soon, too quickly, married a worldly, romantic man, Bill Ticen, who I met while we were both singing in a musical. He was a VP at Burlington RR and we lived the high life, even honeymooning in Tahiti. We lived in a world of fantasy based on passion and glamour. Bill wanted the martinis mixed when he got home, and me in a negligee.

Every day I went from the fantasy of my life with him to the even more intense hard-driving and challenging world of insurance sales, and back again. As an agent with Lincoln National Life Insurance Company, I was driven by my need to prove myself. I was told by the General Agent that hired me that I would never succeed because I was just cotton fluff. But he needed to hire a woman because of EOC and, by the way, too bad I was not black, because he could "kill two birds with one stone". Imagine saying that today. I proved him wrong and became one of the top agents in the country.

My dual passions were all-consuming. I had no time for introspection and spiritual growth. The fatigue and pain got worse. When I began to complain and compensate for my symptoms, my husband refused to understand. His fantasy world did not include a sick wife. He wanted only the unencumbered, unspoiled fairy tale. He started having an affair with someone else that he was currently singing with and made excuses to be gone much of the time. I saw her in a dream and indeed saw her again at opening night of the play.

Bill mistreated my daughter, as well as my sons on their visits. Susan had to be in bed before he came home. He had no tolerance for her. If my sons were there and we were gone, they had to be locked outside so they wouldn't hurt anything in the house. That was intolerable to me. They had been through enough rejection. Our differences became irreconcilable, and I then found myself locking another door. Again I left, feeling unloved, unappreciated - and a failure.

Single again, I submerged myself in a mindless round of furious work and pleasure, interrupted only by ever-lengthening bouts of pain and numbness. I was determined to squeeze the most I could out of life. The more I experienced, the more I wanted and the more I wanted, the less satisfaction I received. I jammed my life full. I sold million dollar policies of insurance, became a top agent with Lincoln National Life and got many pats on the back. All the while, the men in the Portland Agency tormented and harassed me constantly. When I came in with a big policy, they would say, "Were you on your back when you got that signed?" I was a big threat to them. But, I loved the process of meeting new people and finding the right products that fit their needs. Lincoln even flew me to home office in Fort Wayne, Indiana to make training films about me to be used to recruit other women like me. They tried to figure out the personality traits that made me successful. If they only knew that what drove me was the belief that I was not good enough and I was out to prove myself every day.

I began feeling good about my success, though not about myself. I was advancing myself to a severe stage of Multiple Sclerosis. My left leg was almost constantly numb. I seemed to hurt all over, but especially in my legs, chest and back. It felt like burning molten lava running through my nerves. I had periods of deep fatigue when I could not get out of bed. My eyesight became severely affected, and I realized my memory was failing.

PHASE 4: SURRENDERING TO ILLNESS & DEATH

One morning, I awoke to find that I could no longer even move. Overnight, I had become an invalid. I went into the hospital and after tests, specialists, conferences and more tests, the doctor was able to "pronounce sentence." I had an incurable disease: Multiple Sclerosis. My body was breaking down. I also suffered with heart disease, Myocarditis, and had a hysterectomy for cancer of the cervix.

I felt myself swallowed up by an all-consuming fear and panic -- trapped in an invalid body. Next came rage, an anger screaming to be released. Then a helpless, hopeless sorrow. Then, something strange began to happen. I felt almost relieved-- as if a giant burden was lifted from me. The pain was still there like an irritable old friend, one that you tolerate because of familiarity. I had lived with it for a long time, and now in some curious way, I began to find my situation comfortable.

Financially secure with insurance and my illness to buffer any demands that could be made of me, I was totally "safe." I had built myself a maximum security prison. I had constructed it to protect me from the world. My life seemed to consist only of pain and pills. Intermittently, I became fiercely angry at myself, my fate, the people around me, the very world in which I was living. When my daughter had to leave me and live with her father, it was as if everything I had ever owned, loved, cherished or wanted was now taken away from me. Self-pity tugged at me and sapped my remaining strength.

To say now that I enjoyed that life sounds very strange. As bleak as it was, it seemed the only alternative to the "normal" life that had made me a mental and spiritual invalid. By comparison, the life of a physical invalid was an easy one. A fellow agent and friend, P.K. Williams, moved in, cooked, cleaned and lovingly cared for me. It was a perfect arrangement for he hated insurance sales and he loved being a "wife". It served both of us. I had the financial means to pay our bills and we were comfortable. Lincoln had made us all buy disability policies in addition to group disability insurance. I cannot say enough good things about Lincoln National Life and their support through those tough years. They sent flowers, fruit and paid personal visits to bolster my spirits.

Fortunately, rather than trying to think, to analyze, rationalize or justify - I then began to breathe - to meditate, to look within at my spiritual self. Prayer is the request; meditation is listening to the answer. Meditation and the Breath revealed that I still had one valuable treasure - TIME. I had time to stop, to get off the roller coaster, time to discover what my life really was, who this person inside me really was. I had time to discover that what I thought was

God's punishment was actually grace and love calling on me with its beckoning for growth.

When I opened myself up and surrendered to my spiritual growth, I soon connected with others who were committed to their spiritual journeys. I met a powerful and wise woman named Ama, who was with a group called *Subud*. *Subud* essentially means *right living manifested in your life through surrender and worship to God*. *Subud* is based on meditation, incorporating cleansing and purification practices into daily living. Ama shared her love, wisdom and spiritual teachings with a small group of us who wanted to live a spiritual life. When my time of initiation with Ama was complete, she sent me and the others away into the world to do our work. Ama foretold that I would be a writer and would influence many people. I never saw Ama again and I suspect that her time was finished here on earth.

There were others who influenced me and assisted me in healing. I had one dear woman who came and did foot reflexology two or three times a week. She put her love into the work. It was a powerful therapy for me. Just to receive love, freely given, is quite a lesson for most of us. We find it harder to receive than to give, especially if we believe we are "not good enough."

In the ten years of Multiple Sclerosis and three years of being an invalid, there were two experiences that have forever changed my reality. I experienced "death" twice. The first time I experienced "near death" I had had a complete hysterectomy to remove cervical cancer. After that surgery, I had an extreme reaction. Although the doctors were never able to determine the reason, I suffered an explosion in my brain, which catapulted me into a semi-coma with bouts of unconsciousness for three weeks. In that near death experience, I went to another dimension -- a place I longed for and had a faint memory of, from long ago. I was taken down a long tunnel faster than the speed of light -- the noise was deafening. The light at the end came faster and faster. I exploded with a loud noise into another dimension, a place where there was no form, only energy, THE EYE OF THE SUN, where there dwells only perfection -- a place of perfect peace, joy, all-knowingness, unspeakable love, freedom, full knowledge of Divinity. The music and colors can only be described as celestial --not able to be experienced on this earth.

I wanted to stay forever. This was the place I remembered deep in my cells - the place I longed for from whence I came. In my knowingness - I was told I could not stay -- I was not ready to return. I must complete my life on earth and fulfill my mission. I had come to earth with a purpose, but had not accepted it. I was to bring that great compassionate love - become that love - and bring people home to that love within themselves.

I was sent back into my physical body, which I hated more than ever. I didn't see the gift I had been given, but felt cursed because I wanted to be here less than ever.

About a year later I was taken down that same tunnel again. In the second "near death" experience I literally choked to death when the muscles of my throat and esophagus stopped working instantaneously. This episode lasted for about five minutes, but seemed like an eternity.

As I exploded into another dimension, after going down that same tunnel with a rush that was almost deafening and seeing the brilliant light at the end, I was surprised to find myself in a very different place, a different dimension than before. "In my Father's house, there are many mansions." There was form, much like the Garden of Eden - beautiful celestial colors and music of the soul, and throngs of luminous angelic beings. Some I knew, but all felt familiar and loving to me.

The transfigured Christ was waiting for me with that vast, flowing, compassionate presence and the most love I have ever known. There was a river both narrow and wide that flowed in front of me. This time I had a choice. I realized that all I had to do was step across the river, take His outstretched hand, and I could stay. In an instant, my life (past, present, and future) was there in front of me all at once. I was given my life review. I realized that I wanted to fulfill my destiny - why I had come to earth in the first place. I was to **Be the Light** for others to find inspiration and guidance. I must embrace life fully and completely, learn to love life - celebrate life! I **chose to live** for the first time in my whole life. Yes, this was the ultimate invitation.

    I came back to my physical life with a purpose, a surrender and a determination to become master of my life. The Breath and meditation helped me to begin to see clearly. I viewed my life as a gigantic puzzle. I saw each person, each experience, each period of my life as a piece of the puzzle. Each piece represented a lesson I had set out to learn. As the whole came into focus, I came to a staggering realization: <u>I had created it all myself!</u> I saw that what I had been interpreting as resentment of others for degrading me was actually my resentment of myself. All the destructive feelings that I had locked inside were my own destructive feelings toward myself. <u>No one had done it to me.</u> I was my own persecutor because of an unconscious decision that I was not worthy, not equal to others, not good enough. I had spent my life degrading myself. I realized that I had given away my power and abdicated the throne of my own Majestic Being. I had flung the staff of power from my hand by telling one basic, gigantic lie -- that I was unworthy to receive the goodness, mercy, love, happiness and abundance of all good things. I had forgotten my Divinity.

My whole life had been a struggle filled with strife and trouble - a death process. I had accepted pain as a way of life, pain in relationships and now pain in my body. The thought occurred to me that healing would take place when I no longer saw any value in pain. Was the pain serving me? It had kept the love I wanted away from me. All of a sudden, I saw that my sickness was my decision. I had decided on weakness rather than strength. I now decided that I wanted to be responsible for my life. I wanted to live consciously. I wanted to be healed. This knowledge was terribly frightening. It meant that there would be no more excuses.

My ego suddenly sprang into battle with my spirit. "Don't give up the disease," it argued. "Look how nice and safe it is. Everyone takes care of you and won't hurt you. How long do you think you can last in the world with all the stress and pressure?"

My spirit, on the other hand, spoke with confidence. It said, "Yes, being well will be difficult, but being well and whole is the only way you will fulfill your destiny and achieve any peace and joy in your life."

PHASE 5: HEALING BEGINS

I committed myself to healing. Lucky for me early on, I had been led to one of the most authoritative and brilliant doctors on Multiple Sclerosis who was far ahead of others in the medical field with nutritional treatment for the disease. My nutritional program, called the Swank Diet for Multiple Sclerosis (also in book form by the same name), was designed and directed by my devoted doctor, Dr. Roy Swank. It was basically vegetarian, white fish, low animal fat, no dairy, no sugar, with lots of cod liver oil every day, no prepared foods, no additives, preservatives, or chemicals, with lots of fresh fruits, vegetables, and brown rice. Yes, I missed the cheese, the meat, the white flour products and sugar. But this was my life we were talking about. Would I be willing to make this sacrifice in order to live? Was this a small price to pay? Yes, indeed, I was very faithful to my nutritional program. Later in the book, I offer much more information about nutrition and healing.

Dr. Swank was very frank with me about the emotional and mental aspects of M.S. He said, "All of you with M.S. have the same personality traits…you are all critical, overachievers, perfectionists, rigid and insecure. You need to learn how to meditate." I did not know anything about meditation at that time, but he said, "Go find out how". He did not give me instructions but rather a direction." He knew of the inner demons of insecurity and negativity that were at the core of M.S. and could only send me on my journey to explore all those self-destructive patterns set in place in my youth.

Dr. Swank also directed me to other holistic treatments. And wonderful healers showed up in my life. One wonderful woman full of love, came every few days and did foot reflexology for me. I found it hard to receive her love and stiffened when she touched my feet. It was only after months that I started trusting her and allowed the love to flow in. I had no loving touch or hugs as a child. I did not know how to show emotion of any kind. I did not know how to receive. It had been unacceptable to show or express anger, hurt, sadness and especially, joy. I became frozen.....kind of appropriate for M.S. which takes form in paralysis.

I explored many other forms of bodywork -- shiatsu, massage, acupressure, hands-on-healing, and many others. My meditations were simple at first as I had lost touch with the Divine Breath. But, when one starts focusing on connecting with God, all one has to do is open up to the Holy Spirit and it is given. In meditation, the breathing became a very important part of my healing, as well as imaging. I started visualizing myself well, beautiful and vibrant again -- free, running, jumping joyfully, tirelessly in a lush green meadow decorated with vibrant hues of all kinds of flowers. I floated through the grass like an antelope on strong, healthy legs. I began to view my sickly body as something apart from the real "me." I began to let go of pain, guilt and disease.

Three years after becoming an invalid, but improving after the second "near death experience" whereby I could get out of bed and get around, I went to a retreat in Monterey, California where the focus was forgiveness. During a meditation at the ocean, there unfolded before me the chapters of my life and all the people I had lived with in varying degrees of love, hate, hurt and need. As each person appeared, we went into the inner room of my heart where there was only the light of love and forgiveness. One by one I met them, came to terms with them, forgave them, released them and then forgave myself. I had deep grief about buying into the beliefs of this world -- about forgetting who I really am -- a spiritual being having a physical, human experience.

I cried the deep sweet-tasting tears not only of sorrow, but of released anger, pain -- and then God's forgiveness and mercy. As I cried, I began to feel light -- so light that I wondered if I still had a body. Fear returned for a brief second. I dispelled it with these words, "From this moment on, I totally surrender. I choose Life, not death!"

PHASE 6: A MIRACULOUS HEALING

As I clearly saw my spirit, I perceived what I can only call "God" -- Divine Source -- a powerful force of brilliant violet/purple energy, the Violet Flame, that moved and swirled before me. Then with a tremendous burst, this energy crackled and descended through the top of my head like an electrical current surging through every nerve fiber in my body, touching and healing every cell, every damaged nerve, every withered muscle. It moved down and then out with a powerful sound, at the same time both deafening and soothing.

This was the visitation of St. Germain, the ascended Master who is the bringer of the Violet Flame, a powerful healing energy field. St. Germain has been one of my closest Masters and teachers, still showing up alongside Divine Mother when healing is needed.

Instantly, I felt cleansed and pure. I knew that healing is very simple. Healing and atonement (at-one-ment) are identical. To forgive is to heal. I realized that, in forgiving, we return everything to a natural condition of oneness. At the moment of forgiveness, I experienced a total unity of body, mind and spirit. At that moment, I was healed. I sprang to my feet and walked -- without pain or fear or guilt -- to share a miracle with the world.

PHASE 7: HEALTH SOURCES AND PROTOCOLS

I would like to share some of my personal philosophy about the treatment of Multiple Sclerosis. First of all, I feel so very fortunate that Dr. Swank did not believe in the drugs commonly given for M.S. such as Prednisone and other steroids. He felt that by taking the drugs, every exacerbation became worse and the body had less strength to fight the disease. Since I had M.S. in the 70's, many treatments and drugs have been tried – most without much success. Now that I understand about the devastating effects of toxic metals (particularly mercury, lead & nickel) to the nervous system, I truly feel that Chelation and detoxification of toxic elements is the basic and essential treatment for M.S. and other nerve disorder illnesses such as Parkinson's, Fibromyalgia, Alzeimers, Environmental Illness, etc. I explain later in Chapter 2 about how and why detoxification works.

Nutritional supplementation is also essential. Instead of the Cod Liver Oil that I used to take, flaxseed oil (sometimes called linseed oil) is a much more potent and pure source of the Omega 3 fatty acids. Krill Oil is the best marine source of omega-3 fatty acids. However, the oils of many marine species contain toxic fatty acids as well as the effects of polluted oceans that are harmful to humans. While cold water fish is still a better nutritional choice than chicken or meat, the best source of the omega 3 fatty acid is certainly flaxseed. A nutritional analysis of this miraculous food shows that man could very nearly live wholly on flaxseeds. It offers all of the essential amino acids. If just one of the essential amino acids is missing from the diet, the resulting protein deficiency can lead to disease. The amino acids replenish the building blocks of life – protein. Flaxseed is a rich source of the important fat-soluble vitamins: A,D.E.B1, B2 and C as well as the major minerals and trace minerals. Flaxseed is an excellent source of fiber. It also contains mucilage which is the substance which reduces excess stomach acidity, soothes and lines the mucous membranes of the digestive and intestinal tracts and helps move cholesterol along. I use both the Flaxseed oil (High Lignans), as well as grind up the flaxseeds in my smoothies. In Europe it is widely used for cancer, strokes, arteriosclerosis, cardiac infarction, liver, lungs, intestines, stomach ulcers, prostate, arthritis, eczema, brain, immune deficiency syndromes and nervous system disorders. I have grown to love the taste and see it as liquid gold.

I believe that the flaxseed oil is the number one requirement for the treatment of M.S. and I recommend at least 6 tablespoons per day if you are healing M.S. I combine it with ½ cup **low-fat** cottage cheese (contains sulphur-based proteins present in abundance) and add crushed pineapple or other fruit.

Another new discovery is low-dose naltrexone which is a very small dose 4.5mg taken at bedtime and the result is the release of tripling levels of circulating beta-endorphins. No side effects have been observed and the benefit is enormous. LDN clearly halts progression in multiple sclerosis as well as many other diseases. I also think it is a great preventative substance. I like the sense of well-being it provides because the body has had the benefit of a big dose of endorphins in the night. I have tried it myself with very excellent results.It is FDA approved but is normally prescribed in larger doses and you have to get a prescription from your doctor and go to a formulating pharmacy for this smaller dose. For more information on the research and how to get LDN, a great resource to show your doctor, see their excellent and informative web site: http://www.lowdosenaltrexone.org.

I still believe that the junk foods and prepared foods are the very worst poisons we are ingesting that is causing so much toxic overload in our bodies. Certainly, when we are in the midst of disease, we cannot afford to take in any more toxins and have to be very pure with our nutrition. We have to be sure to have the right protein. I still recommend the green powder, usually a combination of many pure greens, and there are many good ones available. Salmon is also a great source of both oil and protein. Make sure it is cold water salmon and not farm-raised. I think the whey protein is also a good choice. Many with M.S. are sensitive to dairy and the rice or almond milk is a good substitute. A great source of protein is **chia seeds** which have become popular and are so simple to incorporate into smoothies, put it in yogurt, and many other ways. They are said to have twice as much protein than any other seed or grain, five times the calcium of milk, boron which is the mineral that helps transfer calcium into your bones, omega 3 and omega 6, essential oils for the body, and much more protein than meat or fish. The soluable fiber in the gel forms a wall between carbohydrates and the body, releasing them slowly into the body. This has been found to be very helpful for people who have trouble controlling their sugar levels like Diabetics. Many use the seeds as a way to control their appetites as you will get the feeling of being full.

While talking about the sensitivity to dairy, there is one blood type that is not - the B blood type. All others are allergic. I also recommend that you read the book, "Eat Right for Your Type" by Dr. Peter J. D'Adamo. I absolutely agree with this theory and it is difficult for most people to accept at first. We see it as having to sacrifice some of the things we love. However, those things are poison to our systems and why would we want to ingest poison. I believe that some foods suppress our immune system if we eat them on a regular basis. B types are allergic to chicken and corn – poison to them.

One of the foods that everyone is allergic to is wheat. M.S. patients are especially allergic to wheat. The bread that I eat is the Ezekial sprouted grain bread, which is in the frozen foods case in the health stores. It doesn't have the allergic reaction that wheat does and it is delicious. Find out what your blood type is and see what are the best foods that will support your life process.

The best guide for food is alive, fresh foods – none prepared. And be sure to have a really good, full spectrum multi-vitamin/mineral supplement that is plant based. Extra magnesium is essential for all of us as our neurological systems are so challenged. I recommend equal amounts of magnesium and calcium – about 1200 mgs per day. I take a liquid plant based mineral mix and find it very compatible with my system.

I will include many more sources, resources and health protocols later in the book which are more detailed.

There is ongoing research for the cause and a cure for M.S. One such example is the work of an Italian, Dr. Paolo Zamboni. Dr.Zamboni has put forward the idea that many types of MS are actually caused by a blockage of the pathways that remove excess iron from the brain - and by simply clearing out a couple of major veins to reopen the blood flow, the root cause of the disease can be eliminated.

Dr. Zamboni's revelations came as part of a very personal mission - to cure his wife as she began a downward spiral after diagnosis. Reading everything he could on the subject, Dr. Zamboni found a number of century-old sources citing excess iron as a possible cause of MS. He immediately took to the ultrasound machine to see if the idea had any merit - and made a staggering discovery. More than 90% of people with MS have some sort of malformation or blockage in the veins that drain blood from the brain. Including, as it turned out, his wife.

He formed a hypothesis on how this could lead to MS: iron builds up in the brain, blocking and damaging these crucial blood vessels. As the vessels rupture, they allow both the iron itself, and immune cells from the bloodstream, to cross the blood-brain barrier into the cerebro-spinal fluid. Once the immune cells have direct access to the immune system, they begin to attack the myelin sheathing of the cerebral nerves - Multiple Sclerosis develops. He named the problem Chronic Cerebro-Spinal Venous Insufficiency, or CCSVI.

Zamboni immediately scheduled his wife for a simple operation to unblock the veins - a catheter was threaded up through blood vessels in the groin area, all the way up to the affected area, and then a small balloon was inflated to clear out the blockage. It's a standard and relatively risk-free operation - and the results were immediate. In the three years since the surgery, Dr. Zamboni's wife has not had an attack.

Widening out his study, Dr. Zamboni then tried the same operation on a group of 65 MS-sufferers, identifying blood drainage blockages in the brain and unblocking them - and more than 73% of the patients are completely free of the symptoms of MS, two years after the operation.

Dr. Zamboni's lucky find is yet to be accepted by the medical community, which is traditionally slow to accept revolutionary ideas. Still, most agree that while further study needs to be undertaken before this is looked upon as a cure for MS, the results thus far have been very positive.

Of course, the emotional issues are at core cause of multiple sclerosis and I do believe there are spiritual lessons as well. This is where the Breath of Light can be of utmost importance. I think M.S. is a result of critical/rigidity of thinking, perfectionism, trying to control life and others, and perhaps an unwillingness to surrender to the will of God. Sometimes these issues are very deeply concealed and are not apparent. Resentment is a key emotion to be healed. The Breath of Light brings all this to light and is able to transmute it to a higher awareness and release. Many decisions have to be made in order to heal this devastating disease. Many relationships have to be dealt with – especially the relationship with oneself. Forgiveness and acceptance is key.

My beloved friends, this is the message. You have chosen the lessons you wanted to learn. These are Initiations. If they were not necessary for your growth, you would not have chosen the earth plane. The soul has chosen a body in order to learn mastery and the right use of it. Our outer bodies are in reality, the true shadows of our inner states of being. On changing the inner state, a corresponding change occurs in the physical body. You are surrounded by these harsh, earthly conditions so that you may learn the strength and power of Soul by handling them with wisdom and knowledge.

I have talked with many of the leaders and teachers in the Consciousness movement and because they are so caring, peaceful, compassionate and loving, one might think that they came into loving and supportive families and they were nurtured and cared for. It has been a little shocking to find out that most of us were in just the opposite families – living with brutality, violence, abuse and cruelty. It is hard to understand why we would choose such hard paths, but we placed ourselves in a lineage to heal all that darkness. Our ancestors have been waiting for someone to "WAKE UP" and bring the Light to them – the transformation for all the past souls and the future souls. It is true that when we infuse our own DNA with the Light of Consciousness – it changes everyone that we are connected with – and it raises the consciousness of the human race another notch. It is quite a legacy that we leave.

How do you feel about the Legacy that you would be leaving if you departed this earth today? Have you accomplished your mission of becoming the Divine Love and Compassion. With every breath we take, every thought, every action, belief we express....we are either adding to the Light of the World, or to the Darkness and Duality of this old earth.

What does it take to become Conscious and Enlightened? Does it take years of therapy and counseling? Maybe. I had some wonderful therapists which I am grateful for. It used to take years of processing to get past that kind of treatment and the patterns and belief systems it caused. It was a long journey home, but I have always been committed to living in the Light. Many of us – maybe this is your story – have come a long way.

I believe we are in a new day with a new edict of Divinity for all who choose it. Many have embraced the dark, evil energies and are beyond our reach. There are many "races" from other universes who are here to destroy and I do not consider them part of the human race. We have to be brave and shine the Light when in the presence of evil, calling it out and being the Light Warriors to unveil and disempower them.

It is time to walk earth back to enlightenment and to our Divine God. Each soul must walk themselves back to the enlightened state…through Initiations where karma is reduced to zero and the ego mind is completely dissolved. It is a decision. It is a commitment. It requires a daily practice and discipline of Breathing and meditation, communing with God.

Why would anyone want to go through Initiation? When we think of Initiation, we shudder and fear invades our whole being. We know it means change and entering the unknown.

What is Initiation? Initiation is the path to become a Master. Initiation is being willing to see through the illusions to truth. They are tests, challenges – which allow you to see the illusions you are living within. What are your attachments...your addictions...that you have given your power away to. It is OK to have things – to have beauty around us...but can we give it all away in the next moment? Can we find happiness without those things...cigarettes...alcohol...junkfood...overexercising... abusive relationships...electronic entertainment – our TV's, computers and phones – ipads, etc. The list goes on and on.

Take care of your body with steadfast fidelity and reverence. The soul must see through these eyes alone, and if they are dim, the whole world is clouded and distorted.

The fulfillment of our senses are what have taken us down to the very depths of existence and we no longer can feel and experience the sweet freedom of Spirit moving through us and allowing us to soar on freedom's wings.

You must enter initiation willingly. You have to make the decision to be fully conscious every moment. Ask yourself if you are awake and aware. If you have confusion or don't know....Breathe consciously, continually. It will automatically bring you to the Light. Invoke your I AM presence every morning. Be vigilant with every thought, word, feeling, action. Ask for help through prayer and listen to the answers. Be peace within. Forgive yourself swiftly if you fall short. Forget...forgive...keep walking...lean in the wind. We are almost there. We hear the Great and Divine Voice of Love inside us...that says..."Call on Me for Guidance...I am always beside you. You are never alone and you are so beloved." Our Beloved is only a Breath away.

Now, in our present time, in perfect Divine Order, we have received a gift of Light from the Heavenly Realms that has moved Humanity's shift into Christ Consciousness forward by leaps and bounds. The Divine Intent of this Celestial assistance is designed to help us reverse the adverse effects of our fall from Grace. This reversal consists of two major steps. The first step involved reclaiming the power that was usurped by our fragmented and fear-based human egos as we descended into the chaos of separation and duality. The second step involves assisting our I AM Presence to reactivate our spiritual brain centers so we can return to Christ Consciousness.

With our awakening and seeing through the eyes of Christ Consciousness, we will see the bigger picture and figure out how we can accomplish our goals in ways that will enhance life not only for ourselves but for everyone involved. With this heartfelt intention based in Oneness and Divine Love, viable solutions will filter into people's conscious awareness and they will realize that functioning from a consciousness of Oneness, Divine Love and Reverence for ALL LIFE is not only life-transforming, it is uplifting and fulfilling in wondrous and glorious ways.

Our soul knows if we are fulfilling our Life's Destiny and purpose. If not, we have a nagging sense of incompleteness and emptiness – we are not happy and dissatisfied with our lives. It is our time to choose the Light or the shadows.

CHAPTER 2   HEALING: AN ONGOING JOURNEY

The very powerful healing experience occurred in August 1979 and was truly the beginning of my healing. Although the healing was dramatic in terms of physical renewal, there was still much healing yet to do in my life - patterns - belief systems - emotional trauma - spiritual immaturity - and all of it was on such a deep, subconscious level that I did not know how to get to it. All I knew was that I was very depressed and unhappy. My whole life was severe and full of struggle. I did many workshops, personal growth trainings, read every book I could get, went to personal therapy and therapy groups. I gained much knowledge and understanding, but I realized that I was still dealing with my problems from a mental place. How was I to get down to the cellular level where this "stuff" must be coming from? I found I continued to <u>react</u> to situations in my life and did not seem to have the ability to <u>respond</u> with any power, or make any decisions from wisdom.

My daughter, Susan, came back to live with me after a painful separation. That was a very happy day for me and for her. I had missed her so much, but could not take care of myself, much less a child during the dark days of my illness. It had not been a happy experience for Susan to live with her father for those years and she lost her self-confidence. John had married a woman with 4 kids and her kids were favored, with my three kids being neglected. It has been very noticeable and made a mark on them with their self-worth.

I moved to San Diego after a brief stint in Yuma, Arizona as I had met Terry Cole Whittaker at Asilimar when I had my miraculous healing. Terry had a Science of Mind Church and it was in its early stages with only about 50 people. I loved Terry's brilliant sermons and felt a kindred spirit with her. There were many classes and opportunities for growth. The energy of the people fed by Terry's enthusiasm was a fit for me. I found a community home.

Someone recommended that I attend Actualizations with Stewart Emory, one of the first EST trainers who left and felt the very aggressive and confrontive training could be done more gently and with more compassion. I did the training and it was life-changing for me. So many of the self-destructive patterns that were driving my life were brought to light and processed with competent, compassionate and firm trainers in addition to Stewart.

One of the trainers, Frank Natale, had founded the Phoenix House in New York City. He was a straight shooter and I had a chance to become his assistant trainer. I had never experienced anything like this in my whole life. I took the advanced trainings and then enrolled for the year-long Leadership training. I had no idea what I was in for. It was a huge Initiation and was designed to go to core, face any and all limiting belief systems, break down and then conquer all the fears that came up. There were 12 of us – 10 guys and 2 of us were female. We met every Friday evening not knowing what would be the test or challenge. We were told to keep our whole weekend free in case it took that long. Many times, we were not able to go home until we completed the test and there was no sleep for days. Those grown men broke down and cried during those processes. One by one, they broke and left. At the end of the year, there were only 3 of us. I remained to the end and triumphantly finished the course. At the end, I knew that I could do anything that I choose to do. There is a price to pay, but I can do it. It certainly gave me a new confidence and the ability to process people with laser like clarity coupled with compassion. I learned about truly "listening " to people on all levels, seeing their energy bodies, watching their body language, and helping them navigate through layers of emotional baggage which had kept them in a self-limiting box. I knew personally about it all.

I reconnected with Subud through the group in San Diego. After a few months, they elected me the leader.

Pak Subuh, who is fondly called "Bapak", the founder, was Muslim because of being born and living in Indonesia, a Muslim country. But, he never encouraged anyone to become Muslim. He advocated for all to stay with your own religion.

The word "Subud" is not directly connected with Pak Subuh's name, but is an abbreviation of three Sanskrit words: Susila, Budhi, and Dharma. In Subud, these are approximately translated as follows: Susila means right living in accordance with the Will of God; Budhi means the inner force residing within the nature of man himself; Dharma means surrender and submission to the Power of God.

Bapak unexpectedly received the latihan for the first time when he was 24 years old. Latihan means "training or exercise". He explained (in talks to Subud members beginning in the 1940s) that he was taking a late-night walk when he had an unexpected and unusual experience. He found himself enveloped in a brilliant light, and looked up to see what seemed like the sun falling directly onto his body. He thought that he was having a heart attack, so he went directly home, lay down on his bed, and prepared to die. He had the feeling that maybe it was his time and that he could not fight it, so he surrendered himself to God.

According to his explanation, instead of dying he was moved from within to stand up and perform movements. It seemed that he was not moving through his own volition but was being guided by what he interpreted as the power of God. This same kind of experience reportedly happened to him for a few hours each night over a period of about 1000 days during which he slept little but was able to continue working full-time. He said he experienced a kind of inner teaching whereby he was given to understand a variety of things spontaneously. As these experiences proceeded, Pak Subuh explained, he gained spontaneous insight into people and situations that he did not possess before. This experience, now referred to as the latihan, is a meditation for purification.

Around 1933, Bapak eventually became aware that he was to pass on the latihan to others. He realized that if other people were physically near him while he was in a state of latihan, then the experience would begin in them also. While still in his early thirties, Bapak's reputation as someone with spiritual insight apparently grew, and people went to him to be opened. In time they also were able to pass on the experience, and the latihan spread throughout Indonesia by word of mouth. In 1957 Bapak was invited to visit England and this is when the development of Subud as an international organization really began. But as Bapak himself put it: "[the latihan] is not foreign. It did not originate in the East and it did not come to the West ... it comes from the Spirit of God, which is nowhere a stranger."

There is much that needs to be put right in us, and this correcting is done in a way that we could not possibly do for ourselves. No teaching, no imposed discipline and no imitation, but only the Power of God, can penetrate to the level within us at which this work must be done. Only God can know what is necessary for each of us. This is why there is no teaching in Subud by man to man; God alone is the teacher. This process of purification is a gradual one and goes according to the needs of each individual, his capacity to receive it, and his willingness to accept it.

The power that works in the latihan is infinitely strong, but it forces no-one against his will. In so far as we accept and submit our own will to the Will of God the process goes forward. It begins on the physical level and frequently results in an improvement in physical health, but its action can never be predicted. All that can be said is that each one receives what is truly right and necessary for oneself, so long as one truly surrenders and submits one's own will with patience and sincerity. The rate at which purification proceeds varies for each individual and cannot be hurried or assisted by any efforts on our part. All that we can do is to accept what we receive and to refrain from wrong behaviour that might undo the work that is being done within us.

The first part is very active, moving, shaking, expressing sounds, and speaking in strange languages. That lasts for about 15 minutes and then the energy changes to a very still and peaceful place. One then sits down and is in a receiving state for information and guidance. Men, being of a more aggressive nature practice the Latihan in a separate room from the women.

The San Diego group was split in a divisive group that wanted to be Muslim and practice that religion. I stood up against that and even wrote a letter to Bapak about the problem. He answered that we should not focus on being Muslim but stay with our own religion. I was not popular with some of the members.

Ama, my teacher who initiated me into Subud, had brought me and the small group of devotees into a powerful teaching and testing process. The tests were given as Initiations to learn about self-limiting beliefs of what we think we can do, but in the process, we learned that our capabilities are much more.

Each time we did food fasting, or sleep fasting, or other tests, we learned that we can expand our energy bodies and experience other dimensions and conquer many fears and belief systems.

Ama was very different than any others in Subud and she did this special teaching with the blessing of Bapak. There came a point when she announced to us that we were complete with her and that we were to disperse and go into the world to share what we had learned with others. Ama was in Washington state when I knew her. I do thank her from the depths of my heart for her strong and powerful teachings and the Initiation she gave me.

PHASE 1: INITIATION INTO THE SACRED BREATH

We got an announcement that Bapak was coming to Los Angeles for the first time to visit the U.S.A. He invited us all from all the states to join him for a national conference and he would do the Latihan with us. It was to be on July 30th which is my birthday. That night in the wee hours, I was awakened with a visitation from Bapak. He said not a word, but reclined the full length over my body, and placed his mouth over mine, breathing deeply into me several times. He said, "I gift you with the Breath". I did not really know the importance of that at that time until much later.

The next day when we were gathered in the huge ballroom of about 1000 women, Bapak came out on the stage and moved over to the right side where I was seated. He immediately locked eyes with mine and gazed into my eyes with purpose and I received his message. He knew. And, I knew. I was initiated into the Breath that day on my Birthday. What an amazing gift.

Soon after, I had to leave the Subud group because of the dissension in the group. I did not want to practice a Muslim life. I cannot be tied to any structured religion, especially Islam and all the laws which demean women. However, I continued for some time to practice the Latihan meditation for purification.

PHASE 2: LOOKING FOR LOVE

I married two times again -- both times short-lived and tragic. My third husband, Tom Kittle, lived on the beach in Del Mar, was a caretaker on an estate and also taught Judo. What I did not realize was that Tom was alcoholic and violent when drunk. He was able to drink quite a lot before he was drunk and then his behavior was altered. We had some fun times at the ocean on his catamaran and picnics on the beach.

He was able to keep his secret for a couple of months. It was Thanksgiving when the incident happened. Holidays often bring up past misery and memories. He started drinking early and left, while Susan and I prepared the turkey dinner. He came back late in the afternoon, very drunk. I was horrified. He was belligerent and started a reign of abuse, first verbally, then physically, hitting me and beat me very badly. He was a big man and physically very strong – a warrior trained in martial arts. Susan called friends and Tom left. They took me to the hospital and talked "straight turkey" to me on that Thanksgiving. I got some counseling and good advice. I realized I would not live long if I stayed with him, and therefore, I left, even though my heart ached with compassion and unfulfilled love for him. I did not understand the alcoholic personality, but did realize that I could not help him. I could only leave. We were married for a very short time – about 6 months. In the meantime, I moved to Sedona, Arizona from San Diego.

While in San Diego, I had started a little cottage based company, *Magic and Miracles Company*, producing a line of Magic Wands which had cards of affirmations for a range of wishes ie: love, health, wealth, etc. They were sold in many gift boutiques nationwide. I even produced a special version for a benefit to honor Mary Martin and the theme was, "The Magic is You, Mary Martin". I was invited to the event and met many stars including Mary Martin. It was thrilling to see all my Magic Wands on all the tables as part of the centerpieces. I then came to a fork when I realized that the necessary expansion would require big scale manufacturing in China and needed an infusion of big money. I was not interested in going in that direction.

Just before I moved to Sedona, I was introduced to David Harris who had orchestrated the Mandala Conference for 14 years and it had become the premier health conference, drawing 4,000 plus attendees. The leaders in the Health and Spiritual fields were the speakers and seminar leaders. It was held in San Diego annually. David was interested in my story about my personal illness, death experiences and miraculous healing. He was guided to ask me to be the keynote speaker and do the healing service for the 1983 Mandala Conference. There would be 4000 people there. This was my introduction to the speaking circuit. I prayed and asked how I could possibly give the audience a true healing experience, not just a nice speech. I received from Spirit to do a multi-media presentation. I had the idea to tell my story to beautiful, mystical photos of nature that would represent the emotional and spiritual journey of my life. Dick Canby, a photographer in Sedona offered his beautiful photos to create a slide show which I set to music. The slides dissolved into each other on 3 large movie theater style screens. I spoke live as the music and slides played. The Holy Spirit descended and enveloped the whole audience. At the end, there was not a dry eye and at the end, people were on their feet responding to my Ultimate Invitation. It was like an old time revival with people shouting and crying. I stood there for 2 hours while a line of hundreds of people came to hug me, touch me and declare their commitment to their life purpose. People still talk about it after all these years. I was asked to return the following year in 1984 for the final Mandala Conference to lead the Healing Service again. Again, even though it was a different program, it was a repeat of the powerful and moving experience for everyone there.

After the conference, I enjoyed some amount of fame and had a whole new group of friends and colleagues. I met Mark Victor Hanson and Jack Canfield, authors of Chicken Soup for the Soul, Jesse Stearn and the Edgar Cayce ARE Clinic people. I spoke at the ARE Conference that next year. I was introduced to Tony Robbins and he actively recruited me to work for him in PR. I hung out with Tony, did his seminars and firewalk, flew to Aspen, for a conference at John Denver's place and spent quite a bit of time together. Ultimately, I did not feel to go to work promoting him. I felt there might be some personality conflicts. I have tremendous respect for Tony as he has helped thousands of people with a powerful program. I was also asked to start speaking on the Whole Life Expo circuit, Focus Expo, Body Mind and Spirit and other expos.

When I moved to Sedona, I started a magazine, *Call of the Canyon*, that became quite successful and was on all the newstands in Arizona. In the beginning, it was a little newsletter with the purpose of connecting all the New Age activities in Sedona. There was a lot going on in the early 80's and Sedona was still pure and not impacted by so many tourists as well as the trendies that trekked there from California. They changed the energies tremendously.

PHASE 3: NATIVE AMERICAN SHAMANIC TRAINING IN SEDONA

Sedona is a place of Initiation. Sedona calls to you and brings you there for healing. When she is done with you, she chews you up and spits you out. But it was an amazing place in the 80's. I met Willie White Feather who became my shamanic teacher and we spent several years together. We went up on the top of mesas out in the canyons, did ceremony and spent all night with the visitations of many spirits. It was not for the faint of heart. He taught me to watch the signs of the birds, the animals. Willie was Cherokee blood as I am, and he was Hopi trained. He knew Grandfather David, who was once the leader of the Hopis and was 103 years old when I met him. Willie had the gift of prophecy and also loved nature and the healing powers to be found there. Willie was despondent over the fact that the leaders of the Native Nations were not able to get along and cooperate. He also felt that many had lost their connection to their spirituality and spiritual life. I was able to visit the mesas and villages, finding that was indeed true. Gangs have infiltrated the reservations bringing the drugs, alcohol and violence. Respect for nature has been discarded. There are still some who are true to their ancient voices and are wise teachers. We found it quite humorous to realize that there is some criticism of whites embracing native ceremony and teaching about the ancient ways. Funny, because as we know, we have all lived before and many of us whites were Indians in previous lives and the Indians were whites. Karma has been paid as we have lived again over and over.

I definitely have full memory of a life as an ancient Indian woman married to the Chief in the Oak Creek Canyon area of Sedona. The Chief started having visions of a flood coming through the canyon. He was hard headed, however, and would not leave. I found it on me to gather my courage and lead the tribe out of the canyon down to the Carefree area just north of Phoenix. The Chief drowned in the flood and there was nothing I could do. Our lives were hard when we moved from our home territory, but we survived. My son then became the Chief and guided the tribe with much wisdom.

I have met Willie White Feather through the years in unusual ways. One instance was when I was in San Diego driving on the freeway with a friend. For some reason I started telling her about my time with Willie and his teachings. I looked over to my right side and saw a red pick-up truck with a canoe on top. I realized it was Willie. We waved wildly and pulled off at the next exit. Big reunion with much hugging and exclamations. We went to a coffee shop and had a wonderful visit. He was going to speak at a conference as he often did. He wrote a book of his prophecies and I always remember that he said that the number 14 is special and to always look for 14 – taking note of happenings on that day. I moved away and in the ensuing years, did not connect again with Willie. I trust that he has been out there living his mission.

PHASE 4: CALL OF THE CANYON

As I got more experience with publishing, the newsletter evolved into a full color magazine, "Call of the Canyon", promoting artists and photographers. I would partner with art galleries to feature one of their artists on the cover and we would hold an Open House for the featured artist. It became the party to go to as we had catered food, music, and lots of fun. I attracted many famous writers like Hugh Downs, Sri Chimoy, Spiritual leader at the U.N., Robert Muller, Assistant Secretary General of the U.N. and others.

My own writing ability was deepened as I realized that the name of the magazine was not just accidental. When I read some of Zane Grey's books, I realized that he was writing through me and had guided me to choose the name of his most famous book. I met with the family in order to get their blessing for the use of the name and they gave me some original photos of Zane Grey that I often printed in the magazine.

The magazine was growing and was on every newsstand in Arizona. I was motivated to move from Sedona to Phoenix in order to do the marketing and advertising sales that was needed to support the magazine. Little did I know what was developing with the magazine.

I walked into America West Airlines office soon after they emerged as an unusual business paradigm of an employee-owned airline. They were guided by CEO Ed Beauvis, and I asked for an appointment with him to do a story for the magazine. He walked right out of his office and was most enthusiastic about me meeting every level of management and employee for personal interviews. We set up a date for those interviews, and also offered me the chance to fly on the airline, anyplace they flew. I chose to fly to Colorado to see my parents and it was a fun flight. My article came out in January, 1984 and they were most pleased. They said they were looking for someone to do their in-flight magazine and asked me to give them a proposal. I put a team together with a top advertising agency, which was essential for international advertising. I was at the top of their list to do the in-flight magazine.

At that same time, I received a call from the CFO of Valley National Bank who invited me to come in and have lunch with some of their management. I was taken to the top floor of their headquarters in downtown Phoenix. They had a beautiful table set for four of us and a lovely lunch was served. They said they wanted to show me their private art museum which contained many art forms from Arizona artists that they had sponsored through the years. Indeed, the whole bank building was decorated with great art from local artists. They had a proposal for me.

The owner of the bank lived in Sedona and had been watching the progress of the magazine. He liked it. They wanted to do a soft PR campaign to reveal their philanthropic projects mentoring artists. They were allied with Carl Eller who owned Circle K's and would put in special display racks for the magazine. They offered me $250,000 to do the project. I asked them what this would be: a loan, a joint venture, an investment? They said it would be what I wanted it to be. They asked me to present a proposal about how I would spend the money. I am still in wonderment about that. I have never heard of a bank doing such a thing. However, I have always had such magical things in every endeavor and have been blessed beyond practical understanding of how things can work. All things are possible. We just have to focus on the end purpose and allow all things to come to us.

However, when good comes to us, the tests and Initiation also comes. We call it all in. It is a strengthening and purifying force in order to become free and fully conscious.

The fourth marriage was truly the most devastating relationship in my whole life. I married Gary Hubbard, who set me up and turned out to be one of the best "con" men ever. The *"Call of the Canyon"* magazine was headed for the stars. I had known Gary years before when I was his insurance agent and we had dated briefly just before my illness retired me. He had been a successful developer and I had faith in his ability as I had witnessed his ability to make millions. When Gary appeared once again in my life, he saw the opportunity that I had created. He convinced me to do the creative part of the magazine and let him take over the business portion, and take over, he did. Although short lived, the long reaching consequences of the damage he did ultimately changed my life. The bank and American West Airlines had based their decisions on their trust and faith in me. They believed that I could do it. But, when they met Gary, they smelled a rat and withdrew after several meetings with him. He did not want me to attend the meetings, saying that men can talk in a certain way when a woman is not present. I felt uncomfortable but let him take charge. Everything fell apart. And, Gary bought a house out in Cave Creek with my money for a down-payment but he never made another payment. He planned it and had a scheme to declare bankruptcy, including the house. I left as I could not be part of his scheme and ended up losing everything. This marriage ended in 1984 after only 5 months, and that was when I knew I had to heal on the cellular level if I was to continue on, alive, here on the planet. I tell you all this to share that I have been there as many of you have, and some still are - in destructive relationships - unhappy and, as it turns out, addicted to suffering and living in a victim consciousness.

PHASE 5: LEONARD ORR AND REBIRTHING

I met Leonard Orr, the founder of Rebirthing, shortly afterwards when he came to Phoenix for a seminar. I felt the rebirthing was my next step in healing. And, Leonard needed an editor to help publish his next book. He invited me to come to Campbell Hot Springs in the mountains above Tahoe, California. I went there to help edit the book, but his assistant quit and I was handed the job of administrator and ended up running the center.

The healing center was a Babaji ashram community and even though Leonard was one of the most eccentric people I have ever met, living in a spiritual community was a wonderful experience. I learned about the importance of having the elements built into everyday life in order to detoxify and heal.

First thing in the morning, we went to the wonderful healing hot thermal springs that flowed into hot tubs set in the open woods and breathed in the hot water. Then we went to temple for meditation. The fire pit which was kept burning 24 hours a day was our next practice and learned the power of purification with fire. It was a great blessing to resolve conflict and anger through the power of fire. We then could go to breakfast which was lovingly prepared by members of the community. We all rotated through the roster of the duties required to keep the community functioning. Even guests at the center were required to do "karma yoga" which were the chores that were accomplished in only a few hours of the day. After that, we were free to pursue our spiritual practices and healing process. We exchanged sessions of energy, massage, breathing, and counseling.

My daughter, Susan, joined me there for a year and she still says that was the best year of her life. She longed for the family experience and we had a big family there. There were problems between the members, but it seems that our environment which was committed to healing allowed the process to happen more naturally. The experience greatly influenced me when I built my own healing resort later in Rockport, Texas

I also met Sondra Ray who was a co-founder of Rebirthing and she taught me the water rebirthing which I loved very much. I did many of her trainings which were more organized than Leonard's. He did not like to interact with people and only showed up briefly at the beginning of the seminars, allowing the students to do the Rebirthing sessions.

After I felt competent to do the work on my own, I moved back to Phoenix and set up a private practice to do the Rebirthing and energy healing work. I also embarked on one of the dearest relationships of my life with Raymond Doss, who was committed to his own healing and spiritual growth. We spent several years together and I count it as one of the best and successful relationships I have ever had. We learned from each other and shared many things, including Rebirthing, detoxing and meditation. I loved Raymond, but my destiny eventually called me and I had to move on. We are still great friends today and acknowledge the journey we have shared.

It was when I found the breathwork in the form of rebirthing that I started to really heal my enormous personal belief that I WAS NOT GOOD ENOUGH! As I facilitated private rebirthing breath sessions with hundreds of people, I healed, also. The breathwork started changing quite visibly -- the first manifestation was that the people I was breathing and myself, as well, started becoming dolphins, whales, looking into the eye of the whale - and always feeling this great loving energy of these wondrous beings. I observed the results of these experiences as being life changing - always profoundly healing. While I did not understand this phenomenon, I had the good sense to "allow" it to happen. The Breathwork kept changing, quite drastically.

PHASE 6: DOLPHINS – MY NEW TEACHERS

I was given a whole new energy and work that was far beyond rebirthing. This was totally related to dolphins and the unspeakable love they embody. The breathwork evolved into a very advanced spiritual, compassionate, gentle process: a process that brings us into the Light and changes the frequency of our being - so that we become a matching frequency of the Light. This particular work brings you home to the love and restores your true identity. I eventually was told that the work I was being given is about Theta and not so much about breath, although Breath is the gateway to Theta. The first stage of my work was called, "Dolphin Breath". Later, I was given the information to name it Cellular Theta Breath of Light. And, as you will read later, Divine Mother changed it to Breath of Light.

I am often asked how my work is different from Rebirthing. In the Rebirthing process, you are kept breathing constantly, through the whole session. This becomes very painful and often has no resolution. I have come to realize that breathing activates the deep cellular unhealed patterns and emotions. We need to get in touch with the emotions and allow them to surface. However, we need to then go into the integration and healing place of Theta. And that comes in the Breathless state, where all the past - all our history - can be transmuted in an instant.

I carry a different energy field with this Breath of Light that is indeed a transmission of Light. As the Breath changed, a different breathing pattern emerged. And the frequency was raised - it has continued to be raised higher and higher through the years.

The dolphins told me that I was to come learn from them and my apprenticeship as an Initiate with the Cetacean Nation began.

I started my dolphin/human interaction/Breath work in the mid 80's and gained quite a lot of recognition as a pioneer with this work. I met many great people including Ric O'Barry who had been Flipper's trainer, but later became the leader of protest movements for the mistreatment of the dolphins by the military and also captivity facilities. Ric has been arrested many times for releasing dolphins that were being held captive especially at military bases. Ric and I became buddies and often spoke together on panels at Whole Life Expos and other conferences. He was committed and caused much public knowledge and exposure of the mistreatment of dolphins and whales. He advised me later on a project that I was working on in Arizona.

One day, I received a phone call from a caller who said his name was Drunvalo Melchizadek. He said, "I understand you are working with dolphins and the breath". I said that I was, and the next thing he said was, "Well, get in your car and get yourself over her, now!" It was a command and I did not even question it. I said, where? He told me that he was just north of Taos. The next day, I was driving in my car over to see him. He had a visitor there from Australia who had this unique very large book that was called "The Legend of the Golden Dolphin" done by the Aborigines and it told in pictures the journey of the dolphins from their universe to this earth. It was remarkable and I will always feel blessed to have had the chance to read that book and to feel the energy that it carried. I learned a lot, and also had much of the information confirmed that I had received from the dolphins.

PHASE 7: DIVINE MOTHER – THE NEW GUIDING ENERGY OF THE BREATH

When I was visiting with Drunvalo at his home in New Mexico, I received a visitation whereby Divine Mother (the feminine aspect of God) came to me and said that she was now the guiding energy of the Breath of Light. She altered the pattern of the Breath and gave an essential piece that opens the heart and the throat. Once again, the Breath was changed and I am only a witness and caretaker of this holy Breath. The Breath of Light is working to restore the feminine energy to the earth and bring both male and female energies into balance. Divine Mother and the host of angels that she brings continue still to direct the work and bless us with the divine compassionate love.

After several years, I received a very direct inner command to start teaching this Breath of Light healing energy to others. I felt the world had to deal with the emotions in order to finally move to the next level.

I developed a training that was designed to train and teach the Breath as a healing modality for therapists. I realized that I could not "breathe the world" by myself. I was assured by my inner spirit that I would be able to impart both the knowledge and this special healing energy to others who were ready. The qualifications were a loving heart, a willingness to serve, and a personal commitment to grow and evolve.

I was speaking at expos all over the country and attended one in Denver with a booth next to a wonderful woman, Karen Stewart who was promoting her company, Kare Products. We immediately connected and she invited me to Boulder to do a Breath of Light event that she would sponsor. She did a marvelous job and the event was well attended with great healing and results. Several of the women who attended asked to be trained as practitioners and we scheduled the first 10 day training there. In addition to Karen, Janet McCabe and Maryanne Hastings were among the committed and became part of a 1 year long leadership training and an integral part of my work for many years. All of our lives were enriched and changed as we journeyed together to the deepest cores of our beings to discover the truths and untruths held there in cellular memory. They were the first to go with me to swim and interact with the dolphins in the Bahamas. They assisted me in further trainings in Boulder, Tucson, Florida, and Mexico. They have many fun stories about me if you are ever to talk to them. I must admit, I have to laugh at myself as well.

About this time, I was shown a vision of a project I was to develop. Part of that vision included human interaction with dolphins. It was a powerful vision and was called "The Desert Dolphin Project." The original vision showed dolphins in the desert -- thus the name. I realized that there were once dolphins where there is now desert, because it was all underwater eons ago. The vision was a transformational project. I spent many years swimming and diving with dolphins in the wild, as well as at many of the facilities in the world, especially in the Bahamas, Belize, Roatan, Florida and Mexico's Sea of Cortez. I also took scores of adults and children with me, and they were all impacted by this most incredible interaction with dolphins. Many were healed, and all of their lives were changed in some way or other.

When I first started learning from the dolphins and doing human/dolphin interaction workshops in 1986, it was not the "fad" that it later became. There were the facilities in the Florida Keys, which provided the opportunity for visitors to get in the water close to dolphins. A good one was The Dolphin Research Facility and had fantastic programs with autistic children and dolphins. Also, they provided a good facility for the dolphins and allowed us to come in with set boundaries to protect the dolphins. We had many good experiences there.

One of the things that has always remained a curiosity to me and others is that many of the humans in charge of the dolphins at the captive facilities are very dysfunctional, off-balance people - some even bordering on cruelty and violence in their personal lives. One would think that the caretakers of the dolphins would be the kindest most healed people on the planet. In fact, many of the people in "dolphin kingdom" are among the most competitive and non-supportive that I have encountered, frequently denying the intelligence and sensitivity of the dolphins, and considering the dolphins as simply toys or "property."

The only explanation that I can come up with is that these caretakers have put themselves in the position to be with the dolphins because they need the healing the most. In close contact with the dolphins, they have frequent opportunities to learn about love, forgiveness, and cooperation. As the old saying goes, we teach what we need to learn the most. I know that I have continued teaching healing because of my continued commitment to my own healing.

I have also known dedicated, open-hearted caretakers who truly love the dolphins and serve as ambassadors of the dolphins' teachings. Many of us have realized that **we are to be the new dolphins – to be that dolphin energy!**

I began going to the UNEXO Facility on Grand Bahama Island, and observed the process that Mike and Jeannie went through to train the dolphins to go out into the open ocean to dive with divers. I was privileged to go on some of the first dives. On one of the first dives, a whole pod of wild dolphins came in, curious to see what was going on. Mike would have held his breath if he had not been diving - for fear that his dolphins would take off with the wild pod. It was a great interaction, and in the end, the dolphins chose to stay with him. I have wonderful video footage of that happening.

At first, I went alone, by myself in order to receive the teachings from the dolphins that I was to share with others. I took my daughter, Susan and also, Logan, my son for the experience with the dolphins. I am sure that has impacted them their whole life. Then, I took many groups for the dolphin/human interaction trainings that I did in the Bahamas, staying at the Grand Bahama Hotel, going to UNEXO for our dolphin adventures. Many people of all ages went there with me for awesome experiences. We combined the Breath of Light with our ocean adventures with the dolphins. We would Breathe and go into theta in order to communicate with the dolphins since their brain waves are in theta all the time. They would send me a hologram of where they would meet us, how many of them, and how long before they would be there. The captains of the boats that I chartered were in doubt and then awe when the scenarios unfolded just as I was instructed to tell them.

There were many instances when the dolphins would sonar me and infuse me with their consciousness. They taught me of their mission to come to earth from their own universe of love and take on the dense forms, first in the shape of a four legged, much like a dog, but could not bear the density of the earth. They were allowed to EVOLVE to the ocean- to the water which gave them more freedom. I can totally understand that and I, too, love being in the water and on the water more than anything. That is where I am most comfortable and happy. At least, I need to be by water somehow.

On one expedition to the Dolphin Research Center in Florida, one of the women was rammed by one of the dolphins who was never aggressive. It was serious enough that she was sent to the emergency room for an X-ray. There was a large tumor right in the area where she was rammed. It might not have been discovered had not the dolphin pointed it out to us.

I took many expeditions down into the Caribbean and these were some of my most rewarding and fun experiences. In my estimation, the best facility in a "captive" category is in Roatan. *Anthony's Key* is a diving facility with the dolphins' habitat in a very large bay of the ocean. The facility has an honest-to-goodness educational and research focus and I liked the people in charge there very much. They stood out as unique amongst all the caretakers that I have personally met.

PHASE 8: MOVE TO MEXICO

During my dolphin journeys, I discovered a beautiful villa on the ocean in a little fishing village, Puerto Penasco, in Mexico. The villa became my healing center and training facility for the Breath. I named it Delphi Sea Sanctuary and since we were on the Sea of Cortez, I chartered the first dolphin expeditions with the local fishermen. I quickly became "infamous" as they thought I was "loco," going into the open ocean and calling in the dolphins to swim with us. This had never been done in the sea there. But the dolphins had taught me how to call them in by sending them a holographic image of us and the boat, and then breathing into Theta to connect with them. Always, before entering the water, we did the Theta breathing and because of that, we had highly successful encounters -- The dolphins always told me how many of them were coming to see us, and where they would be - directing us to the area of the ocean where we could meet. Therefore, even with the wild dolphins that do not normally connect closely, we would often have hundreds of dolphins show up.

There were times when I would hear the dolphins calling as they were about 200 feet offshore. I would grab my fins and swim out to meet them to play and cavort with them. They knew me and came often. There were many sharks in the area, but I never worried as the dolphins would protect me from them. They have done so many times for people and saving their lives.

PHASE 9: DOLPHINS AND BELIZE

It was hard to communicate with me in those days, as I did not even have a telephone. However, one persistent man did track me down, as he had an important reason.

His name was Al Dugan, and he owned an island, Blackbird Caye, in Belize. Al was diving one day and a pod of dolphins came. He had a powerful encounter in which they gave him a vision and awakened him to who they are. He told his son Patrick about his vision, and Patrick had recently attended one of my Dolphin Breath workshops at the Whole Life Expo in Los Angeles. Patrick told his father, "We have to find Mary, as she is a key to this vision." It took them several months to get a message to me in Mexico. Al invited me to come to his island in Belize, which I did. He had kept it very organic and primitive in order to preserve the natural experience there. After going there and sharing our mutual visions of dolphin/human interaction, I took a group there, and we had an extraordinary trip that we will always carry in our hearts.

The island has a natural barrier reef outside with a small opening that allows boats into the entrance of the island. There is a long dock for the boat and we found it to be a great place to go out and breathe and send messages to the dolphins. One morning, we were rewarded when a dolphin came into the dock. No dolphins had ever come inside the reef before. We jumped into the boat, and followed the dolphin, who led us to his family. His mate and their baby played with us for hours. They, too, had long awaited the connection. Al has shared with me that they continued to have many interactions, and groups have had extraordinary dolphin encounters there.

We combined the dolphin encounter trips with visits to the Mayan pyramids. Much ancient Mayan information and energy is coming forth to direct us in this dimensional shift that we are experiencing at this time. I also connected with a dear sister, Dr. Rosita Arvigo, who was doing important work at her compound, Ix Chel. Located on the western border of the rain forest in Belize and next to Guatemala, Dr. Rosita studied with one of the last living Mayan medicine men and Curandero, Don Elijio Ponti. Ponti made his transition -- but not before giving Rosita the ancient teachings and secrets into her trust for safekeeping. Rosita is a white woman from Chicago and had a Naturopathic health clinic there. She is an unlikely candidate to take on the label of Curandera, but she wears it well. She created the Ponti Medicinal Trail preserving the herbal plants that have healing properties. She showed me a very poisonous plant, but growing right next to it was the anecdote. She said "Nature is like that". Rosita's lifestyle, combining simplicity and beauty, has inspired me to always incorporate those qualities into my life. No matter where I am, I know that I could indeed live in a grass hut with a dirt floor and be happy. We have been so entrapped by materialism and our constant drive for "success" that we have lost our connection with what is really important.

Eating the live food from the garden at Dr. Rosita's was a revelation. The lettuce was so full of life, it made my mouth tingle. I had never eaten vegetables that tasted like those which were organic and just not possible to buy in stores. The memory of my Mama Smith's garden was revived there at Ix Chel and I realized that we have to grow our own food if we are to have real nutrition.

Dr. Rosita also taught me about "spiritual diseases" such as hatred and a critical nature -- with envy being the toughest to overcome. I had an assistant with me on one of my trips who was envious of me. While I knew this, I had no idea how devastating this was, until Dr. Rosita pointed out that the physical problems I was experiencing were a result of this. My assistant, Margarite, wanted to be like me, to be me, to have the "beingness" that I have, and the gifts that come with paying the spiritual price of admission. This consists of constant discipline, purification, and surrender to a spiritually directed life. This initial attraction and desire on her part turned into envy, as she did not want to pay the price herself -- and her ego convinced her that if she could "kill me off" in a sense, that she could have my gifts. Because I loved her so deeply and saw the "potential" in her, I was persuaded that in time, she would make the shift for herself. Dr. Rosita gave me some very important advice on this occasion. She said that once the disease of envy and negativity becomes full-blown, it takes a powerful event in that person's life to heal it. She perceived that this woman would not let go of the envy. Sometimes, we cannot help others to make the shift, and we have no choice but to let go of them.

Many of us are finding this true in our lives, daily. While the results of breaking the ties with these people are often painful, it is the only way to resolve it. They, then, many times, seek revenge - which was true in my situation. You will find that you have to love these people from afar, hold them in your heart, and the Light of awakening. We have to keep going toward the Light and not waste our energy in defending, retribution, or convincing these people, some of whom have been our family or our friends. I can say, with full confidence, that the dark energies or people who are servants of these negative forces will never truly harm us, unless we believe that they can. It is very important to heal the patterns around this scenario, which, are about wanting others' acceptance and approval. We can never come into full empowerment and do the job we came here to do as long as we are on the never-ending roller coaster of these self-destructive and counter-productive reactions. I have had very good teachers in this process.

Most of my adult years, I had very little to do with my Father and Mother as I chose not to accept their abuse. Even with short visits, they always proved to be disastrous as Al was on a mission to destroy me. Every visit was horrendous. He never failed to tell my children that they were no-good worthless pieces of shit. And, I was the whore of the devil. So, on that note, we would pack up and take off. No happy memories for anyone.

Because we are processing many kinds of energies and at times are in physical danger because we are bringing in a different paradigm and the old paradigm is fighting and screaming as it feels the loss of control and power. We need to know that we are protected by the Light and the Ascended Masters are with us at all times, but will show up if we are in a precarious position. I had an experience that gave me the full confidence that this is true.

PHASE 10: ENCOUNTER WITH ASCENDED MASTERS ON A MOTHER SHIP

I was up in Pine, Arizona for a writing retreat and was offered a remote cabin to stay in. I was alone and there was no one anywhere around. The bedroom was a full glass wall looking out at a vast expanse of wilderness and sky. I went to sleep and was awakened at about 3:00 am by a powerful light shining in through that big window. I stumbled out of bed over to the window and looked up, seeing only that light. The next thing, I am beamed onboard and in the presence of Ascended Masters and celestial beings – Elohim, Elijah, Zoran, Jesus and St. Germain. I was awestruck at being in the presence of such brilliant light beings. They told me that they had come to reveal themselves to me and that they would come whenever I was in great danger and needed their help. They wanted me to know them and what their presence felt like. They told me how to call them in, but only in extreme cases as they are very busy these days. Note: I have called them in only when my life was in extreme danger and they came, bringing the force of their power to the situation. They told me that they were going to put me back into the bed and had much to transmit to me about other things. So, the next thing I was conscious of was being in bed, glancing at the clock for the time of 3:15am and then going deep into a state of receiving the transmission they gave me. I am not afraid and know that I am in the arms of the Beloved Ones and they keep me.

I have had to call them in a couple of times when I was in real danger. One time was quite dramatic and there is no doubt that they saved my life. Some teachers say that everything is love and light and there is no evil. However, I can attest that there is darkness in this world and some people are given over to it.

I was speaking at a Whole Life Expo in Boston with 200 people in the audience. Afterwards, people could sign up for a 10 day training with me in Mexico. I did not have a chance to know the people who signed up until they arrived in Mexico. One young man, Michael, was among the group and I had a bad feeling about him. My place in Mexico was remote and had no telephone. On the first day of the training, I chose Michael to do the healing demonstration on as I wanted to handle whatever he was dealing with. Immediately when Michael started doing the Breath, another entity within him was activated and became very agitated. He spoke in a very deep, loud voice and I also was able to see what Michael had been sent to do. He was part of a satanic cult dedicated to destroying the Beings of Light. He was trained to use his hand like a knife and go into my chest, pulling my heart out, destroying me. He had killed before. I knew I could not go into any fear or I was a goner. I called in the Ascended Masters and they came immediately. I also saw the Dark Masters that Michael served and they were tall, hooded beings that were horrifying, emanating evil energy. The Light Beings directed me and I just kept talking to the Michael who once was owner of his body and spirit – just telling him that he was safe and that he could come into the Light for protection and free himself of those dark, fearful beings. After 3 hours of holding Michael in the Light with the protection of the Masters, he finally broke through, weeping and declaring that he wanted to live in the Light.

Michael ended up staying with me for over 3 months as he needed the safety and nurturing that I could offer him in my Sanctuary. I learned the terrible story of Michael's history of being a very young child given over to the Satanic Cult by his mother and being with other children initiated into a life of darkness and fear. Michael just kept breathing in the Light and finally was strong enough to reenter the world. He did continue with therapy when he went home, but he stated that I had saved his life and he would be forever grateful.

We are not victims and can call upon the Ascended Masters for protection and guidance. Just Breathe the Light into your being and enter into the streaming Consciousness of your I AM Presence and make the call to the Brotherhood of Light on behalf of the mankind of Earth. When the call is made, the Ascended Masters can give more assistance to the Sons and Daughters of God than otherwise be possible. We have untold power available to us, and we forget to ask, to pray, and to listen. Breathing and meditating allows us that entrance into the power of the Divine.

PHASE 11: COACHING TO BE A WORLD LEADER

It was through the coaching of my mentor, John Cundiff, that I finally was willing to reconcile these patterns of wanting approval and subjugating my own divinity and power to others. It set me free to become a true participant as a world leader to bring about a change here on the planet. I hired John to be a coach and I thought it was to learn about administrative leadership and business practices. Think again! Little did I know that his goal with me was to take me from victim thinking to an empowered place. And, true to form, because of that, a powerful Initiation was given to me in order to purge my strong desire to have people's acceptance and approval. John was there for me in a great way when the news media did an article that was both slanderous and damaging to me and the project. I had fired one of the principals of the project because he was undermining me and trying to get rid of me with my investors. They were my friends and told me what he was doing. There is no fixing something like that. You just have to get rid of them. But, he responded by going on a vengeful rampage. He called the newspaper with lies and diverted the positive news article they were planning. Many people called the paper trying to get them to not print a negative article, but the media loves controversy and does not care who is hurt.

The article came out with my photo on the front page and 3 pages devoted to dolphin abuse and negative responses to captivity of dolphins. Our plan was to bring dolphins that were already in captivity and damaged by being in terrible environments. Ric O'Barry was working with me to create a wonderful rehab place for the dolphins. We knew they would probably never be able to return to the wild as they were too conditioned. However, the article was misleading and slanted. John Cundiff called me when it hit the stands and asked me what I was doing. I said I was hiding in my closet and never coming out. He said that he had the margaritas mixed and to get over right then. When I arrived he had the article - all three pages tacked up on the wall. He handed me a margarita and said that we were celebrating. "Do you know how powerful you are to create your picture on the front page and three pages all about you? This will be old and forgotten three days from now. They will only remember your beautiful photo on the front cover." He insisted that I go to Unity Church the next day and so I did. People made comments like, "That was a great photo of you in the paper" and no one even really read the article. And, it was forgotten. A waste of energy to buy into the fear and shame that it first brought up. Thank you, John, for being there to hold me up and make me remember who I am.

PHASE 12: CONTRERAS HOSPITAL IN TIJUANA– OASIS OF HOPE

Soon after, I reconnected with Dr. Francisco Contreras at a Cancer Conference and we had a long talk. He could see how the Breath could help his patients and invited me to come join their staff.

When I was invited to join the Contreras staff at their hospital in Tijuana, I left my sanctuary and Point of Light I had set up in the fishing village. Dr. Francisco Contreras was the Director of the hospital and his brother, Ernesto, Jr. was also working there. They were the sons of Dr. Ernesto Contreras, Sr., who was the founder and pioneer of the hospital as well as the research work with laetrile and other therapies for cancer treatment. Dr. Francisco Contreras, fondly known as "Paco" is the most brilliant doctor and surgeon that I have known. He trained in Vienna as a surgeon and he and his wife, Rose, would have stayed in Europe as they loved it and Francisco can certainly be called a renaissance man. He is a most remarkable surgeon, innovative in pioneering techniques such as the lumpectomy rather than radical mastectomies. The family needed him to administrate the hospital as Dr. Ernesto, Sr., was semi-retiring and needed his sons to help him.

Dr. Francisco was also doing work with Live Cell Therapy and rejuvenation therapies having trained with Dr. Hans Nieper and other pioneers in this intriguing field. I was pursuing my continuing dream of building a Spa-Clinic and I wanted to learn from him. When we first met, we had a mutual connection and Dr. Francisco invited me to join his staff there at the hospital to use the Breath with his patients, especially to manage pain. He also encouraged me to put in place a full holistic program of therapies that would support the alternative cancer treatments they were administering. After evaluating the nutritional programs needed for the different cancer protocols, I wrote a manual with menus, recipes, and the shopping lists needed. This was all translated into Spanish for their kitchen.

Massage, Breath Classes, Cellular Theta Breath of Light Healing Sessions utilizing the Breath and energy, Art Therapy, Foot Reflexology, Acupuncture, Cranio-Sacral Therapy, Bach Flower Remedies, Ozone Therapy, Colonic Hydrotherapy, Detoxification Program, Nutritional protocols for the Hospital kitchen, Stop Smoking & Substance Abuse Therapy were some of the health services that I was instrumental in establishing as a Body – Mind – Spirit program. It was so exciting to be able to put into practice in a very practical way all the things that I had trained in and learned about. Most exciting was the support that the Contreras family gave me and the wide range of freedom they afforded me. They were very open to trying new, innovative techniques.

Most of the patients came to us after being told they were terminal – "no hope". They had had every kind of invasive and sometimes unwarranted treatments as well as surgeries, which left them permanently damaged. Even though our treatments for cancer were successful, the patients were left with the results of invasive treatments such as over-radiation. They were just burned up and suffered terribly. In the U.S. when a patient learns they have cancer, they become an experiment. Unnecessary treatments are prescribed in the name of getting the maximum insurance payment they can – while they can. Most doctors see cancer patients as terminal, so why not? However, a famous Arabian physician by the name of Alrazi, during the first century, shared this philosophy with his disciples: *"The doctors must take care of patients faithfully and thoroughly, even if the symptoms forecast impending death, for the body can receive life from the spirit."*

Dr. Ernesto Contreras, Sr. founded the Contreras Hospital with the philosophy of treating the patient, not just the disease. This is only possible when a special blend of science, medicine, faith, hope and compassion make a vital and lasting connection. This can be done only by a total care approach of Spirit, Mind and Body. He said, "We know from our experience that treatment of the mind, body, and soul are consistent with reality. Time and time again, we've seen cancer arrested for years and then come back when an individual has experienced extreme stress or anxiety."

Best of all, for me, was the Breathwork that I got to do with the patients. I offered a Breath Meditation Class twice a week and oftentimes the companions attended as well. Many of the patients were having to withdraw from morphine and had intolerable pain. Morphine steals the will of the person and they have to have their will in order to heal. Dr. Francisco had seen that the Breath would be a great way for them to manage their pain. It proved out to be true. Dr. Francisco exclaimed to me one day, "Do you know what the most important thing the Breath does?" He then shared that it changes the PH balance from acid to alkaline in just a matter of minutes. This is profound. The body has to be in the alkaline PH balance to heal. It is extremely difficult to get your body into that alkaline level. The Breath can help you to manage the PH as you can easily breathe throughout the day.

The other gift it gave to the patients was to allow them to perceive other options and awaken to the real power they had to take back their life. Many were in jobs they hated, dysfunctional relationships, harboring resentment, guilt, deep-seated anger which all led them to death and disease. When they became aware that they were responsible for their condition, they started making changes, which led them out of their valley of shadows. Sometimes, a patient did not want to make the life changes that make healing possible, instead clinging to their ego driven pride – not forgiving – not letting go of whatever or whoever. They would rather die than let go. And sometimes they did. Others were given the vision of a higher life and meaning, choosing the Light. They started on their healing journey. Other factors in their lifestyle change often meant incorporating more alive food, to their nutrition, adding exercise, putting more fun in their lives and of course, breathing for relaxation every day. I can truly say that I felt greatly fulfilled and rewarded more than I ever had. The work there at the hospital blessed so many and healed scores of patients. It also enabled many in their transition as they passed over to another dimension. It was also a great source of strength and comfort to their companions and families.

While my work continued to evolve more into the Holistic healing field, partnering it with the more medical models of treatments there at the hospital, I was more convinced than ever that we have to treat the whole person – not just the symptoms.

While in Mexico, I was sponsored in a very special individualized program that allowed me the privilege of getting my Naturopathic Degree. Some of the training was in Merida at an institute and some of it was hands-on apprenticed training under the tutelage of wonderful healers and the doctors at Contreras Hospital. My previous training in many modalities was incorporated as it was all pertinent. It was a great time in my life and I was so blessed by all my teachers.

During those years in Mexico, I was traveling to Belize, and Florida to lead Breath of Light Certification Trainings. I was speaking at Whole Life Expos and other conferences from coast to coast. I met a wonderful friend in Key West, Dawn Chorley. She and her husband owned a beautiful private resort called *Kelapa* – which became a perfect center for teaching the Breath of Light Training to healers . While in Florida, I chartered boats with Captains Victoria, Tom and Simone who specialized in ocean/dolphin experiences.

The first time I went out in Key West waters, a mother dolphin came to me (in the Theta Breathing) and told me she was bringing a whole pod. But they were far away and it would take them 45 minutes to get there after our arrival at the designated place. She also said she would give me a sign that I was on course and everything was being given as needed. The sign would be when she would show me her baby dolphin. She had said to have patience and wait. Captain Tom was growing impatient, but I implored him to stay. Sure enough, they showed up right on time. We were able to get in the water, with one of them coming right up to my assistant, Amy, and me -- looking at us in the face and then sonaring us. After several hours, we finally climbed back on board and then *they* came alongside the bow -- the mother and her baby. They turned over to show their undersides in a gesture of love and tenderness. I knew in that instant, it is all very real - we are doing our job - we are being given all that we need - just when we need it. It was a great confirmation!

There was much spiritual understanding transferred to me when I was working with the dolphins. The main teaching and reason for the vision was to give me the spiritual understanding to share with humanity about the great need for us to evolve to a collective consciousness. If humanity does not evolve to this consciousness and join together for the good of this planet, rather than living self-serving lives dedicated to greed, we will not make it as a species. The other part of the teaching is to stay in our hearts and allow ourselves to feel and express our emotions.

No matter how far we go with technology and science, in the end, we will come back to the wisdom that it was love all along that was truly important. Nothing else matters except this.

"Man was made in the image of God." I do not believe that this refers to the physical image, but to the soul or spirit or mind. Every one of us was entrusted at birth with a precious fragment of the Divine Mind to develop it for good or evil. That we may know how to develop it for good God in His infinite wisdom gave us the pattern whereby we can keep alive this precious birthright -- the Divine spark within us.
Cecil B. DeMille

In the last months of my time at the Contreras Hospital, I was inspired to update and rewrite the first version of my book, *The Last Breath*, and renamed it, *Breath of Light*. I self-published it and printed it in Mexico. The book has been a blessing to the work and helped so many people understand the healing process so much more, giving them insight as to the power of the Breath of Light.

PHASE 13: TIME TO LEAVE CONTRERAS FOR OTHER PARTS OF THE WORLD

After I left the Contreras Hospital, the next chapter of my life led me to one of the most intense, profound and difficult times of my whole life. I knew what was before me was going to be very difficult and challenging. I had no idea how much this would demand of me, and what an initiation it would prove to be. While I loved the Contreras Hospital and my work there, I suffered burn-out. I lived, breathed every waking hour at the hospital. And Spirit finally said, "It is time to go". I did not even know why I was being led to leave, but it was indeed time to take the Breath of Light to the world.

I first went to Phoenix and then Flagstaff briefly. I was so blessed to be with my dear friends, Willie and Jane at their creative studio on a ranch in Flagstaff. I have many fond memories of sitting in front of the fire, snow piling up outside, sharing tea and deep conversation. I felt a sense of family, which is rare and precious. It was a gift to prepare me for the coming venture.

I had some disturbing news while in Flagstaff. My youngest sister, Theresa, was murdered. She was born 20 years younger than me and I did not really know her as I was gone from home. She had lived a very troubled life as an "only child" who was alternately tormented and spoiled.

All of us other girls were already gone from home. Theresa had so much going for her – beauty, talent as a musician- popular-intelligent, but she was so troubled by trying to please a father and mother who were playing out their own sick war games. Theresa wanted their approval so much that she went to extreme lengths to get their acceptance. But, no matter, it never came. She was desperate for love and fell in with pals who were drug users – marijuana, cocaine, crystal/meth, and others. She had graduated from the university with a journalism degree, but was living in total degradation. Eventually, she became a dealer and manufacturer to support her habit. Theresa shorted 3 people $50 in their order. They returned for vengeance and shot her to death. She was 33 years old.

I thought this would be the wake-up call for our father, but he never claimed any responsibility for Theresa's tragic life and death. Mother knew, and suffered deeply and never really recovered. She manifested Renal Cell Carcinoma (kidney cancer) because she was really "pissed off" about Theresa's death. But, their life continued on as usual.

I, next, went to Pah Tempe Hot Springs in Hurricane, Utah, hired to create a spa with services in addition to the healing thermal pool they had. I held a Breath of Light Training there at that facility and met some lovely people from Las Vegas, which led me there for about 6 months in order to meet and train other healers in the Breath of Light.

Again, I met some precious people and the work spread. While in Las Vegas, I met Cherie Smylie from Albuquerque who became trained in the Breath of Light as a healer/practitioner. She, her husband, Tom, and daughter, Jamie, were going to Europe for a year to look at different lifestyles, feeling the need to simplify theirs. Through her encouragement to take the work to Europe, I started opening to the new mission of going abroad in order to heal old dark and deep wounds in Germany and some of the other ancient sites. Germany was the place chosen first because a man who lived in Hannover experienced the Breath of Light through Cherie Smylie, while in the U.S. and wanted to sponsor me and my work there. He promised that I would teach at the Naturopathic School and could stay with him. I took two assistants as we were expecting a full regime of teaching, private sessions and workshops. A week before we were to depart, he stopped taking my phone calls and literally dropped off the face of the earth. I was distraught, but Spirit said to go anyway. Through Cherie's help, we located a woman in Hamburg who was willing to rent us her basement to stay in, and she spoke perfect English.

I went to Hamburg, Germany first in December of 1996. The man sponsoring me turned out to be the catalyst to get me there. Isn't that the way many events and people turn out to be for us in our lives? We think they are betrayals or catastrophic events. Instead, they are closing doors that need to close, turning us in a different direction, or, maybe, even are angels orchestrating a blessing in disguise – gently guiding us in the unfolding of our destiny. And we are tested in order to awaken to all the dark unaware parts of our self, healing and strengthening our human self as well as our immortal soul. I felt quite abandoned and alone when I got there, but I was guided all the way.

I found my way to a metaphysical bookstore, *Wrage*, where the owner, Jurgen spoke English. Jurgen welcomed me with much enthusiasm, but was dismayed that I had arrived in December when they were totally immersed in Christmas promotions and sales. Starting up promotion in December is impossible. But, Jurgen volunteered his workshop room and said he would help by distributing my fliers at Wrage. He was not hopeful that we would have very many people at that time of the year. I knew that if I could get just one person to experience it, they would tell many others. Five people came to that first evening workshop and as I expected, they were absolutely ecstatic – telling everyone. I scheduled the next workshop January 8th there at the Wrage and quickly redid the flier, which we had translated into German.

PHASE 14: GREECE – REVISITING PAST LIVES

I went to Greece for the Christmas holiday season as it was very inexpensive compared to Germany. I also had a date with destiny there as it turned out. The first week was spent in Athens exploring the beautiful ruins and sites, which resonated deep in my cells. I went to Epidaurus and the places where Pythagoros, and Asclepious had been. I remembered so much from long ago and felt that I had come home. I then went to the northeast island of Chios close to Turkey. I had a contact there and a distant relative as well. I fell in love with the land and the sea. I felt that was the place that I wanted to spend more time and started looking for a little villa.

I returned to Hamburg, Germany in time to do the January 8th workshop, which was attended by 28 people. Again, they exclaimed that they had to have another one so they could bring their friends. (The next one in March had 52 people and all of a sudden, I was so booked with private healing sessions and workshops, we always had a waiting list.) I met a wonderful couple at the second workshop, Joachim Blunck and Jeannette Kollien who invited me to come stay with them when I was in Hamburg and also to do the private healings in their lovely home. They were such precious beings of light and tremendous support for me. Later, they took the Breath of Light Training as well.

In the meantime, I traveled back to Greece to explore my connections there. In February, after another trip to Chios and Athens, I felt compelled to travel to Delphi on the bus. There was a very handsome man sitting across the aisle reading a book by Rimpoche in English and as it turned out was from Amsterdam –his name was Paul Splinter. We kept glancing at each other and were very conscious of each other's presence even though he "appeared" to be reading that book. We were the only two that got off at Delphi and struck up a conversation as we walked up the hill. I had reservations at a hotel and Paul was checking out the possibilities. Later as I sat on the veranda of a local restaurant with the sun setting and the breathtaking view all the way down to the ocean, I heard a "Hello there". It was Paul. We shared the sunset and then later went to dinner. We ended up talking until about 2am. We met the next day to tour the ruins and temples together. It was quite an emotional time of cellular remembrance for both of us. I remember being an oracle at Aphrodite's temple and how I hated being drugged all the time in order that they could get their information from the spirit world. I think that is why I am so adverse to any kind of drugs today. I like being fully conscious. I had no life of my own and hated the dark, dank caves below where the ethers rose up that I had to breathe and inhale in order to become "intoxicated". I knew exactly where that cave used to be under the temple. And when we went up to the stadium, Paul's eyes clouded with tears of memory and he remembered the games that he participated in. The memories are so alive in those ruins and one cannot help but be stimulated with ancient memories.

Paul and I were quite inseparable and he had to leave earlier than I to catch a plane. He invited me to come to Amsterdam to visit him and continue our relationship.

I wandered the streets of Delphi ending up at the Xenia Hotel. One of the waiters at the restaurant sat down and visited with me. There was no one there at the time and the staff is so much more casual in Greece. He asked me what I was doing there and I told him I was looking for a place to bring people for a training. He immediately called the owner who was down in Athens and came to tell me that Panos would be there quickly. Panos had instructed him to put me in a suite and make me comfortable. The waiter had given me a tour of the hotel and I was greatly surprised to see a spa facility in the making, but not being used. I was out at the pool when Panos walked up. He was a short, handsome Greek man, full of confidence and energy. I asked him why he had not done anything with the spa and he replied, "I have been waiting for you to come, in fact, I have been waiting for you for 2000 years". The Greek men are so romantic, but so married, too. So, Panos wooed me to help him set up the spa and I also agreed to have a training there and help him market the beautiful hotel. He had built a small amphitheater just below the hotel which looked all the way to the sea with a breathtaking view. That amphitheater is where I held a training later in the year. Panos had me stay at the hotel for awhile and then gave me a villa to live in. I had already located a furnished villa over on the island of Chios, and I found myself back and forth between these two magical places.

In Delphi, I met so many amazing people as I dined with Panos every night. People from all over the world came to the hotel and I sat as Panos' hostess and assistant entertaining them. And on Chios, I had met some lovely people. I fell in love with the villages, which turned the clock back about 100 years and the sea that sparkled like a million diamonds. I met an American Greek woman, Anna, who had actually been to one of my workshops in New York at the Whole Life Expo years ago. She and her family really took me in and introduced me to village life and the customs of the Greek people. I loved the simple lifestyle. I had many rich experiences and got to see Greece in a way tourists never do. Anna loved the Breath of Light and eventually got trained in the work at Delphi. We held meditations and breathed at the sea many times. I knew I was opening a portal of Light there for not only Greece, but Turkey. There is so much old trauma, hate and anger in that part of the world. But, I had to be very careful because there is so much suspicion and fear in the people. Rumors grew about the American blonde witch.

Some of the local women were coming to the meditations and they were being set free from their bondage, and they were changing. Of course, their husbands did not like the idea that they were becoming free and liberated. We had to stop inviting others and were only able to do the work ourselves, quietly. It can be quite dangerous there as a person could just disappear and never be found. I got the strong message that I was in danger. But, the work was done. I met a few more spiritual people, but not many.

The Greeks are very disconnected from their spiritual heritage and are immersed in materialism. I found it very difficult to integrate into the Greek culture, especially being a single woman. The women are very suppressed and because of that, full of resentment and anger. The men all have mistresses and the women just have to put up with it. They looked at me and could only imagine that I was there to take their husbands. They shunned me. But, they are unable to form a real sisterhood with each other, because they are so mistrustful and angry. The men have one thing on their mind when they look at women. Women are not respected for their minds or abilities. Thus, the hotel owner put a lot of pressure on me for sexual favors. I could not deflect this and finally gave up the project as it was too stressful for me. He was not aligned with me in a spiritual focus and it never works when partners of any project are not aligned.

However, I did much good work and experienced amazing events there in Delphi. We had a summer festival in July where we honored a great Greek poet and his wife. Musicians and performers were invited from all over Greece. We had some of the events at the ancient stadium with the full moon rising and the music of Vangelis. I could feel the ancients speaking to us of lost mysteries and great beauty. This will be in my heart of memories forever.

I went back to Germany to continue my work. I made plans to go to Amsterdam to visit Paul, and as it turned out, to open the work there.

PHASE 15: BACK TO GERMANY

I was sponsored in Munich and a whole new chapter opened as people flooded the workshops – the very first one had 52 people there. Again, I was hardly prepared for the flood of people that came for the private healing sessions. Many of the people that came were the children of the Nazi's or had relatives that were connected with the holocaust. I saw that we were healing the deepest, darkest, wounds of this century.

I was invited to the Hotel Gutshaus Stellshagen, a bio hotel, on the North Sea owned by Gertrude and her husband, Dharma. We did a wonderful Breath of Light training there and I loved the place so much. I was invited to come, stay and work, but I knew my destiny was calling for me to spread the work everywhere.

I was asked to come to a thermal spa hotel in Bad Sulza (formerly East Germany) and I took a group for a detox retreat experience. They had built an indoor thermal/saltwater pool which had speakers in the water for sound, and the most incredible thing, - lights, colors, dolphins and whales swimming across the round ceiling creating a multi-media, multi-sensory experience. There was a recording studio connected which I went into while the couples were breathing in the water, and led them on a mystical journey with sound and music. It was a marvelous experience and led to a series of return trips to Bad Sulza.

Again, they wanted me to come reside there and do my work. I met Elaine Thompson there, from England who pioneered a very powerful work using sound vibrations from your voice and determining which notes were missing. When the missing notes were given to you via a cassette that you listened to for a period of time, those patterns were healed. It was like the missing links were given to you. I had an analysis done by her and then later by Veronika Pennekamp, her assistant. It was very powerful for me and they found that the missing notes for me were the notes of my father. I think that was a huge revelation for me. I listened to those notes for a long time and I feel there was a huge shift in me towards my father. I do not need him anymore, nor his acceptance. I am complete with my own father/mother energy.

I spent much time in Munich as my base. I was so fortunate to be offered beautiful places to stay while the owners were traveling. I lived so beautifully there and met the very best people who were seekers and certainly here to heal themselves and the planet. I thank Steven Barrett and also Helga Macko, who were instrumental in making sure I was in lovely homes and took such good care of me always. I stayed with Steven most of the time and he became such a wonderful friend. We toured Germany together and he opened the beauty and history of that country to me. Steven and I have continued to visit through the years and have had amazing adventures together, both in Europe and in Texas. He became my assistant and translator at all my events. Steven was a dancer at the time that we met and was with a professional group in Munich. He was deeply committed to his healing and spirituality. More than that, he had such a beautiful spirit and heart, and he became a dear spiritual companion who I love deeply to this day. There are those rare beings who come into our lives with such a strong connection that it can only be called Divine, and Steven is one of the ones who has touched my life in a powerful way. He now teaches Yoga and uses the Breath of Light in Munich. He gives his testimony at the end of this book.

We had a training in Munich with about 12 people. Many of this group have been ardent supporters and completely committed to bringing this work to all of Europe. Another wonderful woman, Henny Van der Horst who lived in Holland, was a loyal supporter and was among the group that came to visit me in Texas. She stayed with me at the Sacred Sanctuary and helped me put in the garden and other projects. Henny loved to work – especially close to the earth.

PHASE 16: AMSTERDAM – GREAT WORK AND A GREAT ROMANCE

I finally made my way to Amsterdam to visit Paul. It was wonderful to see this marvelous man in his homeland. He loves Holland and had a great time showing me his country. I was told about a local bookstore, Oibibio's, which was sponsoring workshops. I went there and met the owner, Ronald Jan Heign. He had a huge vision and was happy to promote me as a healer that would benefit Oibibio's platform. I was booked for a workshop a few months later. And it gave me a reason to return and see Paul. The work exploded in Holland, demanding that I return often to do the private sessions as well. I did 52 private healing sessions in a 6 week period. It almost killed my physical body as I had to process so much energy and hardly had time off to recuperate. A wonderful networker, Jill van Maasdijk, Publisher of the *Shield of the Command News*, was very moved by the work and did a wonderful job of promoting me in Amsterdam. She kept me booked with the work as well as arranged for many workshops.

A lovely Dutch woman came to me after one of the workshops and said that I was the "one they were waiting for." She explained that a very beloved healer was critically ill and dying. I knew immediately that it was the "dark crystals" that had been implanted in Atlantis and had remained with her etheric field through many incarnations but had been activated because she had raised her frequency in this lifetime. When activated, they are designed to stop the person by manifesting as illness and even to destroy the person by death. They were implanted in the ones who would come back to bring the new paradigm of Light and Enlightenment to humanity. The Dark Ones knew that we would return one day to finish our work.

I have had full memory of that lifetime in Atlantis where I was a very great and beloved healer in a temple where we used crystals, energy and many other technologies as well. We were a triad of healers. I was a female with two men and we started playing games with each other and it graduated to sexual seductions. There is no place for those deviations and distractions in a healing temple. We sunk to such debauchery that we lost our focus and started making mistakes, harming our patients, and then some of them died from the mistreatment. We were so deviant that we were unable to be clear and mentally stable. We decided to hide and bury our "mistakes" in the catacombs below our temple. That is how crazed we became. But, the city fathers decided to do excavation in the catacomb system and discovered our evil deeds. We were brought before the Tribunal Council, stripped of our healing ability and nobility. We were then given to the Dark Ones in the Catacombs and lived a very pitiful life. We were also implanted with the Dark Crystals as they knew we would come back to redeem ourselves at a future life. A friend was able to carry me out to a monastery where I died shortly afterwards.

A dark crystal activated when I became a healer and started raising my frequency. I was in so much abdominal pain that I thought I might have to go to the hospital. But, my inner voice said that was not the solution and I called a friend who was also a healer. She came and we started breathing deeply and bringing in the Light energy. We were both shown what it was and then the Dark Ones appeared as they were guarding the crystal and making sure it was left intact. We had to bring in the Light Angels, St. Germain, Archangel Michael to help us and Metatron showed us the formula to remove the crystal. We followed the directions and removed it, with immediate relief from the pain and anguish I had been consumed with. Afterwards, St. Germain anointed us and bestowed upon us the Authority to remove the dark crystals in other Lightworkers. And, that was the situation with the healer in Holland.

So, of course, I was happy to get on the train with Connie and go across the country to see the healer who was dying. Connie explained that a healer had come from Peru and had seen the crystals and started to remove them. But, she also saw the Dark Ones appear and realized that she did not have the authority or power to remove them. But, she saw that there would be a woman healer that would come and remove them. When I walked into that healer's room I knew that she was critical. Her kidneys and liver had shut down and she was days away from death. I did not know if she would survive. I was only able to remove 3 of them that day as it is like psychic surgery and it is a shock. I told her that I would be back in 2 weeks to remove more. She actually did survive and I made two more trips to remove all of the crystals. She recovered fully.

I did much of this work for the people in Holland and Germany. It is extremely taxing for my own energy to do the removals and it almost took my own life after years of the work. I have been led at times to do this life-saving service for some of my beloved healer friends.

PHASE 17: CORPUS CHRISTI - THE SEASIDE SANCTUARY CLINIC AND RESORT

I met so many wonderful committed people who wanted to do the work. I knew that I was to bring the people to the dolphins in Corpus Christi, Texas. I had been receiving from Spirit that it was soon time to return to the U.S. and that my work in Europe was almost done. I knew I wanted to be on the Gulf Coast close to the dolphins and the water. I visited Corpus Christi, which is aptly called, "The Sparkling City by the Sea" and fell in love with it. I felt more at home there than anywhere I have been. I was drawn to the little towns across the bay such as Port Aransas, Mustang Island and Rockport. There were no really adequate facilities to do the trainings, but I did find a very large beach house at one of the resorts in Port Aransas which would suffice. I was also exploring the bay and interacting with the local dolphins. I have been many places to meet dolphins, but these were the friendliest and they were more abundant than I had seen anywhere. Must be because they are Texans. The people were also very friendly and dolphin-like. I knew that this was going to be home for me.

I did the first training in Port Aransas in December of 1998 with a total of 20 participants – almost all of whom were from Holland, Germany, Belgium and a few from the U.S. I had 3 great friends as assistants, Dawn Chorley from Key West, Cheryl Smiley from Albuquerque and Steven Barrett from Munich. Irene LeRoi was in that training and would become a wonderful assistant and healer. She eventually moved to the Sanctuary and helped me clear, dig, and build on that wild, raw land. I value her friendship forever.

This training was a most successful, easygoing and life-changing for all of us. And, I probably had the most challenges I have ever had during a training. I only returned from Europe four weeks before the training in complete burn-out from that tour. I went to New Orleans for several workshops and private sessions. I returned for one hour and found out that my mother had been rushed to a hospital in Dallas by ambulance with a life-threatening brain tumor. I caught the next plane from Corpus Christi and arrived in time for the surgery, which went very well. They traced the origin of the cancer to her left kidney. They scheduled the surgery to take the kidney out in the middle of the training (my worst nightmare fear). First of all, I would have preferred to have a chance to treat it alternatively, but many times, our own family is our biggest opposition to believe in alternatives. I stayed after the brain surgery and started juicing, doing special tofu/whole food nutritional drinks to counteract the effects of the radiation to the brain that was being administered for 5 weeks.

When I returned to Corpus Christi to prepare for the training, it was at Thanksgiving and my three children were flying in. Two days before, the owner of my condo I was leasing showed up at my door with a court order to move back into the unit – part of his divorce settlement. So, my property management company helped me find a new house the same day, still close to the ocean – on a canal with a boat dock. I stayed up all night packing, moved the next day, stayed up all night unpacking and picked up my kids the next morning for Thanksgiving. WOW! I surely did a lot of breathing to get me through that intense time.

A few days after my kids left, people started arriving for the training from Europe as they came early to rest up from jet lag. I was running to the airport as well as all my friends to pick up 23 people. When the Leadership with my assistants began before the training, I was completely in overwhelm. I knew I could not do the training in that shape. I breathed and surrendered. The angels moved in, my assistants rallied, and the participants all took 100% responsibility for their process. Not one person projected any negative energy to me or anyone. This was the first time this had ever happened. There is usually one person that wants to play out their victim game. I can only say that I feel blessed beyond belief to have experienced this and feel something shifted in me for this to have happened.

Another miracle happened. We, (the participants in the training) all prayed that Mother's surgery would be postponed. I got the call the first night that the surgery was rescheduled for December 28th. What a gift to have the chance to be together Christmas with Mother, Dad, and all my sisters, and to be free during the training of that concern. There were many miracles in that training for us all.

After Christmas, Mother had the surgery and I stayed to rebuild her immune system. I knew I had my work cut out for me. It was far from over. Because the cancer traveled from the kidney to the brain, it was certainly in the blood and could reappear anywhere. I was hoping with the alternative treatments, we could cut off the blood supply to the tumors and also strengthen her immune system. I pulled out all the stops. I got shark cartilage suppositories from the Contreras Hospital Laboratory, added the Wobe enzymes, pancreatic extract, juicing, lots of supplements and a few other herbal remedies. I know that it all contributed to her recovery.

I feel it is a blessing to get a chance to heal many things as we work with family. It is certainly a big challenge emotionally. I am sure all of you are experiencing this. We also have to let go of many of our loved ones in the coming times as the frequency is intensifying and all is changing. We are being strengthened and prepared to lead many of the awakening human race into the new era. We do not have much time to prepare ourselves for the lifting of the veil. As this happens, it will cause tremendous chaos and awakening for the human race.

Another dream was fulfilled when I returned to Amsterdam to do more work. I met Letitia Kingsford who is a documentary producer and is also a wonderful spirit. She volunteered to produce the video, which I had been dreaming about for some time. I knew it would be important for people to be able to see the Breath of Light demonstrated and taught. I can say that she did a remarkable and professional job. She produced a mystical set at the beautiful estate of Maggia and Rik Swets (where I later stayed in their guesthouse) and we all did the breathing beforehand. When I was able to deliver it in one take, the whole crew was astounded. But, the Spirit of the Breath directed us all to produce a fantastic tape.

PHASE 18: PRODUCTION OF BREATHE THE LIGHT- A GUIDED MEDITATION CD

One of Letitia's good friends, Magda Buining, knew of my desire to produce a CD that would be a guided Breath of Light healing journey with beautiful music. She took me to meet Jan de Roos, a musician who dreamed of a long piece rather than the commercial jingles he normally did. I thought he would compose the music and I would go in and sing to it as well as record the mystical journey meditation with the Breathing. After some weeks of working on it, Jan called me and asked me to come out to his studio. He said that he had tried and tried and it would not come. What he felt was that I was to go into the studio and just let the singing come through and he would compose the music around it. My first reaction was complete and utter fright. But, after I took some deep breaths, my own inner spirit said that he was absolutely right. I was told to go into the Breath of Light and Spirit would sing through me. And that is exactly how it happened. Again, I did the spoken meditation in one take and then just allowed the music to come.

It was one of the most awesome experiences that I think I will ever have. To be able to tap into the highest Creative Energy Source is a remarkable gift to us all. It is available to any that are ready to surrender to it and can be found in the Breath. I have always been concerned that the CD would not just be a lovely music experience, but rather transmit the frequency that the Breath of Light is. It was promised to me that if I did listen to the directives of Spirit, and keep raising my own frequency by being faithful to all that is given to me to do, the gift would surely be given.

I am grateful beyond any words that I could utter for the power of the CD, which is named, *"Breathe the Light, The Journey Home"*. I sometimes keep it playing 24 hours a day because it does transmit the frequency of Light. It keeps me connected when I hear it and even if I cannot hear it, it is broadcasting the frequency into the atmosphere. I listen to it when I go to sleep and do the breathing in order to go into Theta and do major healing work on myself during the night. If I am stressed, I find myself drifting toward the recliner by the CD player, just sitting down and connecting with the frequency – letting all my burdens go. Sometimes it is only for a few minutes and sometimes it is longer that I can give it over to the release and transmuting process.

I am quite sure that doing the music for that CD has changed Jan's life forever. After some months, he was able to come up with the first cut of the CD, which was wonderful. But we all recognized the need to have more of my singing on it and he went back and rearranged some of the music and included more of my singing. He was finally satisfied with it and when he sent it to me in January of 2002, I, also, knew that it was complete. After Jan did my

CD, he wrote a little commercial jingle for Nissan and so many people were singing it, he was asked to do a full piece. That new piece hit the #1 charts in Holland and stayed there for months.

This book and the *Breathe the Light* CD are designed to be a complete package for teaching, and giving the experience of the Breath of Light. While I would like to introduce it to each of you personally, I cannot. This is a safe, complete way to share the work with you and get it to the masses of seekers.

As I was spending most of my time in Holland and Germany, continuing to do a very heavy load of work, I was starting to hear the voice of Spirit whispering to me, "Your work is almost done". I took it to mean that my destiny and purpose was fulfilled. I became even more dedicated to fulfilling the work before me. My physical body was suffering, but I never faltered. I led several more trainings in Port Aransas with many from Europe attending. I knew the Breath of Light work would be continued after I left by the many healers that I trained. And while I really cared for Paul, he was committed to living in Holland, and I knew I was to return home to the U.S.A. He was a beautiful support and wonderful friend to me. I thank him for his love. But for some of us, relationships are secondary to our purpose and mission. Sadly, we say goodbye, but with very fond memories. I will love him always.

On one of my return trips home, I was reading a Thrifty Nickel advertisement for real estate. I saw a little ad for 10 acres in Rockport, covered with Live Oak trees. The agent that showed it to me was named, "Angel". I knew it was a sign. And when I stepped onto the property, I felt such energy and peace that I knew this was the place. The place for what? I thought it was going to be my gift for being faithful – a place to live out the rest of my days. And it was in the county, which had no restrictions as to usage and building. I also checked on the history of the land, and amazingly, there had been no one living on it in recorded history. The Carancahua Indians who were nomadic fishermen had camped along the coast. But no one had homesteaded here. I purchased the land and then started spending time there in order to commune with the nature spirits. I needed their support and permission to be there. I also needed them to tell me which trees were willing to go – where to build the buildings – where to drill for the well. The nature spirits told me they were so happy to finally have humans come as they had been lonely and wanted to share their healing energies. It was part of their purpose and they had been waiting for a long time. They welcomed me and they guided me step by step.

While I thought that the land was for my last days, the land had a far more powerful effect. Working with nature healed my body, mind and spirit. I started revitalizing, coming alive again. My mind was able to start dreaming again. I knew that if this place could heal me, it could heal others. Indeed, whenever anyone comes on the land, which I named Sacred Sanctuary, they experience healing. I used all the principals of healing with the elements: earth, fire, air, water and community. I used Feng Shui as I placed sacred spaces.

At first, all I had was my little air stream trailer and a very large 26ft. teepee that we did the trainings in. I had to have water around me and I had two ponds dug. They became very beautiful with many frogs, water lilies, fountains, and fish. Later, I acquired 20 ducks that loved being out on the ponds.

I had many wonderful hands that helped me do the initial clearing and work out here. Henny Van der Horst came from Holland and stayed 3 months several times. Irene LeRoi spent many weekends out here. We built a sweat lodge, a medicine wheel fire pit, did extensive landscaping with beautiful flowers and tropical plants. I brought in a mobile home to live in, built a tropical shower house, public toilets, a large dining room/kitchen that allowed for many people to cook and eat together. I built four bungalows and added another travel trailer besides the original Airstream as an additional bungalow. And later, I built the training room and chapel. The teepee became fragile and finally the wind took the cover. All that was left were the two painted buffalo which became medicine shields at the entrance to the land and at the medicine wheel fire pit.

I felt it was a sign of new direction. I had already been receiving the information that I should concentrate on universal sacred spaces rather than only Native American sacred spaces. While I still honor the teachings of the tribes and medicine men/women, they are of the past. The new sacred spaces are of the future. I changed the colors at the medicine wheel from the traditional red, black, white and yellow to green, blue, purple, and white which are the higher vibrational colors. There are many universal laws that are found in all sacred space order and formation that are ageless such as sacred geometry.

The Sacred Sanctuary project was started early in the spring and in the short time that it took to build, it seems miraculous that it was so extensive. Everywhere I looked was a miracle because I knew what it took to create. I never even saw all the property as it was so thickly forested and I only cleared about ½ of it. There were many sacred meditation sites and we had ceremonial places such as a Long Dance.

At the very first Long Dance on a full moon in November, we had a huge tatami drum and was disappointed to see that a huge cloud cover had come in cloaking the full moon. We had a wonderful sweat lodge first and we prayed that we would be able to see the moon during our night long dance. We started dancing and totally focused on our goal. In about one hour, a huge hole opened up just so that we could see the moon. It held all night and proved to us how powerful we are when we believe and focus our energy.

One of my most memorable times at the Retreat Center was when Helen Stembridge who I met in Houston, called and said she was guided to come down and that we should do a special blend of essential oils in honor of the Breath. Her business is *Earth Angel Oils* and she has gathered the purest oils from all over the world. I told her how busy I was and she insisted that we take a few hours to do this. I yielded and she traveled the 4 hours down from Houston. We went into my 50 foot teepee which had a sacred altar and breathed together first. She spread out hundreds of oils and we continued to breathe and allow Spirit to guide us to pick the special oils to blend together. Instead of one oil, we were given 3 different blends, "Lifting the Veil", "Dolphin Breath", and "The Anointing" which are all quite different and quite extraordinary. Helen and I Breathed and inhaled those oils for a full day. At the end, I think we could have ascended, we were so full of Light. Helen is a very devoted Master with the oils and I have always enjoyed my times with her. You can go to www.earthangeloils.com/148 to order any of her oils with my personal link. Be sure to tell Helen I sent you.

Some of the important healing retreats that I have developed and have focused more and more on these past years are the detox/cleanse programs. All healing is based on these principles whether physical, emotional, spiritual or mental. And when we cleanse one body, we must detox all the others as well. I have had several of these week-long retreats and they have been so very successful and rewarding for all who participated. I do my own personal detox program several times a year and encourage others to understand the importance of healing ourselves. I will give a few of my favorite "remedies" later in the book.

I had held the vision for more than 40 years of a healing spa/clinic that does true healing – not just a surface band-aid –feel good approach. That vision was clarified when I was at the Contreras Hospital in Mexico. I saw the many alternative programs whereby most incorporated a detox aspect. Certainly all required nutritional support of one sort or another. I feel very fortunate to have been exposed to so much knowledge and experience with these concepts as they are key to true healing. I know that this is my specialty and I combine live-raw, organic foods, juicing, nutritional supplements, which are all good medicine and can create the body chemistry and pH balance for a healing environment in the body. Emotional-mental-spiritual healing is included in all my healing protocols.

Another program that was offered at the Contreras Hospital was Chelation IV Therapy. In those years, it seemed the major focus was on dissolving the arterial plaque and clearing the arterial system with Chelation. I was not so aware as now that it is essential for detoxing the heavy metals from our bodies. I did not realize how toxic even minor exposure to the heavy metals such as lead, mercury, and nickel can be. The main ingredient in the therapy is EDTA (Ethyls Diamine Tetraacetic Acid) which is a synthetic amino acid and has an unusual lock that attracts the heavy metals and arterial plaque, chelating it out into the urine. EDTA may act as a major anti-inflammatory or anti-oxidant agent. Heavy metal toxicity inactivates enzymes needed for day to day cellular processes. It depresses the immune system and free radicals take over. One study shows that there is ninety percent reduction in cancer mortality after Chelation IV therapy.

Chelation IV Therapy was a standard treatment for years until the bypass surgeries, stints in the arteries, angioplasty, etc. became the standard protocol as they were much more lucrative for the medical doctors. With all the recent double-blind studies published about the effects these metals have on the nervous system, I have realized that even though I had a spiritual healing years ago of the Multiple Sclerosis, I still had heavy lead, mercury and nickel in my body. This was proven with a simple 24 hour urine test after a Chelation IV which forces the metals into the urine. I have undergone extensive Chelation IV Therapy to remove those metals. As long as anyone has them in the cells of the body, the immune system is depressed, and the nervous system is challenged. The diseases of the Nervous System such as

Multiple Sclerosis, Alzheimers, Fibromyalgia, Parkinsons, Chronic Fatigue, Neuropathy and many others are caused by the toxic metals.

I felt a Chelation IV Therapy Clinic was essential for healing and had a desire to have one available. Several of my friends who were going to Mexico and traveling long distances for the chelation treatments encouraged me to open a clinic in Rockport. I knew that I had to have a medical doctor as a partner to oversee the patients. I had met a nurse that had experience with Chelation IV's, but where was I going to find a medical doctor who was holistic in their approach and did not have an attitude and an ego to match. I kept asking everyone if they knew anyone who might be open to working with me. I was finally led to Dr. Dorothy, a M.D. who had a chelation clinic in Texas City. She agreed to be my medical director and let me use her license in order to do the IV's. She was not able to come but once every couple of months. So that meant that I had to get trained and be capable of overseeing and administering the IV's with my nurse's help.

I went to the classes and trainings sponsored by ACAM. One of the doctors that made a huge impact on my work was Dr. Sherry Rogers, author of "Detox or Die", a very powerful book about detoxification methods. I highly recommend the book which has many resources available. I met many other teachers who were doctors and very willing to share their knowledge of formulations. I absorbed everything that was being taught about IV Therapy and all forms of detoxification. Dr. Sherry Rogers believed that one of the best forms of detoxing, even plasticides, is a Far Infrared Sauna so I installed one. I had learned about the power of hydrogen peroxide IV's, Ozone, colonic hydrotherapy, and other IV formulations. And, nutritional support is essential with cleansing. I have been given very important resources and understanding of even more detoxing protocols which I will elaborate on in a later chapter.

I was informed by some of the doctors that I studied with that there are two kinds of EDTA, the chelating formula. One is paid for by insurance but does not clear the arteries of the plaque. It chelates the heavy metals which are toxic. Dr. Dorothy was prescribing the EDTA which was covered by insurance since she was doing the billing for me. But, the heart patients that were coming to me needed the other one. I was furious when I discovered this. She had deceived me and my patients had been mistreated. I immediately went to my patients who had cardiac problems and offered to treat them for free to make up for the wrong treatment. It did no harm, but they deserved to have the right formula. I also fired Dr. Dorothy as my medical director. She was furious and it was a fire storm at first. She kept all the money that she had billed for me and I was left without much money for a period of time. I had to go get a loan to pay the overhead and keep my doors open.

I was sent a wonderful doctor friend, Dr. Meg Quayam, who said she would pinch hit for me until I found another medical doctor. She was very generous to me and saved the day. I did soon find another Medical Director who was with me until I closed the clinic and retired.

I opened a second Environmental Medicine clinic in Corpus Christi and called it Seaside Sanctuary as it was by the sea. I found a marvelous old historic, run-down building called Gaslight Square which was utterly charming. It was built around a square containing a huge oak tree and a beautiful big fountain brought from Italy. The buildings were in such disrepair that they had to be taken down to the studs and sometimes completely removed. The owner really wanted a showcase business there and liked what I was proposing to do. He bankrolled me for the build-out and the lease reflected the cost, but it was an amazing opportunity for me. I got to design the 5,000 sq. ft. clinic and it was extraordinary. I had small ponds with fountains at the entrance enhanced by orchids and ferns. We had lovely meditation music playing all the time and there were comfortable recliner chairs for the patients to get their treatments in. We had massage rooms, colonic hydrotherapy, exam rooms for our Medical director, a spa room for skin treatments and other spa protocols. Patients loved coming as it was a sacred healing space and you felt it the minute you walked in the door.

It was a true healing place and we offered many protocols which are now being called "integrated medicine" – combining holistic with more conventional methods. We addressed body, mind, spirit, and emotions in all our treatments.

PHASE 19: FINAL YEARS WITH FAMILY

While I was in Corpus Christi, I felt that I wanted to try and create some good memories with my aging parents who were living in Sulphur Springs, in East Texas. I proposed that they sell their home and I would help them move to Corpus Christi. They were getting elderly and as the oldest, I felt compelled to have them close by in order to address their aging needs. They agreed as they were experiencing ill health.

I went to Sulphur Springs, in East Texas, cleared out their huge storage shed, the attic and all the excess in the house for a moving sale and donating. I was encouraging them to downsize, but that was almost impossible because my mother was attached to everything she had as if it represented her very reason for existence. She had 5 mix-masters and I asked if I might have one. She said that she really did not know....maybe if they did not sell in the garage sale. I gave up a whole month to work constantly to pack and sort through their stuff. I still did not get a mix-master. Nor really any thanks for my hard work.

Attachments to stuff can be so ugly. Another very visible lesson about how addiction to materialism can stop the love.

We found a lovely home in Corpus Christi that was only slightly smaller, and I managed to get every stick of furniture that they insisted on keeping arranged in the house. It was crowded, but they were in.

I had dreamed of being able to heal our relationship and wrongly thought they had mellowed in their aging years. I think they might have even gotten more vicious. My sisters, Paulette and Charlotte, told them that I was only doing all of my good deeds so I could get their money. They even persuaded them that the healthy green drinks and smoothies that I was buying organic fruit, green powder, vitamins, minerals, etc. were poisonous. Later, I found out that they were waiting until I left the room and were dumping the health drinks that I was so lovingly making for them. Plus, I was paying quite a lot for the ingredients. It would be a dream come true for someone to make green drinks and smoothies for me. But, their unconsciousness allowed for all manner of mistrust and their paranoia grew, fed by my sisters who were plotting. They were joined by that step-cousin, Raymond Bearden, who wanted to become Al's son and usurp my place as the eldest. He spent every minute with him and played the role. My father was over-joyed at having a son and Raymond played the role well.

Those last few years were so painful as Al made it his mission to make me miserable and try to destroy my life. He would wheel himself into my clinic, full of patients and start ranting and raving, calling me terrible names too terrible to say. He would call my medical director and any other doctors that I was associated with and tell them strange and crazy stories about me. He turned me in to the A.M.A. making claims that I was mistreating patients. They then started sending in undercover agents. That did break my heart when I found out that he had gone to that extent to destroy me. He could not stand that I was successful – more successful than he had ever been. He also would not allow me to be with mother unless he was in the room. Sometimes she would call me and whisper my name and then I would hear a click. He kept her from me. He did not want her to be happy either.

I finally had to cut the ties from him and also my mother because I could find no way to get to her around him. I was able to hear about how she was through their live-in caretaker.

In August, I took a cruise to Alaska and that was the best vacation ever – to get away, but also to return to my home state that I loved so much. To be in that wild and still natural nature was rejuvenating and inspirational.

When I got back from an Alaskan Cruise on Sept. 11th, 2005, my father had died that night. Al Meadows was dead at age 91. When I returned, I had a call from my youngest sister, Kathy and she was very distressed. It seems that Charlotte had come down to stay with them and she and Al got in a physical fight. She pushed him down and he broke his hip when he fell. He had surgery and Charlotte called Paulette to come down. Raymond joined them. They put their plan into action.

I did not mourn my father's death. I think I had mourned him for so many years that there was no more emotion left. I just felt relieved that he was no longer here on earth and would not be terrorizing me anymore. A huge burden was lifted off of me and I felt at peace. Free at last!

As things evolved, I had to step in and become guardian of my mother who had been put into a nursing home to die by my sisters, Paulette and Charlotte. My sister, Kathy, begged me to rescue Mother and take care of her saying she would share her portion of the estate with me. I was the only one that had the money to pay for all the expenses that were involved. And, as it turned out, I spent a great deal of my personal funds taking care of Mother.

Paulette and our half-cousin, Raymond Bearden, had tricked Mother into leaving me out of the will altogether. They took a notary into the nursing home, took mother's hand and made and X for her signature on a new will they had made up.

I had been alienated from mother and daddy because Paulette and Raymond worked overtime to make sure that was the case. And, daddy hated me because I refused to cooperate with his lifelong quest to control me and make me subservient to him. He tried to separate all of us from each other and pit one against the other. He, most of all, wanted to keep mother isolated from me. I was strong and he did not want me to influence her to stand up to him. So, it was an easy thing for Paulette and Raymond to create a wedge between me and daddy as well as mother. Raymond came from an impoverished, ignorant upbringing and always envied our wealthier lifestyle. If he only knew how miserable that our life was because of the materialistic emphasis both my parents worshiped. Raymond wooed daddy to become the son that Al had never had. Al gave Raymond his motor home, his boat, and many other things. Most importantly, Raymond replaced me.

Mother stayed with daddy because she believed she would not have anything if she divorced daddy. So, we all paid a terrible price for all those material things which meant nothing in the end.

I believed Kathy was on my side and never believed she would betray me for the money. I thought she was a better person than that. In the end, she chose the money. She had wanted a Tummy tuck and I guess that was more important to her than being true to her sister.

I brought Mother home in Corpus Christi, Texas after having to go to court and become her Legal Guardian. I had to post a bond and pay all the attorney fees/court costs to do it. I hired a live-in caregiver, Lila, who had been Mother's caregiver previously, to help me. I had planned to move to Flagstaff and had bought a home there. But, I had to take care of mother who was semi-comatose from a stroke, and had a feeding tube. She was not expected to live but a few days or weeks. However, I had faith that I could help her especially with a special healing supplement, glyconutrition. I started her on a therapeutic dose, along with other products, which I knew could assist the body to heal. Because she had a feeding tube, I was able to put massive amounts into it which would have been impossible for her to ingest. But, it extended her life and even helped her to come to consciousness so that we could have our special time together.

Taking care of her was the hardest thing I have ever done. She had to be turned every 2 hours and fed through the feeding tube every few hours, as well as diapered often. And, I had to fight my sisters all the way. Paulette called Social Services and reported that I was abusing mother. After, the investigator came out, he said that he could only wish that everyone treated their parents half as good as I treated mother.

In the beginning, I had Charlotte living at the house to help with Mother's care since I was back and forth from Flagstaff. She convinced me that she could be a big help as long as I paid her and supported her. But, Charlotte admitted later that Paulette had made a secret alliance for her to be there in the home in order to carry out their plan. They had bragged to a few people that they had killed daddy by giving him a poisonous tea made from Oleanders. I later found a book there at mothers' that was about poisonous herbs including info about oleander. After my experiences with the two of them, I am inclined to believe they actually did it. They fulfilled daddy's worst fears by putting him and mother in a nursing home and then, most likely, caused his very demise. He called both Kathy and me on his cell phone begging us for help and to rescue him. Paulette took his cell phone away from him and he could no longer call anyone. The people at the nursing home said that he was ranting and raving saying that "they are poisoning me". He was perceived to be a crazy old man and no one paid any attention to him. Mother was in the same room with him and when he died, the nurses asked her if she wanted to spend a few minutes to say goodbye to him. She loudly said, "NO!" I guess she had had enough of him for a lifetime and was happy he was gone. So, he lived out his nightmare, dying alone and in a place that he had made all of us promise that we would never send him to – a nursing home. Karma is the great equalizer and payment can be terrible.

After a couple of months, mother started waking up and communicating. She was able to eat some by mouth and talk with me. We had our whole lifetime of alienation to heal. She finally told me she loved me and asked me to forgive her. So, I got the Blessing I had yearned for my whole life. But, she was so weak and her organs kept getting septic as they had shut down for some time. I could get her back to some extent, then she would crash again, and I would have to take her to the hospital for IV antibiotics and stabilization. So, we were in and out of the hospital many times. I learned about the worst that one can imagine about hospitals and nursing homes. I found that I had to sleep at the hospital and stay with her all the time as there was so much incompetency and they just did not care. I decided to move her to Flagstaff so that I could be with my daughter and newborn grandbaby (born in December). My Rockport property sold in December which freed me to move. And I could take care of mother as well. So, I cleaned, organized and packed mother's things and moved her in an ambulance van with the moving truck in tow. It was a nightmare getting medical personnel in place in Flagstaff, and again we were in and out of the hospital with mother finally going comatose again.

She died on May 8th with my daughter, Susan, granddaughter, Tatum, and me to help her make her journey with love and peace. I anointed her with oil, played her favorite hymns and when Amazing Grace came on, she looked at Susan with the brightest, vibrant, bluest eyes I have ever seen, then looked at me for a long time, and then looked up – I could see her angels there welcoming her home. I saw my Mama and Papa Smith, sister Theresa and others. Al Meadows was not amongst them. She took a deep breath in and closed her eyes. Her body pulsed for a few minutes as her life energy flowed out and then her body was just the empty shell that she was so ready to leave. She was weary and I know that she stayed as long as she did in order to complete with me. She also knew how hard it was for me and that she was a great burden. That whole experience was one of the great blessings of my life.

There is a whole lot more including the fact that all of my sisters betrayed me, and Kathy too. She chose to keep the money that she said she would share with me since it was all my money which paid for Mother's care and the lawyers' fees to fight Paulette, Charlotte, and Raymond, who all banded together to betray Mother. They put her in a terrible nursing home and it was their goal to make sure she died as soon as possible. Mother was mistreated and even abused in that nursing home. I couldn't stand by and knowingly let that happen. It would haunt me my whole life to do that. I am so different from my sisters and chose a very different path from a very young age.

I have thought about our ancestors and the heritage that they left for us. Most of them left heritages of evil, hatred, victimhood, terrorist, and only a few of them left a heritage of love and support. My greatest champion was my Mama

Smith – my mother's mother. I have drawn on her loving support throughout my whole life. It was our choice of which heritage we wanted to perpetrate and embody through our lives. I have always known that it was my mission to change the flow of evil and betrayal of the human spirit that was so prevalent in our parent's lives. Daddy was the epitome of evil and mother betrayed us by allowing us to experience his terror. She chose it and it was up to each of us girls to choose it or reject it in our own lives. I thought Kathy understood how important it was for her and me to make the choice for good and redemption. This would affect our whole ancestral lineage for all time. Kathy, Charlotte and Paulette made the choice to carry on for daddy and mother. They became the perpetrators of betrayal and evil. I have found this so incomprehensible that I can barely stand to even think of it. I cannot even imagine being in their bodies and their lives - there had to be huge consequences for betraying me. They gave up the right to all the benefits of heaven's goodness and instead, chose greed - of money that was not rightfully theirs –especially Kathy. I know that Mother would have wanted me to be included as her daughter. She absolutely knew that it was me who was caring for her, protecting her and loving her. I would talk with her during those last months of her life and she would cry – tears rolling down her cheeks. She would squeeze my hand and I knew she heard me.

The next phase began when she died. Paulette, being the executor, took over her burial and funeral arrangements.

She had threatened me and Kathy. Paulette had been arrested twice for acts of violence and one of those involved her shooting a gun. She has a history of drunken violence. We took her threats very seriously and after much consideration, decided not to go to Mother's funeral. I was seriously afraid of what would happen at the funeral.

Funerals cause people to act out their worst emotions of hatred and resentment. It happened at my Mama Smith's funeral with all of her kids (my mother and her siblings) "duking" it out right there at the funeral home. It was a terrible physical fight with them rolling on the floor, hitting each other and acting like animals. I knew that Paulette, Charlotte and Raymond would like nothing more than to get the chance to really hurt me. I chose not to go. I do not regret not going to Mother's funeral as it would have turned out very badly. I had my time with Mother when she was still alive. I had held the vision of Mother recovering enough that we could sit out on the patio, having a glass of iced tea, and just enjoying being with each other. Daddy had kept us apart at all costs. He did not want us to have a chance of any kind of loving relationship. By that time, Mother did not have the strength and power to stand up to him. She might have been able to earlier in her life and it has been so difficult to understand why she did not stand up to him and protect her daughters.

When mother died, I thought I had reconciled the very hurtful relationship I had with her and my father. I did not mourn his death at all. It was a relief that he was finally gone and no longer able to torment me. But, when mother died, I went into the deepest grief and pain I could ever imagine. I cried for a whole year until I thought I could cry no more, and then it would start all over. Mother never became the person that she was to be. She sold out for materialism. We all lost so much by her choices. Through my tearful, mourning process, I feel something has melted within me that had to melt and be transformed. I know that I emerged as a whole different person. I am resolute with what is most important to me. I am committed to being a loving grandmother and supportive mother to my kids and model an exemplary life. I appreciate each day and love life, knowing how blessed I am.

Yes, it does seem to be a release and a reconciliation emotionally to write about the events of my life. It is interesting that as I am writing it from my heart, feeling it personally, I also notice the Observer at work giving me feedback later as I evaluate it. I expect the Observer helps me to reconcile it all. I know that after all of this saga, I have come to that place of peace and forgiveness so I can be free.

The only reason to look back at my history is to realize that I "made it out" and to look at how far I have come. I stayed true to myself and my mission. I battled my father, my tormenter and terrorist, and passed the Initiation. I have released all of the pain of my earthly family, knowing that they were unawake and chose to stay asleep. None of my sisters made it out. They have carried on the terrorism, materialism, hatefulness and vengeance of Al Meadows. They may even be worse than he was.

I recently read the trilogy by Steigg Larsson,"The Girl With the Dragon Tatoo", The Girl Who Played With Fire", and "The Girl Who Kicked the Hornet's Nest". I then watched all three movies. They absolutely held me transfixed and I realized that I identified with parts of the story. *The girl's father had beaten her mother until she ended up mentally incompetent and the girl tried to kill him for his violence to her mother. Later, her own father shoots her and buries her but she was not dead. She digs herself out of the grave.* I realized in daddy's last years, how much he hated me. He lived every day figuring out ways to make my life miserable.

Raymond was a frequent visitor during those last years and Lila, who was Mother's caregiver, told me that Mother hated him because he was trying (and did) take my place in their lives. Daddy would drag out the steaks and treat him like a king. Lila also disliked Raymond because they would talk about me in very degrading conversations. Daddy continued to abuse mother and talked to her like she was a worthless dog, berating her and telling her that she was stupid and to shut up. Raymond just sat there and grinned while daddy was acting like a complete idiot. Raymond would do anything to get in daddy's good favor. He should have stood up for mother. Daddy made him promise that he would not let anybody put him and mother into a nursing home. And, that was the first thing that Raymond and Paulette did. I was the only one that would have made sure that their wishes were honored - if daddy had not alienated me, he would have had a real protector in me. He chose the wrong allies who were really his enemies. And he had to die alone in the worst place he could imagine, helpless, in terror, fulfilling his worst fear of being in that nursing home.

He forbade mother to see me. Lila told me later that mother would confide in her that she only wanted one thing - to come and live with me. She would try to call me, but daddy was ever vigilant and did not leave her alone except for the few minutes that she would be in the bathroom. And, he only allowed her a couple of minutes alone because he knew that she would try to contact me. She was a prisoner. One of the last things he said to me was, "I am going to come back from the grave and get you". He certainly tried. I had to exorcise him from the house because he wanted to take mother with him. I could always sense when he was in the room. Mother would get really agitated. He would play with the thermostat and cause motion detectors to go off. But, I was determined not to let him get mother or me. Finally, after using sage and camphor, praying and chanting, he finally left for good. We were free of him and his misery .

I was an orphan, really, with no champions except the infrequent times I got to go up to Mama & Papa Smith's farm. I think that Mama Smith always was on the girls' sides and felt more for us over the boys. I know she had been through so much heartache in her life But she had such wisdom and gave me a feeling of safety with her. I loved going with her to the creek to fish and then picking blackberries. Then she cooked up all that delicious food on that old wood stove. I can still see her throwing out the feed for the chickens and talking to them. I can see her churning the butter after milking the old cows, sitting on a little stool. I can remember the walks in the garden with her, picking tomatoes and eating them right on the spot. And those watermelons they picked off the vine, just eating the heart and throwing the rest to the pigs. Yes, those memories of my Mama Smith bring such warmth, sweetness, and love.

I did love mother but I also know that she had that side of her that did her in - her love of material things - and her imagined security with Al. He convinced her that she would get nothing if she left him. I tried to tell her that it was not true. She just could not put her girls' and her own welfare as a priority. I believe that as a young girl she was quite innocent and had a good heart. But, all those years of abuse from daddy made her mentally sick. She lost herself. I know that things were different back then, but women did leave their husbands even then, and she certainly had great cause and justification to do so. I can only imagine what our lives would have been like if she had left him. That she would side with him when he was abusive to us is beyond me, as a mother myself. I would never let a man abuse my children – their father or otherwise.

After mother died, and going to court with Paulette and Raymond to get reimbursed for my personal money that I spent for mother's care that last year, I was never fully paid for the $57,000 dollars I spent from my personal funds. I only got about $7,000 due to Paulette's vicious attack and attorneys making their deal in the back room. My attorney took $5,000 and left $2,000 for me. Justice is not so easy to get in our courts. I just had to let it go knowing that I did the very best I could, and got my blessing from my mother.

After that long, exhausting ordeal, I was ready for a vacation. I went to Costa Rica with a friend, Gloria Parker, who published "Aquarius Rising" in Atlanta. She was going there for dental work and I wanted to explore the possibility for my own dental work. I was smitten and totally in love with Costa Rica. The people were so lovely, the tropical beauty was everywhere, the food so awesome....what not to like? And the dentists, Drs. Eduardo Castro and Antonio Anglada were very professional and trained in the U.S.A. They also had state of the art equipment and their clinic was impeccable. It was an easy decision to go forward with them for the massive amount of dental work that I needed. It took 5 trips to complete all the work as it could not be done in one trip. That was absolutely ok with me as it was a great excuse to go back. Gloria and I had so many glorious experiences in Costa Rica, even thinking of opening a medical recovery center there. We had a great adventure together.

I went to the east coast and to the west coast which was a much more developed beach with many resorts. But, by far, my most favorite part of the country was the north where the Volcano Arenal is still active. It is like paradise there with gigantic tropical plants, but the real draw is the heated river that flows down from the volcano and pools in grottos at several resorts there. They vary in temperature and you can move from one to another just soaking up that amazing mineral water.

What a marvelous life I had. I had worked hard for so many years and built my future with the Clinic and the health retreat which I sold at the top of the market. I had wealth and leisure time for the first time in my life. But, what to do with all that money? My strong intuition was to invest it in a business rather than the stock market. And, I kept looking for a business that would have a positive impact on the environment and thus, on our health. I kept looking for that special business, but no one seemed to have the right fit with mutual funds or other stock offerings.

I was speaking at a meeting in California on health and healing. The cameraman, John Ballor, was very excited about my experience with healing and said that I must meet his partner, Jerry Nezat, who was in Kalispell, Montana. He said that Jerry was working with Stem Cells for 50 years and that he was brilliant. I had worked with Dr. Francisco Contreras on Live Cell Therapy in Mexico, but that work had been shut down by NAFTA. So, my interest was hooked. John got Jerry on the phone and we talked for some time. They invited me to come up to Kalispell and all meet to talk about the project. John also told me that they were developing a research project that had to do with fuel supplementation with hydrogen to create a clean burning fuel with significant savings in fuel usage. It was especially important for diesel fuel in the trucking industry as they were being given stiff regulations by the government (CARB) to meet new carbon emission limits. This really appealed to me as it would help clean up the environment and have a huge impact for trucking costs, saving the industry. This spoke to my heart. I felt that I had finally found the business to invest in. We made plans to meet in Kalispell in early October as I had another trip to Costa Rica planned the end of October.

I flew into Kalispell, Montana and Jerry picked me up at the little airport in his old beat-up van. He looked as bad as the van in ragged clothes and looking like a homeless person. He had no personality and could not look me in the eyes, only glancing at me sideways. I thought that this was going to be a hopeless situation as he seemed very eccentric. We went to the house which was a huge concrete dome house and matched Jerry and the van as it was in total disrepair and unfinished. The land was beautiful with the mountains rising all around the area which was heavily endowed with huge pine trees.

Dixie, Jerry's wife, was welcoming and had an exuberant personality, but was obese and wheelchair bound. Some other people who were working with Jerry and John were there as well. We sat down to a large table for dinner and vivacious conversation. They wanted to know all about my work and my trip to Costa Rica. I wanted to know about their beginnings in the hydrogen project.

They had cleared out one of the bedrooms for me to stay in. As I looked around, I realized it was quite a project as the whole house was packed floor to ceiling and wall to wall with stuff. They were hoarders. It also smelled badly – moldy. I would have preferred to go to a motel, but there was no choice.

In the next three days, John, Jerry, and I talked about their grandiose vision of getting an injection mold for large scale production as they were positive that they would be swamped with orders as this was a pioneer field that was just getting ready to burst. The time was right and the idea was right. They painted a vision for me that showed me solutions and the chance to do something magnificent. I left after my 3 days there convinced that I wanted to invest in their project and help create a real business. I could see that neither one of them had an ounce of business sense and that I could organize as well as administrate the marketing that would have to be done. I was in a place of freedom in my life where I could easily move there and work.

Before I left, I did some beginning research and drove around the area looking at condos and rentals that were close by their house in Bigfork. It was beautiful. I could be happy there because of all the nature that I could connect with once again.

I went back to Phoenix just in time to depart for my beloved Costa Rica. This was the last vacation that I was to have in Paradise for many years. It was truly wonderful and I made my usual trek to the Volcano Arenal to soak in those healing waters. And, I finished up the intensive dental work that culminated in beautiful teeth and a healthy mouth. I went home to Phoenix to prepare for the move to Montana that would change my life forever.

I drove up to Montana arriving December 5th, 2008, having shipped up clothes, bedroom linens, books, and the personal things I needed.

When I decided to move to Montana in December to work with Jerry, I intended to rent a condo in Bigfork on the lake. I had seen the house that Jerry and Dixie lived in and it was uninhabitable as they were hoarders - it was piled with junk, was moldy, the floors unpainted and uncovered, no adequate heating, and the floor in the central atrium had fallen in and was dangerous. The 20 acre property had potential as it had 2 streams, 2 wells, 3 septic systems and is in a desirable area. The house was a monstrosity, a concrete dome house with the roof never finished over an atrium. There was no insulation, very limited heating, and unfinished in many ways.

Dixie died in the interim in November before I moved up to Montana. Jerry became extremely agitated when he found out that I was not going to move into the house with him. He argued the house had two master suites and I would have complete privacy. And there was room for a temporary office as well as a lab. I had strong doubts about the idea of living and working out of that house because I knew it was going to take a lot of work, money and energy to get it in shape to live in, and to work in. And, as I suspected, it turned out to be a nightmare. Jerry had no money. I spent a huge amount of my own personal life savings to pay workers, buy supplies, pay for new electric wiring, heaters, furniture, carpet, rugs, etc. It took months of work and also living in that mold which was throughout the house, giving all my energy to clean and fix it up. I had to hire crews to clean up the outdoors of the property which was piled with junk.

When I realized how much I was spending on the property and how much work I was putting into the repair and renovation, I expressed to Jerry that I needed to be compensated for it. He said that if I was willing to do all that work and spend thousands of dollars, he would put me on the deed and we would sell it, splitting the proceeds 50/50%. He did the legal documents to that agreement as he wanted to sell it and move on. We did start the business there at the house, but when we were offered a contract for 1000 hydrogen systems per month, it was apparent that we would have to rent a plant and hire people.

I found an 8,000 sq.ft. plant for lease and bought equipment for both the offices and the plant. I hired a crew of employees, contracted an expert to train the workers and was ready to go into production. The injection mold was arriving from China to start production. I bought the truck load of steel, and plastic for the mold production. We were ready.

However, it was all not as it appeared. Jerry and John had conspired with a couple of their pals to conjure up a fake contract. I was in over my head and had not dealt with sociopaths before. John was drinking heavily and revealed to us that he was a camera man for a porno film company. That did it for me. I told him that I would not work with him and asked him to leave which he did. I had made a large original investment that John took to pay off all his debts and credit cards. That left Jerry, who did not have a clue about business and was a fake inventor. I did not know that about him at that time. I just thought he was incompetent but there was much more to be revealed.

I had done enough research on the proof of concept by NASA and other research facilities on the effectiveness of hydrogen infused diesel and had a deep belief that the technology would work. There were other companies producing systems that claimed great results. So, I decided to push on and make it happen. This was a huge mistake as this was not my field of expertise and training. I was very vulnerable because of my ignorance. That was the first time that "The Voice" spoke to me and told me to cut my losses and close it down. But my ego could not admit defeat and I had put way over $200,000 into the business by then. I was determined to make my investment pay.

In the meantime, I continued renovation on the house in order to list it and sell it. I moved a truck load of my beautiful furniture, art collections, and furnishings from Arizona that would make the house both livable and saleable.

In the beginning of meeting Jerry, I was fooled by his "mysterious façade" as an eccentric inventor and he had quite an act. But, I was to discover that he was a swindler. Initially, he offered to share his stem cell research with me to have an experienced doctor as a partner and open a rejuvenation clinic. I was enticed by him to invest in the hydrogen research/development that he was doing. Both ventures were total frauds as I later discovered. My illusions about him fell away and I saw the truth. He claims to be an inventor, but he steals his ideas from others, from the internet and from patent searches for patents that have expired. He is no inventor, just a clever thief.

I was not attracted to Jerry as a man and a romantic interest. I only wanted to have a business and friendship relationship with him. But, he was obsessed with being with me and pretended that we were married, often telling people that we were married. In the very beginning, I thought that maybe having a companion in my golden years might be a possibility and it "seemed" that Jerry and I shared a lot of common ideas and philosophies. As time went on, it became more and more apparent that Jerry was spinning a myth as to who he is and what he has done. Things were not adding up.

He was obsessed with the fact that he was impotent and I found that he was getting prescriptions for that. I was horrified as I have been celibate for many years and not interested in being involved in that way with Jerry or anyone else.

One of the main reasons I moved to Montana and agreed to work with Jerry is that he claimed to have a stem cell therapy that he would share with me and we would develop it together. He said he had been working with the same strain of stem cells for 50 years and that he had healed a lot of dogs, horses, and people with injecting it. He was very secretive about it and promised to reveal it to me after I had been there for a while and he knew he could trust me.

I heard him on the telephone placing an order with a pond supply company. He said that a package would be coming and he had to watch for it every day because it could not be left in the mailbox because it would freeze. The package came and I observed that he put the little minnows which were inside into an aquarium with a light bulb over it in the back room. After about 4 months, he took me into the kitchen and announced he was going to reveal the stem cell process to me. He took a dish down out of the cupboard and put it on a used, non-sterile cutting board. He brought out 3 of the little fish which he said were mosquito fish and took his pocket knife out, slitting their little swollen bellies full of eggs. He squeezed the innards of the fish into the dish and mashed them up with his knife, pulled out a big syringe and suctioned the mixture up. He then handed me the syringe and said, "You can inject it now". I stood there flabbergasted and horrified. I knew then that he was a complete fraud. He had not been working with a same strain of stem cells for 50 years. Those mosquito fish are toxic, scavengers that eat mosquito larvae. I told him that he was out of his mind and I was not going to inject that toxic stuff into my body ever! I was so distraught and knew that I had lost all trust in him. I believe he knew it too. And, on top of that, I had been rejecting his amorous advances, becoming more and more disenchanted with him.

He claimed that I tricked him into putting me on the deed. He was in full mental capacity when I met him but, he is a liar and swindler. His erratic behavior may be in part, related to his self-induced diabetic state. Jerry was diabetic when I met him and he and Dixie, had been eating enormous amounts of sugar, pies, cakes, donuts, fudge and candy. The house was full of them as well as the freezer. He was on metformin and insulin – his glucose tests were off the chart -and high blood pressure medication. When I lived in the house, I cooked nutritious food with no sugar. When he stopped eating all that sugar and junk food, he started losing weight, his diabetes became non-existent, and blood pressure normalized.

I asked Jerry to change our partnership agreement because he was not contributing anything to it and indeed was doing things that were very detrimental to the hydrogen system. It was apparent that he really did not know how to improve it or make it work. He had only copied other people that also did not know how to perfect the hydrogen systems. He got very agitated and said for me to take the whole business. I believe he knew that the jig was up for him and that he had been exposed for the incompetent fraud that he is. I showed him all the hydrogen plans that were already invented and being marketed that he was claiming to have invented. He signed the agreement for me to take over the business of hydrogen systems as it was completely funded by my money anyway. He said he would develop his other inventions- his imaginary inventions.

In the night, I woke up with him on top of me trying to force himself on me. I had my own bedroom suite at one end of the house and his was on the other end. I kicked him clear across the room and screamed at him to never come into my room again. I had to lock my door and he used to pace outside my door all night. He stalked my every move – if I went to the bathroom or kitchen, he was right there wanting to know what I was doing.

PHASE 21: POISONED – ALMOST MURDERED

I started becoming very sick with abdominal pain, gas and bloating, acid reflux and had blisters in my mouth, throat, and all the way down my esophagus. I had to sit up in the recliner chair in the living room and Jerry would sit there and stare at me.

He had been bringing me coffee in the mornings and he stopped drinking it which was very odd. But, I did not think about it in the beginning. He also made some smoothies which were very bitter and I refused to drink them. After several months of suffering terribly, I heard a loud voice from a very big angel and it must have been Archangel Michael saying, "You are being poisoned." He had a pint of potassium hydroxide (lye), which we used in the hydrogen activation, mixed up in the pantry, and he put just enough in my coffee, that over a long period of time would kill me. When I realized that he was poisoning me, I got to the emergency room and they started tests, and referred me to a specialist for further testing. I had extensive damage to my whole digestive system. I was lucky to be alive.

I have been naïve and have always seen the positive aspects of everyone and wanted to see only the good. I have made excuses for bad behavior. And, this scenario was out of my capacity to conceive that someone would actually poison me and try to kill me. I have since come to a new realization that there are evil people who will do this without batting an eye or feeling any remorse. I experienced it firsthand and it is very frightening.

My rejection of his advances and losing faith in his abilities, knowing that he was a liar and a thief made him very angry. He ranted and raved, was drinking heavily and I was afraid of him. He is unconscionable and will do whatever he wants to get what he puts his sights on. I was in imminent danger. I knew I had to get away right away. That very day, after leaving the emergency room, I found a condo rental and went home to quietly pack some suitcases with clothes. That night, I sneaked the suitcases outside and loaded them into my car. I left in the middle of the night, driving like the wind out of that place.

I filed a police report stating that Jerry poisoned me. But, the detective just sneered at me and showed Jerry the report. So, he then claimed I poisoned him. I have medical records that verify that I was ill and suffered long-term effects that will take some work to heal. The detective threatened me and said that they were going to make my life miserable and they "would get me". Kalispell is a "good ole boy" town and outsiders are not treated kindly. I started understanding just how dangerous it is to be on the outs with the locals.

I moved back to Phoenix in March, 2010 for my personal safety and to get my health back, after being poisoned. Even though my health was compromised, I was determined to keep the business moving forward and make it successful.

Jerry claimed I tricked him into putting me on the deed and that I had set my sights on his house before I moved up there. He says he did not know what he was doing and I deceived him. I invested about $75,000 into the house. He put zero dollars into it. He filed a lawsuit in court to get my name off of the property. I did not have the funds by then to hire an attorney and I decided to choose peace. So, I agreed to give him the deed if he would ship my personal things down to me. I wanted my furniture and personal effects out of the house. But, as I suspected, he sold and disposed of almost all of my beautiful and irreplaceable art and furnishings. He has no conscience and just takes whatever he wants, believing he is above the law. But he did send my FIR Sauna down and I placed it in a chelation clinic for them to use for detoxification.

PHASE 22: RECONCILING MY CHOICES – LESSONS LEARNED

It has been difficult to reconcile that I, as an enlightened person entered into the nightmare with Jerry, as it only brought sadness, stress, and the loss of my life savings. We always have to look at ourselves in these situations. Jerry is who he is. What happened to me?

I know that I went into the situation with such a high level of honorable intentions. I wanted to do something really good with my money and make the environment of this world a better place for our health. Looking back, were my antennae out there actively looking for the warning signs and did I just ignore them? I have not identified any karmic payoff. Was I to learn about hydrogen energy for some reason to be used in the future? I abandoned my spiritual work during this time and concentrated on the technology. It does remind me of Atlantis as that was the reason that Atlantis perished. The people abandoned the Spiritual life and the heart of love in order to embrace technology to such an extreme that it destroyed them.

I have full memory of Atlantis and as one of the Twelve Keepers of the Crystal, trying to bring the people back to center and embrace both technology and spirituality. I was unsuccessful and when Atlantis started sinking with the great tsunami that came as a result of their abuse of power, I took the Crystal of Knowledge out and transmitted it to the dolphins. They took the Knowledge to the whales and they have been the keepers ever since. The whales are also the keeper of the grid of this earth from the very core to the outer layers. I remember going down in the deep waters as Atlantis sank, and the dolphins came to take me home. I did not survive but many did, migrating to other European and land countries. Maybe, Jerry was one of those old Atlanteans that were without heart and soul. He definitely has acted out in this lifetime as such. I have had difficulty in forgiving myself for allowing myself to be involved. I am finally reconciling these events and am content with my life, feeling peace in my heart and mind. Again, another initiation taking me further into the mind and heart of Christ, detaching from the things of this material world.

I feel it important to recount all of this to you in my willingness to be transparent and totally honest with myself and you, the reader. None of us are exempt from going through hard experiences and distressing emotional experiences. It is important to ask the question of what is this about and what is the meaning? It can be tricky to know if it is a karmic debt being repaid or is it an initiation to transcend and go to the next level.

I can say that there were signs that I ignored and felt I could make the project work regardless of the circumstances. That is certainly an act of the ego. I love creating and manifesting. Renovating that monstrous house into a beautiful and livable place was a creative project which I did love the end result.

There were many parts of the hydrogen project that was also creative and fun. But, the negative outcomes outweighed any balance with the positives. I think another thing to learn is that if you give a person time to reveal their true self, they will. They can only hold a façade of lies for so long and then their real selves show up. I did not wait for that to happen and invested prematurely. And, after I had invested, I did not want to walk away and lose the money. I was determined to save my investment and continued to put more money in.

I have realized that I did not want to be a failure as a woman. That is unthinkable and betrays my sisters. If a man fails, it is normal and acceptable. But, women are not allowed to have a failure. The shame is monumental. I did not listen to that inner voice that whispered to me to stop the research and close the business.

PHASE 23: BACK TO PHOENIX

When I moved back to Phoenix, I started looking for a new team. I needed an engineer who could produce a real hydrogen electrolyzer system that was effective and efficient. I was introduced to Shields who claimed to know all about hydrogen systems, to Howie, who had been active in sales, and Rich, who was a financial planner. They caught the vision from me and we opened a new plant and offices. After some months, I realized that Shields was not able to produce an effective electrolyzer and actually, all of his experimental models which were examined by engineers were deemed to be ineffective even by high school chemistry standards. The trio had been looking for investment funds and at the same time, plotting to take the company over. We had a little Friday team meeting whereby I sent those three conspirators on their way. I did listen to my inner voice and was willing to be aware of the reality of what was being played out. The trio thought they could pull one over on me, because I was a woman and seemed soft because of my spirituality.

The City of Chandler was opening the Innovations Technology Incubator and inviting in some technology companies that they could foster and help them grow. After an interview with Chris MacKay, Director of Economic Development for the City of Chandler, they invited me to house my hydrogen technology research and development company, H2 Pure Power, at Innovations. I was given a state of the art laboratory and an office. I contacted an engineer that had some true hydrogen experience and I felt that he could develop a true hydrogen electrolyzer system. Jim Clements and I went to work and we came up with a very excellent system which got exceptional hydrogen output. I tapped into Divine Intelligence and the training that I had from the Master Teachers in the labs on the ships for all those years. I remembered all just when I needed it.

Jim had the solid engineering foundation which is needed to design technology. But as all engineers, he was locked in a box and had difficulty understanding metaphysics and quantum physics which I often employed and used to enhance the system and make it work better.

I went to two World Hydrogen Energy Conferences, the first one was in Vancouver, Canada and met Nigel Williamson, an engineer, from the U.K. The second one was in Toronto where I was privileged to present our technology. Most of the projects were hydrogen fuel cells and they had experimental cars and buses at both conferences. Canada and Europe were far ahead of the U.S. in the focus of funding and development of this energy of the future. Nigel was impressed that I actually had a working model that I was marketing to put on vehicles. We talked about perhaps working together in the future. He was currently working for a leading hydrogen manufacturing and research company as their head engineer in the U.K.

In 2012, I was honored at the University of California, Fresno at a Green Energy Conference as a Hero in the Energy Age with all the contributions that I had made with the development of my technology.

I felt that the enhanced diesel fuel system that I had developed was a bridge between fossil fuel and the hydrogen fuel cell vehicles. The problem that I and others were facing was that the system worked wonderfully well on older vehicles which did not have the computer systems that started being installed in 1995. On computerized vehicles, the hydrogen would be allowed for about 200 miles and then the computer would kick back in and relearn, adjusting the air-fuel mixture and not allowing the hydrogen to work. One loyal customer, Roger Moss, had an older truck which we installed the system on and it improved his gas mileage considerably even after several years. He has been a wonderful advocate and supporter for me.

We tried everything to overcome the computer systems with chips and other devices. Sometimes, we had success and other times, none. It was hit and miss with the success. The hydrogen system worked, but adapting it to the different vehicles was a challenge. I started realizing that the secret would be to work with the automotive makers of engines and computers to allow the systems to be integrated.

Jim moved on to another job as he was discouraged with the results we were getting. Nigel said he had left his company and now he wanted to tackle the improvements to my system that he thought would make it far more efficient and effective. I was very happy at our collaboration. He had a partner with funding and I went into a dormant state while I waited for him to do the research and see how to adapt the systems. He kept reporting to me that he was facing the same problems that I had with the computers on vehicles.

PHASE 24: DISABLED BY CIPRO

In the midst of developing the hydrogen technology, I became very ill with a serious intestinal bacterial infection which I am sure was MRSA, and suffered with it for 4 months. I was so utterly spent from it that I agreed to call a doctor that a friend knew and over the phone, he called in a prescription for Ciprofloxen. The doctor did not run tests or examine me, but I had heard of Cipro and knew that it was a common antibiotic. Two weeks after I started taking it, my feet froze up and then "burst into a million shards of glass" making me literally an invalid. I could not walk, and had to crawl to my bed. I was in agony. I also had a severe rash. I could not figure out what had happened to me. It dawned on me to look at the side effects of Cipro and the warning said that the major side effect is ruptured tendons and tendonitis. There were other side effects which are all classic Cipro warnings.

I went in to see the doctor and he denied that Cipro could have that effect. He did an X-Ray which did not show anything. He just dismissed it as nothing is really wrong. I changed doctors and was sent to a foot and ankle surgeon who did a MRI to confirm his diagnosis of a ruptured tendon in my left foot. He scheduled me for surgery and I was so relieved as I thought the surgery would bring my foot back to its complete normal state.

The surgery was so intense that I had to go into a rehabilitation center for 21 days and then after that, a wheelchair, physical therapy, a walker, a boot and even after three years, my foot has not completely returned to normal. The Cipro also had the effect of tendonitis throughout my whole body causing spasms and charley horses when I stretched. Cipro affected many systems causing diabetes, high blood pressure, hypothyroidism, high cholesterol and other things which I had never experienced. I had the severe effects of acid reflux, gerd and digestive issues due to being poisoned, but I had worked very hard to be healthy and had achieved very good body chemistry. I had been doing Zumba exercise and aerobics. After the ruptured tendon, I was not able to exercise and gained weight which adds to ill health.

Those of us who are in the process of changing the density of our bodies to those of Light, moving into 5th

Dimensional energy, cannot take these drugs. This experience with Cipro has taken me to my knees and humbled me. There are several reasons that I have been through this and I know this is a huge Initiation for me. First, it was the giant sign from the Divine to close the hydrogen business and to return to my true mission of health, spirituality and healing. I did not listen to the Voice which had come to me several times and I ignored it with my strong will taking over. I did not want to fail at this business or any venture as I have always had the strong desire to be a model for other women to enter fields that were reserved for men. It is totally ridiculous that women cannot be successful in any field that a man is in. This has to be resolved and is in process. I wanted to succeed so very much.

The other part of the Initiation was that I needed to learn more about healing and all the elements of healing, returning to the simple things of nature and all the elements. I have been called back to my shamanism and herbalist training to bring forth the ancient teachings of Earth, Air, Fire, Water, and Community. So many herbal remedies, formulas, and treatments have come to me in my search for my healing. It is thrilling to discover and rediscover many wonderful remedies. I will address them in a later chapter.

I had a renewed commitment to the Breath of Light during this stage of Illumination and Divine Insight. I did not Breathe as I should have during the test of the Montana saga. I allowed myself to be disconnected from the stream of

Divine Intelligence. But, now, I had the time and the deep desire to Breathe deeply in the Holy Spirit and resurrect my body, mind and spirit. I had gone through a death in some ways of my Self. Who was I going to emerge as this time? I knew that closing the door on the business and technology was going to change my life drastically, but I did not know in all the ways it would change. I just knew that it was the only thing to do or I would truly die and leave this earth. I had to complete my mission and give my gift of the Breath of Light to the world.

Since I had invested all my funds in the hydrogen project and the house in Montana, I found myself left with meager funds of Social Security. It was interesting to have to manage on so little and learn to live simply, very simply. But, things were uncomplicated and I learned that it is not about the money. I can have money or not have money, but I can be at peace and happy, even in bliss as long as I am Breathing, meditating, letting go of the past and just in joy about the present. So simple. So difficult to come to that place, but I am in the deepest gratitude possible for being able to achieve this state of grace. I am in love with my life and all that it is, every moment.

I read for the first time, The Nine Faces of Christ, The Quest of the True Initiate by Eugene Whitworth, and reread, The Life and Teachings of the Masters of the Far East by Baird Spalding, and found my old well-worn copies of the Alice Bailey Esoteric Teachings which I have been devouring these last years. I am so lifted up and able to transcend all of the physical and material concerns with putting myself in the Mind of the Divine.

PHASE 25: BACK TO THE BREATH OF LIGHT AND MY TRUE MISSION

I felt called to start teaching and sharing the Breath of Light meditations and classes on Initiation with the Elements. I have been offering them in the Phoenix area and in Las Vegas at Unity there. The work is expanding and I know that I am being prepared to take the work to a whole new level. The Fifth Dimension that we have entered demands it.

During this course of my immersion into spiritual practice and doing my preparation work for Ascension, I received the very strong vision that I must get all my materials done to help others through their Initiation. First, my book had to be rewritten and updated with all the new information and understanding. And, I was to do a whole new series of meditations focused on many different themes. I made a sacred contract with myself to complete this project and it has energized and lifted me up even higher. I am being transformed as I write. It is cathartic and I am healing on all levels. I know when I have finished with the book I will be healed and changed in a dramatic way. My other DNA strands are being activated and I am aware of being able to perform alchemy and miracles. All of this is possible for us all. We just have to do our work and commit to daily spiritual cleansing as well as physical detoxification.

Meditation is essential to connecting with the Mind of God, the Divine Intelligence and becoming transcendent of all our attachments. I am setting aside two days every month to do a personal meditation retreat – turning off all communication and just communing with the Divine. We are now being downloaded with the new frequency, information, DNA activation and cellular healing. It is a great gift to ourselves and the world to commit to this Spiritual practice. Our only work now is to BE the Light and the great Compassionate Love of the Christ. I have been a Doer and now it is time to just BE and radiate the Presence.

Another decision that I made was to cultivate friends and have a personal life that included spending time with my children and grandchildren, other women friends who are treasures, and being in nature more. I have worked very hard for so many years and have achieved a lot, but I have not had much fun and laughter. That is important to me.

In seeking a way to detox the Cipro, which was systemic, out of my body, I found the Sunshine Clinic, a chelation clinic offering hydrogen peroxide and glutathione IV's which I know to be very effective from my own clinic. I exchanged my FIR Sauna for the IV's and they brought me a quantum leap with detoxing. I can say that I am being healed and know that I will return to radiant health and complete recovery. I wholeheartedly recommend that you find a Naturopath or IV Clinic wherever you live and get the

IV treatments as they are far more effective than any oral protocols.

My beloveds, we are being called to the Ultimate Invitation to become Christed and step forth out of the addictions of the physical existence and become Bringers and Wayshowers of the Light.

CHAPTER 3 BREATH OF LIGHT: BREATHING INTO A NEW DIMENSION

Breathing physically detoxes the body. Therefore, when used correctly, the breathing system is one of the most powerful systems to heal the body. Unfortunately, most of us stopped breathing correctly when we were very young, maybe even as infants. Often, when a baby is born, the first breath is traumatic as the lungs may not be cleared of the fluid, which can cause searing pain. Because of emotional suppression as children, we hold our breath or breathe shallowly out of fear. It seems the only emotions that are reinforced for us as children are shame, guilt and fear. Most often it was not acceptable for us to be joyous and alive -- at least with the lot of unhappy parents that I have observed.

So as adults, we have to retrain our breath to breathe deeply enough to be effective and heal our bodies. The breath can change our pH balance from acid to alkaline in one session. We know that we have to have an alkaline system in order to heal. The breath takes in oxygen to the red blood cells, which then carry the toxins out through the exhale. We also know that if we can get enough oxygen in our bodies, no disease, virus or bacteria can exist in the oxygenated systems. Mentally, the breath clears our brains with the added oxygen (carrying off toxins) so that we can have clear and positive thoughts. When we accumulate toxins, it is impossible to stop the negative thoughts from permeating us. We all have a "Board of Directors" in our heads. They never seem to stop with their yammering -- mostly critical, terrible thoughts about ourselves and others. This is just part of the "human condition." Our minds can be our best friends or our worst enemies. We have to come to a place of quiet and peace in order to commune with the Divine and our higher selves. Breathing is the most effective way to correct negative thinking. Negative thinking dumps toxins and acid into the body, which leads to disease and death.

Emotionally, the breath allows the emotions to come up gently and be released, as well as integrated into our bodies. We are emotional beings -- we are human beings. We are in human bodies to purify off the emotions. The only way we can experience emotions is in a physical body. They are a very tough challenge. Not too many of us have conquered our emotions. They are the very thing that is keeping us in the low consciousness that we see on our planet. If we want to move into new and higher dimensions of spirit, we have to heal the emotions and no longer be at the effect of them.

Feelings and emotions are different. Feelings are the higher range of emotions that have been transmuted and transformed into another energy form such as love, peace, joy, compassion, and acceptance. Emotions usually include anger, jealousy, envy, fear, guilt, resentments, etc. When we have these emotions, they dump massive acid into the body. When we have the higher feelings, endorphins are released, which heal the body.

The Breath relaxes the body, brings in a very high vibration of love energy, clears the negatives from the mind, and stimulates very powerful healing. As you feel love that accepts and forgives all, washing away guilt, pain and fear, the emotions are released. Sometimes, old emotional trauma is remembered but is now observed with a higher perspective than when it happened. The emotions are then released and transmuted, leaving the person cleansed and alive, being set free, as it were, from the devastating density of negative emotions.

The body is the best learning facility we have. The body is fully instrumented. It has millions of instantaneous feedback circuits. It contains more information than all the libraries in the world for it codifies, in its structure and its genes, evolutionary experience that goes all the way back to the first living organism and before that, to the Light.

The body is all time remembered. At the microscopic and submicroscopic levels the body holds even more information - a catalogue of crystals, complex molecules, simple molecules, atoms, a quantum of pure energy. They link the time and space self to the birth of the universe when time and space themselves were born.

The Breath of Light is indeed an "Awakening" -- a catalyst for those ready -- for new beginnings -- to heal old self-destructive patterns -- to clarify purpose and action in your life. As an Initiate into the Breath of Light, all of the circuitry of one's body is connected and allowed to fire, thus permitting the life force to flow freely through the body, which has long been disconnected. This Breath of Light carries within Its frequency the codings that will activate the Divine Blueprint contained within the messenger codes of our RNA/DNA - the blueprint for our Unlimited Physical Perfection, the blueprint for our Light Bodies. Our personal healing work at this time is very specific. We are to surrender all of the dense, unascended energy of our physical embodiment to the Great Healing Light in order that we become matching frequencies and vessels of Light. We can only be in Service when we have come into this state. We are to be restored to our Divine Will and Mind of our Father-Mother-God and empowered to do the work we came here to do. We are no longer to be imprisoned in the "veil of maya" believing that we are lowly human victims doomed to a karmic wheel of suffering, fear, pain and sacrifice. We are initiated back into the Light of the Great Central Sun brought by Divine Mother and the Celestial Hosts of Angels.

Through our bodies, we gain access to a treasury of knowledge and guidance. We need to know that bodily feelings and movements can inform, as there is wisdom in flesh. Tuning into another's body - healing another or yourself - is simply paying attention to messages from within. You realize you are connected, and energy passes between yourself and others continually in a flow.

I know no better way to experience this communing with yourself, with others and with God than with the Breath of Light. I see the Breath as the Holy Spirit, the compassionate presence, the great comforter and lover of our soul. We don't take time for this life-giving process of meditation and learning from Spirit. Is it any wonder that so many are tired, weighted down and despondent from carrying such a heavy burden by themselves?

The Holy Spirit comes on the wings of the Breath and brings with it the awakening or a quickening into the Light. We came from a great Light and a love that is so vast we cannot experience it lest we go there through spirit. With it comes the release from our addiction to suffering.

The Breath alters the brain waves and takes us down out of our functioning Beta state(measured at above 12 hertz) to the relaxed state of Alpha(measured at 8-12 hertz). There are many levels of Alpha, but it is considered meditation and relaxation. As we go into Theta, our brain waves are slowing down to about four to eight hertz, and there are also levels within the theta state. When we go lower than 4 hertz, we are in Delta - deep sleep (unconsciousness). This is also the state where we die and are born.

Theta is the deepest level of altered states of consciousness. It is also called the "dream state." The sleeping period is marked by four or so times a night when the sleeper's eyes move rapidly under the lids. It is during these sleep periods, known as rapid eye movement or REM sleep, that we naturally go into Theta.

Little has been known about Theta. Research studies are now gaining more information about this mysterious state - how it works, what is affected, and the benefits of Theta. The following research findings substantiate the scientific basis for the brain's activity - though the body and conscious mind are asleep. It takes tremendous activity in the subconscious to deal with emotional traumas that the conscious mind will not acknowledge.

REM sleep is brought on by waves of nervous activity. It begins in the brain stem, the top of the spinal cord, where it juts into the brain, and travels up to the geniculate nucleus. This is a region of the higher brain where visual inputs from the eyes are processed.

Since these sleep-inducing waves thus activate the visual-processing parts of the brain, it is not so surprising that dreams are primarily visual in nature. The first stream of brain stem waves usually begins about 90 minutes after the onset of sleep, and the fourth (or last) about 30 minutes before waking up. During each of these REM periods, the brain is even more active than it is while awake. Because the muscles are paralyzed, the body lies quietly.

The new research being done is focused on mapping the two opposing circuits and the transmitter chemicals they produce, as well as related circuits.

Researchers have discovered that the transmitters in the sleep-inhibiting circuit arise from two particular clumps of cells in the brain stem, called the dorsal raphe and locus coreleus. A major function of REM sleep may be to let these cells rest and replenish their chemical stores during the night. This may link to the process of chemical reactions stimulated by emotional responses that happen during waking hours.

Another research group at Harvard reports that another nerve cell circuit connects to the place in the brain stem where movement such as walking and running are triggered. When a group of cells in this region is activated by an as-yet undetermined chemical signal, the stimulation helps to bring on the muscle paralysis typical of REM sleep. At the same time, glutamate, a brain chemical that excites neurons, is active. This might explain a paradox of REM sleep, when the eyeballs move and the body twitches even though the dreamer cannot move his sleeping body.

These findings offer more important data from which researchers hope eventually to fully understand the role of

REM sleep. I believe that the state of Theta will be revealed as one of the most powerful healing states we can experience.

We know that you process the deeper problems of your life (stored in the subconscious mind) during your dreams. If you don't, science has proven through research that you go insane. These are problems you could not get to with your conscious mind. Perhaps they are too painful. The idea that unfinished emotional business is the stuff that dreams are made of has found support at *Rush Presbyterian - St. Luke's Hospital* in Chicago. Dr. Rosalind Cartwright has been studying there the dreams of 214 men and women going through separation with the intent to divorce.

By waking people after each REM (rapid eye movement) cycle in the sleep laboratory, Cartwright is finding out how often emotional subjects appear in dreams over time. In most dreams, she said, a central issue is carried through the night, and from night to night, from one REM episode to the next, until the person begins to work through the problem.

So it is very beneficial to go into Theta at will - especially if you are in a healing crisis and trying to release any emotional traumas held in the cells of your body. I believe that most disease (probably about 80%) is caused by emotions. The rest is environmentally caused, but there may still be some emotional cause that would allow your immune system to accept disease.

TIME MAGAZINE (June 1996) reveals in an extensive review of Faith and Healing --*Recent research demonstrates that these stress hormones also have a direct impact on the body's immunological defenses against disease. "Anything involved with meditation and controlling the state of mind that alters hormone activity has the potential to have an impact on the immune system." says David Felten, chairman of the Department of Neurobiology at the University of Rochester.*

It is probably no coincidence that the relaxation response and religious experience share headquarters in the brain. Studies show that the relaxation response is controlled by the amygdala, a small, almond-shaped structure in the brain that together with the hippocampus and hypothalamus makes up the limbic system. The limbic system, which is found in all primates, plays a key role in emotions, sexual pleasure, deep-felt memories and, it seems, spirituality. "The ability to have religious experiences has a neuro-anatomical basis," concludes Shawn Joseph, a neuroscientist at the Palo Alto VA Medical Center in California.

When you are approaching Theta, your breathing will slow down and may even stop altogether for several minutes. This is safe and highly desirable, as Theta is a very still state. We know that all healing and change take place in Theta.

An observer would see that the body is pulsing as it doesn't need to breathe anymore. Though the body remains almost as still as in death, within it much is happening. The person will have REM, and there is a certain vibratory rate you can sense if you are intuitive. People in Theta often experience visions, commune with loved ones who have died, receive messages and information to heal their lives. Sometimes, the person does not remember what happened at all. And sometimes it feels like shadows passing - you can almost see something very important, but it is processed before you can actually see it.

The great meditators and masters have sought this holy state of Theta for years. It was given only to a few. Because we have to accelerate our growth and need something very powerful to get through the emotions, this is a new healing energy being revealed to us on the planet. We are very blessed to have the help of this healing vibration in the form of the Breath of Light - it is so very easy if we have a desire to heal and live.

As we take that last breath, going into the breathless state of Theta, we can finally look into the face of the Divine. We can finally know that we are His beloved in whom He is well pleased. We can know that Love is eternal and will never forsake us. We will bring heaven to earth, spirit to density, and receive Initiation into the new dimensions of spiritual consciousness.

There is another special thing that is happening to many of us as we sleep, allowing the body to restore and rejuvenate. That is when we are able to leave the body and travel to other places and even other dimensions. I am very aware that I am visiting other areas of the world and am conscious of who I am with and what we are doing. I do not know these people but have vivid recall of them. I have been in the Pacific SW and Colorado lately, building projects and doing other work. So, we are very busy during our sleep times. I also have visitations from others as well as my beloved, Joe. This is part of the gifts to us of entering the fifth dimension. We are dwelling more in Spirit and able to do things that we have not thought possible and are considered miracles.

Jesus came to show us this ability and teach us how to do the miracles that He did and much more. Our time has come. Just have faith and believe.

CHAPTER 4 HEALING WITH THE ELEMENTS – EARTH, AIR, FIRE, WATER AND COMMUNITY

All organisms, human or plant or animal, are composed of a multitude of tiny individual living units called cells. It is these cells and the manner in which they are organized into specific tissues and organs that form the physical body. This organization -- the very life of these individual cells and, therefore, the body as a whole -- is dependent upon a continuous source of energy to rebuild and replace the dying cells. This is a highly efficient, organized process governed by a sophisticated, computerized system -- our brain. And directing the whole process is our mind, not to be confused with our brain. The mind is our higher spiritual self - our oversoul that reaches into spiritual dimensions, communes with the Divine Source and the Holy Spirit in order to bring wisdom and learning to our human experience - which is physical, emotional, mental and sensory.

Within this organized stability, there is constant change. Every seven years, all cells are replaced. Every few months, all proteins are replaced. Every few days, the epidermal layer of skin is replaced. Every second, 2.5 million red blood cells die and, at the same time, 2.5 million new cells are born.

The body is more like a flame than a lump of clay - burning yet not consumed. The substance, of which it is made, changes. The essential form persists.

Even the body's solidity is an illusion perpetuated by our limited range of visual sensitivity. If we could take a voyage into the body, entering cells, molecules, atoms, we would find no static substance at all - only pattern and pulse.

We have to start listening to our bodies. In addition to our physical body, we have an emotional, spiritual and mental body. We must gain awareness of these bodies and know that our physical body is a very accurate gauge reflecting what is going on in all the rest of our bodies.

We have been given everything we need to heal and rejuvenate ourselves, from the Creator of all things. We do not have to devise some new, artificial, medical treatment! Nature always creates the antidote for disease and disorder. All that is needed is to purify off the toxins using the elements of Earth, Air, Fire, Water and Community.

The Native Americans have always understood this and lived in harmony with nature and the elements. I have studied with many of the wise teachers from several Native American tribes. Cherokee blood flows in my veins and, with that, brings a cellular memory of ancient and natural healing practices from my ancestors.

Our ancestral heritage is brought through the cellular memory and is more powerful and influential than we realize in governing our behaviors and thoughts. We may have to purify and heal our lineage of past "sins." We come into this life to heal our mother and father (male and female). We can do this in several ways. Sometimes we have to do the work only from within ourselves if our parents have passed over already. If we are lucky enough to have our parents still living, we have an opportunity to put this work into living action. We must put pride and ego aside - see the past as just that - **the past.** Yes, it happened. Yes, it was painful. But it is time to get on with our lives. If we are able to purify ourselves at this deep cellular level, we actually can heal the past -- and the future as well. As we heal ourselves, we prevent those cellular patterns from being passed on to the future through our children.

We can also benefit from our ancestors, calling on their ancient wisdom to help us. The Theta breathing brings forth these memories and the wisdom, as well.

So how do we harness the continuous source of energy we need for the body to heal? And what is energy?

EARTH – FOOD IS NUTRIENTS FOR OUR CELLS – ENERGY

We usually think of the food we eat as supplying our energy needs in terms of a certain amount of carbohydrate, protein and fat. However, these nutrients have to be converted into a form that can be used by our cells -- otherwise they are useless sources of energy. We say that we burn carbohydrates in the body, but what do we mean? If carbohydrates are being burned in the tissues, doesn't this hurt? Why doesn't fat sizzle, and where does the smoke go?

In a fire, energy is released as heat and light. The reaction involves the burning of carbon-containing substances. The end result is the formulation of carbon dioxide gas (CO_2), water and ash, along with the release of energy. The energy that is produced when something burns quickly is manifested as heat and light.

The heat energy in a fire or explosion can be used to drive a machine. The automobile engine is powered by the rapid burning process of gasoline exploding in a chamber.

How do our bodies harness energy? Cells must have energy, but they do not run on explosions. All living organisms are fueled by a furnace that releases energy by combining fuel with oxygen.

The fuel that we use comes from the carbohydrates and fats that we eat. It is combined with oxygen, under very special circumstances, to keep it in a form that is both useful and safe. That is why the reaction takes place in tiny subunits within the cell called mitochondria. These mitochondria contain a series of specialized protein molecules or enzymes called the cytochrome oxidase system. This system takes the energy, released from the oxidation of our food, and transfers it to an energy storage molecule called adenosine triphosphate or ATP. Found in biological systems throughout nature, ATP may be thought of as the basic unit of energy storage for cells. It has the ability to produce energy within the cells of the body. This, in turn, maintains the chemical reactions necessary for the cells to function normally.

One of the most important things I did for myself during those years of healing was to implement my nutritional plan. There are so many theories concerning what to do with nutrition that it gets very confusing. Indeed, I have refined and changed my ideas about diet through the years since my healing, and even since the previous printings of my book.

One thing that I do know is that nutrition was crucial to getting my body into a heightened state of energy and clarity so that I could also receive input from my meditations and thoughts with clarity. It also gave me the energy to heal. *SWANK'S DIET FOR MULTIPLE SCLEROSIS AND*

OTHER DEGENERATIVE DISEASE by Dr. Roy Swank was the basis for my diet when I was ill. Dr. Roy Swank was my personal physician and I count myself lucky that I had a doctor who believed that diet was a determining factor. Mostly, the Swank Diet contains low animal fat, no preservatives or additives, no dairy, along with the addition of cod liver oil (pure Norwegian) every day. I went several steps farther, eliminating the sugar and becoming more vegetarian than even Dr. Swank recommended.

If you are ill, it takes incredible energy to heal your body. If you are taking your energy to turn around and process bad energy foods that you are eating, then there is not going to be enough energy to heal yourself. When you are ill, you have very little energy - certainly not enough to squander.

Because of my concern to share as much knowledge as possible with those who are working to heal themselves, I have continued to research and experiment with nutrition. The one thing that is for sure: nutrition is critical. I find myself becoming more and more committed to living foods. I am going to share some of the things learned and researched that are crucial for healing. And NO, it is not particularly easy to get into the lifestyle necessary to eat this way. It is a process that keeps evolving and moving more towards the purity that we need to truly heal. However, how important is it for you to be well and enjoy good health the rest of your life?

If you are dealing with a healing challenge, physically, then you are going to have to be very pure with your diet. I have found that, for myself, I have moved more toward semi-vegetarianism. When I am in good shape, which is most of the time, I do better with a little fish, a little organic poultry, and in a "blue moon" a little bit of organic beef. But most of the time, I eat steamed/sautéed vegetables and live foods. When I do eat some sort of "meat," I always supplement with enzymes and amino acids, to aid in digesting the protein. I am supplementing with powdered greens such as spirulina, wheat grass, green barley, etc. These greens are the highest protein source on the planet. And, we need more protein at this time of the shift. I have been interested to talk to healers, teachers, spiritual leaders around the world, and many have felt it necessary to change from strict vegetarianism at this time. And, not to say that we very well may return to that dietary regime again. I don't think any of us can be so severe or fanatical at this time that we are not able to hear Spirit's whisperings to each of us as to what is needed in the moment.

And I would like to speak about severity. I have certainly been severe in my own life. I have felt that I needed to suffer in order to prove some sort of worthiness to be here and alive. How could I enjoy life when so many were suffering in the world? I have come to realize that for me to buy into suffering and embrace it into my life just added more suffering to the world. And remember, when I had the second "near death" experience, I was told that I must learn to celebrate life here on earth before I could leave. I believe the only way we can inspire anyone else to seek the Light is by our own personal witness. Everyone wants to know that these principles work, and we have to be authentic. We have to live the truth, be the Love, and share joy. So, sometimes, I "sin" a little. But I do watch what state my energy is in, and check my systems to see whether I am weak. If I am, I stay to a strict diet. But if I do choose to eat something like a dessert or meat, I make it a celebration and enjoy it to the "max"! I think when you add the joy factor, you transmute a whole lot.

Now, for those of you who will take a mile if I give you an inch, this is not an excuse or permission to go out and eat anything or anyway you want to all the time. We do have a real responsibility to choose a healthy diet most of the time, and stray only once in a while. I see so-called "spiritual" people eating junk food, smoking, drinking, doing drugs, overeating, etc. And I am here to say that we cannot just sit around, think it, or talk about it. We have to be congruent and authentic. Otherwise, we are frauds, and are no different from the "world" we are trying to change. We are going to see a lot of people diseased and dying in our own "spiritual communities" because they are not living by the spiritual laws. We have to change our dense frequency and shift up into the higher resonance, which is taking place right now. And food is one aspect of that purification that must take place. When our body is suffering and diseased, our mental abilities are affected. There is a veil between us and our connection to Divine Intelligence. It clouds our ability to receive clear guidance and direction. Our emotions color our thoughts and the toxic energy poisons us on all levels.

A definite relationship exists between food and life expression. It is plain, scientific fact that the two greatest dangers in our food consumption today are animal fats and refined carbohydrates. I believe that a third danger is the preservatives and additives put in meats and prepared foods. These may be the biggest killer of all. A vegetarian diet, followed scientifically to include all the basic requirements of proteins, vitamins, minerals, enzymes and the right kind of fats and carbohydrates will inevitably prolong life, strengthen vitality and increase resistance to disease. Disease cannot exist in a normal metabolism, and a normal metabolism can be achieved and maintained by following the principles of scientific vegetarianism.

Yes, I can identify with your resistance to becoming a vegetarian, because I resisted it for years. It seemed a difficult lifestyle, and I would have to "give up" so many things I loved. However, the things I "loved" did not love me back. It takes much soul searching to make a decision to love ourself enough to see our body as a temple, and put only life-giving things in this instrument.

I regard abundant health and vitality as the normal condition of man. Our goal is health, a perfect, balanced development of body, mind and soul in harmony with the eternal laws of nature. The quality and quantity of food have an effect upon moral development as well as upon physical well being and happiness.

To understand how diet can so definitely affect all of life, it is necessary to know how the body is constructed and nourished. The body is made up of living cells, continually disintegrating and continually being renewed. These cells require food in order to live, and the food they require is not just any substance the individual may put into his mouth and swallow (like junk food), but rather foods that supply them with the exact materials they require. The function of food, then, is to 1) build and renew the cells, 2) yield energy and 3) regulate body processes.

The cells that compose the body are made up of water, protein, sugars and starches (carbohydrates), minerals and vitamins. The food that will fulfill the needs of the cells must, therefore, be composed of utilizable forms containing these same elements. The science of biochemistry has determined what foods will supply the needed substances in the proper proportions and in the particular forms from which man can obtain the most adequate nourishment. We are now understanding the importance of balancing body chemistry. Food does not have all the necessary nutrients that we need and we have to supplement. I would like to share about some of the newest keys to longevity and health. One of the new stars is Glutathione which is a natural protein made of three amino acids: glycine, glutamate and most importantly the essential amino acid, cysteine. It turns out to be essential to living systems and without we age and disease faster. More than 3000 published articles have been published and the application of this knowledge will change medicine and disease as we know it in the next decade. According to research by French scientists, almost 50% of people have lost a 10KB fragment from their DNA that is responsible for glutathione function. This means that half of the population has no defense against environmental toxins if they don't avoid exposure or supplement with extra cysteine and glutathione. This protein causes major biochemical reactions in the cell. It acts as the major cellular detoxification enzyme to environmental agents including prescription medications and alcohol. It is the antioxidant that recharges vitamin C and E, which recharge the substances that if left uncharged, lead to arthritis, inflammation, thrombosis, atherosclerosis and many other conditions. It is the cellular substance that makes the immune system fights disease. In addition, genetic damage from internal and environmental stresses are dependent on cysteine and glutathione for successful repair. Lack of these substances lead to degeneration and mutations that can lead to cancer and aging diseases. The transport of simple protein hormones, such as insulin, sex hormones, and adrenal hormones are dependent on it to cross from the blood stream into the cell where the actual work gets done. So, if 90% of disease is based on low glutathione function in our body, how can we raise the levels safely? Oral glutathione supplements in any form are not well absorbed. I believe glutathione administered via IV (intravaneous) is the best way for the body to absorb it. I get glutathione pushes after chelation or hydrogen peroxide IV's. There are several products that provide this important nutrient such as NAC (N-acetyl cysteine) which has been used safely for the last 20-30 years as an antidote to tylenol overdoses and many other conditions ranging from acute myocardial infarctions, cancer, colon polyps, lung diseases, arthritis, hypertension and other toxic conditions. It has been discovered that the NAC potentiates whatever supplements you are taking and therefore, does not require so many or at a high dosage.

Another very important supplement that I consider essential is flaxseed oil. It is also called linseed oil. I wrote extensively about it in Chapter 2 and in my Health Protocols.

Certain elements besides foods are necessary for the human organism to exist. These include fresh air, water and sunlight. Fruits, vegetables and grains store these elements in a form that can be utilized by the body in the highest degree. It is for this reason that we give an exalted place to these foods in the diet.

Fruit represents the highest form of vegetable life on the planet. Man's organs and senses both undergo progressive improvement on a fruitarian diet. Man was entirely a fruit eating animal, according to science, when he inhabited the earth prior to the Pleistocene cataclysm. Man's physical structure indicates this, having the teeth and digestive system closely akin to the monkey family. Eating nothing but fruit, monkeys have teeth and digestive systems very different from the carnivorous, the herbivorous and the omnivorous animals. Man has no sharp pointed teeth like the carnivore for tearing flesh. His incisors are not developed for cropping green herbage, like the herbivore. His molars are quite different in form and in enameling from either order of animal. From these physiological facts, it can be assumed that man's body was constructed to subsist on fruits, his natural diet being fruitarian.

However, for the last few thousand years, he has eaten other foods for which he is not structurally fitted. His organism has learned to adapt itself (in a measure) to these other foods. He cannot therefore immediately change back to a fruitarian diet. The race habits of several thousand years cannot abruptly be broken without causing an imbalance in his system. Only when we have reached a somewhat higher stage of evolutionary perfection can we safely return to a diet of fruits alone. In light of this, vegetarianism does not advocate that more than 50% of the daily diet should be fruit. At least 30% should be fruit. However, I used to recommend eating only fruit until noon, although if you have blood sugar problems, you may not need that much. I find that I need protein in the morning. When I eat fruit in the morning, it sends my blood sugar soaring. I have shifted to eating fruit in the evening, or as a snack in the mid-afternoon.

New research is showing that intermittent fasting which allows the digestive system to rest and recover over a longer period of time is a very healthy thing to do.

Fasting is a challenge to your brain, and your brain responds to that challenge by adapting stress response pathways which help your brain cope with stress and risk for disease. The same changes that occur in the brain during fasting mimic the changes that occur with regular exercise. They both increase the production of protein in the brain (neurotrophic factors), which in turn promotes the growth of neurons, the connection between neurons, and the strength of synapses.

"Challenges to your brain, whether it's intermittent fasting [or] vigorous exercise . . . is cognitive challenges. When this happens neuro-circuits are activated, levels of neurotrophic factors increase, that promotes the growth of

neurons [and] the formation & strengthening of synapses. . . ." American Journal of Clinical Nutrition

Fasting can also stimulate the production of new nerve cells from stem cells in the hippocampus. Fasting stimulates the production of ketones (an energy source for neurons). Fasting also increases the number of mitochondria in nerve cells; this comes as a result of the neurons adapting to the stress of fasting (by producing more mitochondria).

By increasing the number of mitochondria in the neurons, the ability for neurons to form and maintain the connections between each other also increases, thereby improving learning and memory ability.

"Intermittent fasting enhances the ability of nerve cells to repair DNA."

A study published in the June 5 issue of *Cell Stem Cell* by researchers from the University of Southern California showed that cycles of prolonged fasting protect against immune system damage and, moreover, induce immune system regeneration. They concluded that fasting shifts stem cells from a dormant state to a state of self-renewal. It triggers stem cell based regeneration of an organ or system.

This means that fasting kills off old and damaged immune cells, and when the body rebounds it uses stem cells to create brand new, completely healthy cells.

There are many ways to implement intermittent fasting, but the most recommended one by nutrition experts is waiting to break the fast until about noon and limit your eating to just 6-8 hours. Adding reduced calorie intake can result in weight loss. But, the health experts are recommending fasting as a health regime. Some are fasting for a full 24 hours every week. There are many variations and you can google it for more input. I do not eat and break the fast until about noon and try to keep my food intake to 6 hours. It feels easy for me and each one has to find what is your natural rhythm.

What I currently do personally to break the fast and recommend is a health protein smoothie which includes the following ingredients: 1 cup almond milk or coconut milk, whey protein powder, strawberries or blueberries, ½ banana, 1 Tabl. flaxseed, 1 Tabl. coconut oil, 1 Tabl. Flaxseed oil, ½ cup plain Greek yogurt, 1 Tabl. Brewers yeast, 1 Tabl. Nutritional Yeast, ¼ teasp. MSM, 2 Tabl. Dried greens (spirulina, barley green, wheat grass), 2 Tabl. chia seeds, and 1 Tabl. non GMO sunflower lecithin. I add stevia for sweetener. This is chock full of nutrients and I can guarantee that you will not be hungry for many hours after this.

For a mid-afternoon snack, I have about ½ cup low fat cottage cheese with 2 Tablespoons of flaxseed oil and ¼ cup crushed pineapple. This is an anti-cancer recipe (without the pineapple, but I like the taste and digestive enzyme) from

Dr. Johanna Budwig of Austria. This has had excellent results as an anti-cancer treatment both as preventative and during active cancer. I absolutely love the taste of it and I think my body is requesting it. I have an afternoon slump and can feel fatigued, but if I have the cottage cheese and flaxseed oil, I am given the boost that carries me through.

Note about Soy: Just recently, information has come out about soy products and how toxic they are. Only fermented soy is safe. Soy contains anti-nutrients that deplete necessary enzymes, precludes absorption of much needed minerals and increases aluminum consumption by 10%. Aluminum is very toxic to the nervous system. This was another case of the soy industry being able to petition the FDA to lower their standards for fats and oils so as to create a new standard for their products. Another very toxic oil is canola oil which comes from the rapeseed which they used to make poison gas for war purposes. There is no canola plant, but they could not very well call it rapeseed oil, could they?

Please ask someone to muscle-test you, or just breathe and ask spirit to give you your own personal guidance on your body's requirements.

I have become aware of how important juicing is, and recommend that you purchase a juicer. There are many, and the best ones even pulverize the pulp so you get the fiber as juice. Juice should always be fresh, not canned or concentrated, as the enzymes which are the important part of juice, only live for several hours maximum. Canned juice often contains additives and sugar. Read the labels. If you are not able to juice because of time constraints, then buy the Greens powder and use it in a smoothie.

My favorite juice for detoxing is a combination of beets, carrots, apples, celery, kale, cucumber, cabbage and you can add a potato if you are fighting cancer.

Like fruits, vegetables have accumulated certain specific energies of a solar and cosmic nature. The optimal diet will include about 30% of fresh vegetables in the daily ration as well.

There are many vegetables that have unusual healing ability. I will share with you one of my most favorite cures. If one has any infection or pain in their lower body, especially the legs and feet, then this is the remedy for you! Shred about ¼ head of cabbage into a pan. Pour boiling water over it and let set until cooled enough to put your feet in it. Let your feet soak for about 20 minutes. You will need to do it for several days, but the results are worth it. I have amazing testimonies from people who have been stung by sting rays, or had infections whereby puss seeped out their toe nails. The infection and toxin is pulled out by the cabbage. Be sure and throw away as it will be toxic and you cannot use it more than once. Cabbage juice is also very potent to get rid of toxic drugs and carcinogens. Cabbage juice stops bacterial mutations and protects against low-level radiation as well. It aids if one has ulcers or other digestive ailments. Foods are medicine – good medicine. I am writing a new book that is both gourmet healthy recipes as well as many of my remedies using foods and herbs. Watch for the release.

For many generations, man has eaten grains and cereal products. A ration of 25% grains and cereals is recommended in the vegetarian diet. The balance of the diet may consist of certain concentrated foods such as seeds, nuts, legumes and dried fruits.

For some, grains are problematic and especially the gluten ones with wheat being the worst. The Paleo diet does not endorse grains in that protocol and mainly consists of meats and vegetables. There are many books that direct you through the Paleo nutritional plan. As we are seeing, many new nutritional plans are being researched and marketed. Again, you will want to educate yourself and meditate on what is best for you. Your body will tell you if you listen.

The objective of correct nutrition is to obtain the highest level of health and well-being of the individual. It has been proven by scientific experiment that faulty nutrition results in ill health. Illness is the result of disobeying natural law.

When man follows the laws of nature, he renders himself immune to infection. Apparently, man is not obeying these laws. Recently published figures indicate that more than one-half of the people existing in the world today are sick.

To have a clear understanding of how health is dependent upon nutrition, it is necessary to know something about the biological processes of the human organism. Nutrition has three functions: the renewal of the body's cells, the supply of energy, and regulation of body processes. These functions can only be performed in an adequate manner when the food breaks down into substances that are usable in the body.

Science states that the vital energy needed for man's existence is derived from the radiations of the sun. Biologists say the solar energies are recovered when man eats foods that have been impregnated with this solar energy. It is through the metabolism of the vegetable kingdom that this recovery takes place. The roots of the plants draw the elements from the earth, the sun, air and water, and change them into a form utilizable by man, thus providing the nourishment for his organism. Through the processes of metabolism in the plant, the inorganic substances it absorbs are so finely triturated that they are taken into the body in organic combinations containing the vital forces of living matter.

This living matter, called biochemical substance, is utilized by the body for the building and maintenance of the cells. This is termed the anabolic process. The process by which the organism eliminates by-products (the material it cannot use and waste products) is called catabolic. The two processes together are metabolism. Metabolism produces the chemical changes in living matter that releases the energy for the vital processes and life activities. When an organism cannot utilize the ingested substances and discard those useless to it, disease results. That is why it is so important to understand balanced proportion of the different food elements in the vegetable kingdom. They are classified into seven groups: water, sugar, starch, protein, fat, minerals, and vitamins. The body needs no other substances for its perfect development, maintenance, vitality and health.

The ingestion of food into the physical body is for restoration and sustenance only. Proper nutrition does not cause or cure. These two functions are controlled solely by the individual's intelligence. It is up to the individual to learn the spiritual cause of disease and allow his wisdom to develop and learn through disease. Through right thinking and right living, the dysfunction can be corrected. Even though the cause and core of the dysfunction in the physical body has been corrected, the damages inflicted on the cellular structure must be repaired and the cells rebuilt by a proper nutritional program. The body can relay messages from the cells to the sensory mind as to what they need to start rebuilding. However, the individual will have to draw from his own higher source the knowledge that constitutes his own truth. When thinking about nutrition, man can defer to this self-knowledge rather than the maze of confusion and contradictions of sense-knowledge. Sensory knowledge stems from the memory cells related to emotions.

At the age of 26, the body starts to degenerate. After this time, we must have an adequate intake of enzymes from food supply or we age at a much faster rate.

This supply of live enzymes must come from fresh, raw fruits, and vegetables. Cooked foods, synthetic products, extracted or processed supplements do not contain live, active enzymes. If the product has been heated over 116 degrees, the enzymes have been completely destroyed. We should get our enzymes from raw fruits and vegetables, as they remain alive throughout the digestive process. The vibratory frequency of enzymes contains pure energy, which then upgrades the negative vibrations of the electromagnetic impulses in the physical structure. The Light that sustains the growth of fruits and vegetables is fused with pure energy from the sun, and has not been exposed to negative or discordant vibrations. The intake of the Light, through raw vegetables and fruits, greatly raises our feelings to higher levels of peace, joy, love, freedom, and naturally creates a sense of well-being. This also brings the enlightenment of consciousness to our bodies, and our minds have greater clarity of thought -- free of low negative emotions.

All cellular structures consist entirely of mineral compounds. They are found in all foods; however, they must be alive to function. While food does not form blood, it does furnish the blood's mineral base by setting free the inorganic or cell-salts contained in all foodstuff.

Again, the reason for ingesting raw fruits and vegetables is that we need the live minerals and Light energy provided by these foods. When we consume food that does not contain Light energy and live minerals, our physical bodies must age and are in the process of dying. When food's Light energy is gone, the food's minerals can no longer absorb electromagnetic impulses (which we are made up of). Nature, immediately starts the process of degeneration from this lifeless material. This dying food then becomes the cellular structure in the physical body - and the body must die. We are constantly rebuilding our bodies with dead or decomposing construction material.

While raw fruits and vegetables with their magic minerals and powerful enzymes are great for repairing and rebuilding the physical structure, they cannot cure disease in the body. Diseases are caused only by the need for cleansing and learning. The greatest value of minerals and enzymes is that they furnish the required nutrition for strong, healthy, new cells to constantly replace the old cells.

The plant kingdom differs from the mineral kingdom in that it contains its own light consciousness with the oversoul of the elemental kingdom. Plants have consciousness to the extent of their function, but do not possess intelligence. Plants are nature and must function within the laws of nature. This is why, when seeds are planted, each variety sprouts and matures as its own kind. It is a law of nature -- like produces like. They have no choice because they do not have intelligence. There are no feeling sensations in the plant kingdom to the extent of electromagnetic impressions -- and no emotional body linked to desire or survival. The plant kingdom is here to serve mankind, and allows light energy to be materialized for human life.

Spirulina, wheat grass, barley green, hemp, and sea algae have the highest Light energy, vibratory frequency, mineral, vitamin/amino acid content, and complete nutritional balance. And the greens offer the highest, most pure form of protein on the planet (much higher percentage than meat). These foods provide perfect assistance for the repair of the immune response system to rebuild and maintain body functions. There are very good sources of greens in powdered form, which simplifies it for us.

The important aspect of nutrition lies in its ability to repair, rebuild and maintain body functions on the cellular level. It is most important to choose "alive" foods that will do just that. Food can reverse the aging process and bring life, light and energy to us.

A critical purpose of greens and fruits is to provide a balanced alkaline system. Another powerful alkaline substance is bicarbonate soda or commonly known as baking soda. It is recommended that ½ teaspoon of baking soda in 8 oz of water will help create an alkaline system. I recommend taking this twice a day, but more often if you are really acid. I can assure you that it does not raise blood pressure and is a very healthy thing to do. The pH of our body is in a constant, non-linear state of flux. This flux hovers within a ph of 7.34 to 7.40. When we get on the higher state of this continuum, the body is required to work to reach a more acidic state. So, it is possible to be too alkaline as well as acidic. Lemon juice is great to use to create the alkaline state. Protein, especially meat, creates acidity.

There are other sources of the earth element such as crystals, rocks, and grounding to the earth's electric field. Many healers use crystals of all kinds to focus healing energy into the body or in a room to process any negative energy. The different kinds of crystals and stones have varying frequencies and are both receivers and transmitters. Indeed, they are used in computers and all kinds of electronics. Himalayan Salt lamps are wonderful transmitters of negative ions which transmute harmful electronic frequencies.

Keeping a salt lamp by your bed and also by your computer are very necessary. A light inside heats the salt allowing the negative ions to be released. Negative ions are what the ocean emits and toxins as well as any heavy, dense energy is pulled away and off of you.

Most crystal people recommend that you always use your intuition to pick the crystal which is meant for you. They indeed call to you if you listen. Crystals can be in the form of a pendulum that you can use for testing to see if a food or supplement is right for you. I love crystals and have used them for many years to facilitate healing and increase energy. I also have them in my home to process negative energy and to emit their healing energy.

Connecting to the earth is important, but our culture with all of the synthetic materials that we walk on, including our shoes with plastic soles, isolate us from the earth's electric field. The earth's electric field transfers easily to the body because the body is mostly water and minerals. It is an excellent conductor of electricity and electrons. The free electrons on the surface of the earth are easily transferred if there is direct contact. In addition to the synthetically soled shoes which are insulators, our homes and office buildings are also insulated and built with synthetic materials.

The earth's electric field is mainly a continuous direct current (DC) producing field. Throughout history, life on the planet has attuned our biology to this subtle field. By comparison, indoor wiring systems in the U.S. use 60-cycle per second alternating current (AC). Alternating current is foreign to our biology unless it is a very low frequency. This, and other forms of man-made environmental electromagnetic fields (EMF's) are being researched as factors in a variety of stress-related responses. Many people are sensitive to EMF's. Living near power lines or exposure to EMF's on the job is related to higher rates of health problems especially cancer.

There are grounding mats that are being marketed to allow the grounding process if you do not have a way to walk on the grass or directly on the earth. One thing I realized at the condo complex where I live is they put toxic substances on the grass and to walk on it would be poisonous to me. So, a grounding mat would be ideal for many of us. We need to connect with the earth every day.

Air -- The Breath

The breath has been called the "Breath of Life" even from *Genesis* of the Bible when it was said that God breathed Life into His creation. The breath seems like such a simple thing, but is actually one of the most complex, profound healing systems in the body.

Physically, one of the greatest cleansing, detoxing systems of the body, the Breath is underused by everyone. We literally have to retrain our breathing in order to get it to function as it was meant to.

In order for oxygen to be available for respiration in the cell, it undergoes an interesting journey from the atmosphere through the lungs and circulatory system, and finally into the cell.

As air is inhaled through the nose and into the chest, it encounters the main airway leading to the lungs - the trachea. This is a smooth, tube-like structure beginning just below the larynx. Thereafter, it splits into two smaller tubes, each one leading to the right and left lung. These airways (called bronchi) branch off like tree limbs getting smaller until they are microscopic in size. After about 15 branching divisions, they terminate in tiny bronchioles and each of these ends in a series of tiny little air sacs called alveoli. These air sacs are so minute that lung tissue actually looks solid and fleshy to the naked eye. In reality, the alveoli are much like bubbles. They have very thin walls - only one cell thick. These cells, too, are very thin and membranous. It is here that the gas exchange occurs.

A network of tiny blood vessels surrounds the alveoli and, when we breathe, O_2 in the air moves down the trachea, through the bronchial system, into the alveoli, where it flows into the blood stream that is within the capillaries surrounding the alveoli.

For this process to take place efficiently, there should ideally be a balance between the amount of blood flowing within the capillaries to absorb oxygen, and the amount of oxygen delivered to the alveoli by breathing. Blood is not evenly distributed throughout the entire lung field. It is gravity dependent. There is far more blood in the lower part of the lung than in the upper. However, the free flow of gases into and out of the alveoli is greater in the upper portions of the lung. This process is not necessarily as efficient as it appears at first. The way we habitually breathe can increase the efficiency.

When the alveoli become injured (as they do from smoking), the lining of the many tiny alveoli is broken down and the tremendous surface area in which oxygen comes into contact with blood is significantly reduced. This results in a condition known as emphysema. The person suffers shortness of breath.

Of great importance in maintaining health is the quality of the breathing process - the manner in which air is inspired and expired. The word breath comes from the Latin word *inspirare* which, means "to inspire, inspiration." Certainly when we realize the full impact of breathing fully, we can understand how this would inspire other people, as well.

Whether breathing is diaphragmatic or thoracic, continuous or interrupted by pauses, rhythmical or irregular, can be of major significance in determining one's physical and emotional state. Everyone, at some time, has had some experience with a disruption in breathing pattern associated with pain or powerful emotions. A sob of grief, a startled gasp, and the deep trembling breaths of one in anger are well known examples of the effects of the emotions on one's breathing. Reciprocally, a change in the breathing pattern can also alter one's emotional state, as well as creating physiological changes in the body.

Being aware of your breath and the way you breathe is an important first step when you begin. The breath is perhaps the only physiological process that can be either voluntary or involuntary. You can breathe, making the breath do whatever you wish, or if ignored, the breath becomes automatic. The body cannot function without breath. Breathing falls back to control by primitive parts of the brain, the unconscious realms of the mind where emotions, thoughts and feelings become involved, and they wreak havoc with the rhythms of the breath. Breathing becomes irregular and haphazard when we lose conscious control of it. When we make the breath part of our awareness, we begin to wonder how we ever managed to live when ignoring it.

Although breathing is partly under voluntary control, it is regulated by the autonomic nervous system. Any attempt to breathe consciously in a manner that threatens survival (such as holding the breath beyond one's capacity) is overridden by this regulatory system. Responses to many emotions are also involuntary. The symptoms of acute anxiety, the sudden rush of fear, or a fit of rage are expressed directly by the autonomic nervous system and often bypass conscious control. We all react to emotions from time to time, and the breath is affected. The breath, being related to emotions, is much more complex than dealing with a set of muscular movements. It becomes a potential tool for the interruption or release of undesired emotional response patterns.

It can be said that the Breath purifies toxins in the physical body by bringing enough oxygen to the blood to cleanse it. However, the Breath can be used to cleanse the emotional body of toxic emotions that have caused death and degeneration to set in. As the Breath in the form of oxygen and energy goes to the cells, whatever is held there in the form of darkness and lifelessness is released by the Light of Breath. Wherever there is Light, darkness is dispelled. The cellular memory, which holds all past emotional traumas and spiritual disorder (both remembered and suppressed), is activated as the Breath enlightens the cells. Because the Breath is the Holy Spirit, the great compassionate, loving presence, the surrender to it is gentle and easy. The process of release is instantaneous, as we feel that great unspeakable love from whence we come, and with which we are one.

While modern scientists give importance to breathing exercises only from the viewpoint of respiratory therapy and oxygen intake, Breath is a science that will someday be recognized as related to energy. The ancients have studied Breath as energy and have a Sanskrit word, "pranayama," which translates as the science of breath. Prana means energy, that is, the vital energy of the universe, and ayama means expansion or manifestation of. One who has learned to control prana has learned to control all the energies of this universe - physical and mental. He has also learned to control his body and mind. The human body is sustained by the same prana that sustains the universe. It is through the manifestation of prana that all body functions are possible and coordinated. This could be an important application when working on healing a certain ailment.

The Breath directly affects the autonomic nervous system, which is divided into the sympathetic and the parasympathetic nervous systems. These two subsystems work in seeming opposition to each other, yet the net result is harmonious regulation. There are only two known ways of having conscious control over our involuntary nervous system. One is the breath and the other is through will power. When the mind is focused intensely, it strengthens the will power, and thus the autonomic nervous system functions according to our direction. Thus, there is no such thing as an involuntary system if one learns to control and regulate the motion of the lungs. By doing so, a vast portion of the system is brought under control.

By consciously making the breath deep, even and regular, one will experience a noticeable release of tension and an increased sense of relaxation and peace. The body has to come into a relaxed state in order to heal. If the body is tense, there can be no healing. Respiration is the most important function of the body. It is the source of all energy and life to the living being.

There are many breathing methods: rebirthing, pranayama, Holotropic Breathing by Grof, Breathwork, etc. All of it is good as awareness of the breath is created. Many of these methods use a very directed approach and guide the process. The focus is on control, emotional release work, and remembering past traumas. While these are important, I believe there is something different that I bring with the Breath of Light work that is essential to healing.

I do not direct the process but rather, turn it over to the person's higher self and the Holy Spirit, who know exactly what the person needs. My job as a Breath Therapist is to allow myself to feel so much love and compassion for the person, that I hold him in the wings of comfort and complete safety. I behold the spiritual being that he really is, while filling both of us with the golden white light. I ask the blessing to ascend to us through the Breath. My personality falls away. I can only feel a blessed state of grace and a release from this world's density and negativity. The intensity of the love felt brings the memory of whence we came. The sharing of this wondrous love brings the person into his own remembrance of all that was and is. The person may experience great grief at having bought into all the nonsense and lies taught when we were children and have continued to believe through adulthood. We have wasted many years - living lives that are demeaned, without dignity and power.

No wonder so many people are checking out and dying. There is despair, grief and apathy as people perceive themselves as powerless. They seem to lack any influence over their physical lives - much less the ability to think for themselves or live lives free of other people's control. Few people want to take their power back and take responsibility for becoming world citizens and leaders, helping to bring about the changes that are necessary. The Breath can awaken you to who you are, help you to regain your power and decide to truly live.

We cannot talk about air without discussing the poor air quality and inhibited oxygen available to us. The air is toxic and it is important to have an air purifier especially an ozone air purifier. With limited oxygen, it becomes more important to do deep breathing – often. If possible, look for a place to live that has purer air. There are areas that are preferable for air quality. At least, visit these areas – especially close to the ocean as often as you can.

Fire -- A Powerful Force to Burn Off Anger

Why has man had such a fascination with fire since the beginning? Why do people insist on having fireplaces that are not functional and do not even give off any heat? And why do we love candles so much?

These are sources of fire -- which bring up anger in our bodies to burn it off. As vegetation is burned in a fire, so are impurities. Fire manifests and purifies anger hidden deep inside us. That is why we feel so good after sitting around a bonfire. We all should be sitting with a large fire for several hours per week for our healing. Candles are good, but it is more effective to have the larger fire.

Even though we have the problem of the thin layer of ozone, we also need the energy from our energy source -- the sun. Sit in the sunlight for a few minutes every few days, especially if you are feeling a little blue or rundown. It is guaranteed to make you feel happy and restored.

The Spiritual Law of Purification encourages us to maintain a clear, pure aura, as well as to direct our efforts and light energies towards purifying our Earth.

Just sitting by a burning fireplace can purify your emotions. If you have a fire outdoors, even the smoke can be useful to clear your auric field. Throw in a handful of aromatic dried herbs and you can have a wonderful body, mind and spirit experience.

Fire cannot be contaminated as the other elements; it purifies itself burning while it purifies other things. Most of us have held sticks over a fire to sear and thus purify them before adding a wiener or marshmallow.

In some cultures, fire ceremonies test the strength of religious convictions and speak of the concentration of higher consciousness. Fire ceremonies are the root of the saying, *trial by fire.* The tradition of firecrackers was originally to drive off evil spirits. Other cultures conduct fire ceremonies to honor deity and most churches burn candles for their services. Even the horrific Burning Times may be a malicious and convoluted tie in to the tradition of Santa Lucia, a young girl whose purity was believed to have kept her untouched by candle fires. During the witch hunts, it was believed that innocent (pure) woman would not burn.

If you aren't fortunate enough to have fireplaces indoors or outdoors or even a place for a campfire, candles will also purify the air as they burn. Of course, the larger you can safely burn, the better and if you include some natural incense, you can easily purify your home, while enjoying the aroma and relaxation of candlelight. Candles can be placed with regular spacing through the perimeter of your home, creating a clearing circle. If you feel the land your home sits on needs clearing, a beautiful string of luminaries can serve that purpose.

Another fire purification experience is the Native American sweat lodge, which is truly transformative and healing. Many Native Americans also burn sage and other herbs, standing in the smoke in order to purify their physical and spiritual bodies. You can pick sage or buy it in many bookstores to burn.

Mayan Curanderas burned copal resin gum from a tree in Central America to create a sacred smoke which worked as a purification and cleansing of any negative attachments. I have participated in this ceremony at Dr. Rosita's Ix Chel compound in Belize and found that it was extremely powerful.

Glorious Fire Purification brings you to a new hope of life because this energy helps you to rebirth, helps you to rise and stand up again from destruction - to begin again - and gain an inner peace. This fire energy helps in purifying from negativity, your anger and destructive emotions which day by day- big and bigger- drive you to suffering.

Our goal is to transform that which no longer serves us, such as our negative history, and allow it to be transformed into new clean beginnings. We can go inwards to connect with our ancestors from the aeons, release negative energy, leave old habits behind, learn to forgive, let go of fears or limitations and grieve losses to free our mind and body. Those connecting with your ancestors can call upon them for their guiding spirit. Let us banish our burdens in the flame and make way for balance and peace to be created from the ashes.

Other methods of Fire Purification are fire-walking, Far-Infrared Sauna, Light from the Sun, Cremation and Light technology often combined with colors. Smudging with burning sage or sweet grass and allowing the smoke to penetrate the room to cleanse it or to pass over the physical body to purify the impurities and negative energies that attach to our bodies. Being with other negative people can rub off on us. Our own negative thinking and emotions can ooze out of our pores. When we are angry, the best solution is go build a fire and sit with it for hours until we are released.

Water -- The Great Conductor and Healer

Water, as a conductor, carries away the toxins and "washes away impurities." Bathing in mineral water, ocean water, or vinegar water changes the pH balance immediately from acid to alkaline. Herbs can be added to the water as well as mineral salts to aid in healing.

You can wake up feeling terrible, but the pelting water of the shower soon changes how you feel. Quickly you are rejuvenated as the death is washed away. One should always take a shower or bath in the morning before eating, as many cells die during the night and cover your body.

Other ways of healing with water are colon-hydrotherapy or commonly called colonics, and enemas, as they carry away toxins from the body. As the colon becomes encrusted through the years, it cannot absorb nutrients through its colon wall to the blood, and toxins build up. Many times, a cleansing fast and colonics are the only things able to restore it to optimum function.

Coffee enemas are administered as part of a cancer treatment protocol and the coffee stimulates the liver to produce bile and eliminate toxins. We did the coffee enemas 2 x daily at the Contreras Hospital in Tijuana and I can attest that you feel wonderful after the cleanse. The coffee enemas are beneficial even if you do not have cancer.

Most importantly, we need to be drinking an abundance of pure water that has been restructured through magnetic therapy. This corrects the direction of the poles from positive to negative. Otherwise, free radicals will be created in the body, resulting in cancer. When water is run through just 12 inches of pipe, it becomes destructured and reverses the poles. Such water is not only useless, but destructive to our body. There are magnets and other devices one can purchase to restructure water. Water needs to be purified with a quality purifier before drinking.

The cells are surrounded by water. Indeed, the body is 85% water and that water has to be constantly replenished, as its job is to carry off toxins through perspiration, urine, etc.

Water is an essential nutrient vital to most body processes.

Water is vital for life and is an essential nutrient. Nutrients are substances in food and drink that are utilized by your body in metabolic and/or sustaining functions. Essential nutrients are those that must be consumed regularly, as your body does not produce the amount needed without utilizing external sources in the form of dietary intake. Deprivation of water will kill an individual faster than being deprived of any other nutrient. This important liquid is a vital component of most major body processes.

Lubricant A primary function of water is to serve as a lubricant. For example, it is found in saliva and is a substantial component in the fluid surrounding joints. Water is also in and surrounding body structures such as the brain, spinal cord and eyes. The water layer helps protect and cushion these vulnerable areas from shock and trauma that could otherwise cause significant damage.

Body Temperature Regulation Water is an important agent in body temperature regulation. The human body cannot function unless this is maintained within a certain range. Water helps achieve this in two ways. Since water is slow to change temperature and is efficient at storing heat, the amount of water in the body composition, 60 to 75 percent, is a natural temperature regulator. Another way this nutrient is used by the body for this purpose is through the process of perspiration. As water evaporates from the skin, the body is cooled.

Chemical Reaction Protein and carbohydrates are two nutrients necessary for healthy body functioning. They provide energy and are vital for growth and development. However, these two substances are useless to the body without water. Water enables a chemical reaction to occur which results in protein and carbohydrates becoming absorbable and usable by the body.

Transportation Water is essential in the body's transportation system. Nutrients and other necessary elements must be sent to all parts of the body in order to ensure functioning of every single body process, from respiration to muscle movement to digestion and waste removal. Without water as the movement medium, the body would not function.

Taking a soak in an apple cider vinegar or Epsom salt bath is very wonderful.

Water represents the feminine energy and one can identify this with the water's function to carry away and cleanse the body.

Community --

The Greatest Purification Challenge

Relationships are the most challenging to our self-purification. We only have relationships with ourselves, no matter what the appearance. People can serve as reflections of ourselves - they may present a mirror so that we can observe and look at a facet of ourselves that we might find hard to see on our own. Many times, relationships set up reactions that show us where we are in our development and learning. Trust, intimacy, respect for ourselves and others, self-love, giving, receiving, truth, empowerment are all issues we learn best by being in relationship.

Because our deep cellular patterns and belief systems are enforced by the ego (whose job it is to kill the body), we have the need to be right rather than happy. We try to prove ourselves superior to everyone else in order to somehow convince ourselves of our worth and our power. All the time, underneath, we have self-demeaning thoughts and low self-esteem. We know that we are living a lie. That is why it is so hard to allow someone to become intimate with us. If they really knew us, how could they love us? And to add to the confusion, we have created a facade that others believe to be our true self. How can this kind of relationship have any hope of succeeding? How long can one keep up the false image?

Of course, the ego builds on this. It whispers, "How can you be worth anything if you do not even have enough courage to tell the truth, to live a lie? This causes so much stress and pain because we have sold out. For what? Approval and acceptance! So much so, that we feel the need to present an apparition that we feel is acceptable and lovable, rather than what we really are.

The ego loves this, because this causes so much distress that we make ourselves sick and die over it. In this condition, we cannot function as effective powerful humans and live purposeful lives.

We have to explore the difference between listening through our conceptual filtering system, which has been taught to us, and listening through the heart. We believe that our feelings/emotions are the same as the thoughts about those feelings. We need to see what it means not to want anything from ourselves, but simply to be, simply to accept. We have to open our filters and just receive it all without judgment. There is a part of us that's always criticizing, pushing, judging, thinking and, always, wanting something more or different. We have learned to respond in superficial ways to very deep feelings. We are afraid to go deep because maybe there is nothing there. Maybe we are empty shells with only a deep, dark void.

We have to allow ourselves to come into the heart, and experience what is there. Allow what is there to become an instrument to reveal what we do not understand. We don't have to understand it. We just have to be with it. First, we have to acknowledge in dignity and humility that we really do not know anything. We know what we have been taught to believe. We believe what we think keeps us safe and helps us to survive. In the end, there is nothing but veils of mystery. We have to disengage from our belief systems and patterns.

As we think about our inner lives, we notice how much time is spent in arguing with ourselves. "I should be somebody else. I should have done it better and differently. I should be somewhere else. I shouldn't feel this way. I should be better than I am. I should know more than I do." There is an undercurrent of criticism, anger, disgust, anxiety, self-hate argument in all our experiences as we assess our actions and thoughts on life.

Who am I? Someone who constantly criticizes my existence and actions? Or someone who is my friend - I want to be a friend of who I am and not an enemy. What we have done in the past can be forgiven and released. What others expect from us can be set aside. <u>Who</u> we are and <u>what</u> we are deserves respect. We have to open up to discovering and then to trusting what we are. From this trust, inner guidance will come. What other direction do we need? We can know that when things are confused and distorted, we will stand true to our own beauty and truth. This brings great power and peace.

We have to learn that it is safe to experience mystery and go into unknown territory - without logically figuring it out. It is safe for us to listen from our heart and not explain it to the intellect. And it doesn't have to make sense. As we realize it is safe to know what it is we really want, the heart starts revealing. Sometimes at first, we can only feel an undefinable reeling moving through us. It is very subtle and feels like a gentle pulse of electrical current. If feels like a wanting, a longing, a remembering, very ancient, but very near.

The heart has consciousness. It listens and expands out from itself in awareness. As the heart feels our desire for acceptance, we notice that the heart does not argue or resist. It does not send us messages of despair or criticism or judgment. There is no suggestion we "should" anything. The heart has no fear, only acceptance and love.

Allow yourself the freedom to say to yourself, "I don't really know what I am. I only know what I think I am. I only know what I have been taught. I am here right now and this is all there is. There is nothing else that exists. I can feel my heart beating and hear my breathing." We feel unsafe if we are not constantly explaining what is going on and the meaning of everything that happens. We have come to believe that our explanations are facts - that our explanation of it is the "truth." We identify with the explanation and interpretation, rather than just experiencing.

All of this stems from a gigantic "I WANT!" coming from our inner self who hurts, needs and wants comfort and peace. Our inner wanting need is translated into the idea that something on the outside can bring satisfaction to a need it does not understand. We are always searching in the world of material form for a way to satisfy this need. This constant searching is an ever-gripping limitation, causing emotional pain.

There is nothing wrong with this wanting need. Currently, it is not in vogue to "need" or be "needy." It is a simple wanting of the heart. But there is part of us that is afraid that the need cannot be filled. We keep taking from outside ourselves in the hope that it will satisfy the wanting inside. We cling to relationships, jobs, some money in the bank, a trip to an exotic place, a new sexual encounter, rich food, and drinks. This is merely an attempt to hold our perception of reality steady enough to satisfy the longing inside for something that never changes and is forever.

Yet, no matter how hard we cling, no matter how tough and tenacious we become, everything and everyone out there continues to change, disappear and dissolve. As that thing disappears out of our clutches, we are left again with a wanting in the heart that makes us all the more anxious. Again, we are left with the longing, but with a shame for wanting more. We work so hard to control our environment and make everything fit into our own expectations. Isn't this our struggle with the world? The shame comes from our deep patterns that we weren't worthy to have it after all. Who do we think we are to even think of having it? Underneath this veil of conflict is something simple, pure and safe. We know that when we find it fully, it will heal us. It will not reject or abandon us.

There is something that never changes even when the body changes, money changes, jobs change, relationships change. **There is a quiet remembrance of something that is real, that does not change, that goes past this illusion we are living in.**

We have come into this world with a simple choice to see our wanting as the lack that breeds shame or a wanting of the heart that transcends this life of pain. We can choose to release ourselves from the methods of dealing with the material world for acceptance and control, and choose, instead, to come to something on the inside - the heart - which is indeed what we really want.

It is love. It is a love that expresses giving and receiving simultaneously. It is a great Divine Compassionate love that can only share itself freely - expanding itself constantly, giving out as only the light of love can. The vastness and power are unspeakable. At one time, ancient though it is, we did not know the distinction between Love and what we are. When we were separated from that knowing, the beingness of that love, it created a terrible wound, the longing, the need, the shame. We have been searching, searching, searching -- an eternity of searching. What a dilemma we have been in, asking for permanent Love from things that change. We have to seek the wound where there is betrayal, fear, pain, dejection. We believe we have done something wrong. It was only our perception and learning born of the human experience here. And of course it was for us to grow beyond all this, and bring us to a place of strength and remembering.

What must I pass through to find that place of safety? I must pass through the wound because the wound is the gateway. How do I find the wound? We go into our hearts and invite all those we have blamed for what we have felt and experienced. We do not have to blame anyone anymore. We can say to each and everyone to whom we have resentment, "I thought you were causing me pain. I thought you did something to me. You were there to serve me so that I could see. I want to know who I am without shame. I want to return to an experience of Love. I want to be healed and safe."

Why should we feel shame for needing God? What shame is there in needing each other? We have only looked for Love where it does not exist. What is wrong with us? Nothing. We have a holy choice. We can believe in logical explanations and beliefs, or we can believe what is truly in our hearts and what is truly there in our experiences.

Each day we have the opportunity to choose how we will deal with the emotions that emerge as a result of circumstances. To make a choice as to how we will respond in favor of compassion, love and trust, we must remember that feelings are not caused by circumstances.

Circumstances call forth feelings and emotions that are already there and then become projected on the circumstance. A new way of responding arises when we understand that we are living in a separated state. Our relationship with God is working itself out in the guise of our personal life and relationships.

The Breath of Light is a great deliverer and frees us from this self-imposed prison. As we start breathing, we soon see that we are not who we try to convince ourselves and others we are. When we remember our beginnings and source of our lives, we can never return to that insane way of thinking about ourselves. Our lives and our relationships all change.

The Breath of Light is the way to communicate and join together with another person without ego and conflict. As we breathe together, we join in spirit of unity and are able to see the higher perspective regarding our situation. When we are in spirit, there is no separation and all conflicts are resolved easily. There is no way we can get to this place through the mind. This place is of the heart. We can talk for years and still not have the ability to achieve this unity. Talking and communicating with each other is very important as well, in order to establish relationship, but the Breath of Light brings us to this Holy place of union with each other and with God.

CHAPTER 5   LET ME LEAVE YOU BREATHLESS

We stopped breathing fully and deeply a long time ago -- probably when we were mere infants. When we are first born, we breathe in a full, connected, rhythmic pattern. However, after being scolded, punished and yelled at with demeaning words telling us, "You are no good!", "Can't you do anything right?", "You will never amount to anything" and so on, we start folding up, holding our breath, freezing in fright, cowering in painful punishments, stooping in bad feelings about ourselves, slinking in guilt.

Maybe Mom or Dad had a bad day and was yelled at by the boss. Perhaps our parents suffered from hearing derogatory comments from their parents and still hear them in a different form as adults. After all, we are all just those little kids in bigger bodies, and still act out in the same ways. Those beliefs and patterns, ingrained when we were very young, do not disappear when we enter adulthood. Even though we become educated, obtain knowledge and strive toward our growth, those patterns are at the cellular memory level. We just cannot get to them from the intellect.

No matter what the reasons were that we got punished or demeaned as children, we took it very personally. We believed our parents. After all, they are the adults, and they know. So we become clever and try many different approaches to win back their love and approval. It took me many years into adulthood and through the Breath to see that it was never about me. I was a very good little girl, an innocent child, and only wanted love, peace and kindness. I tried every which way to be good and to not be noticed as a problem. Of course, adults are caught up with their own problems, and fail to see how important a disapproving glance or a few spoken words in anger are to a child.

So we stop breathing. We paralyze ourselves -- even our breath. Now, we have to retrain ourselves to breathe. You can start practicing and use this time as a meditation. You certainly cannot do too much Breathing, and I find myself Breathing many times during the day for short periods of time. When I am in a stressful situation such as a meeting or telephone call, I just start Breathing and I find my mind clears and my body responds immediately. If you have anxiety attacks, this is a wonderful way to calm yourself. In public, I just Breathe more slowly and gently, but still connect the Breath. No one is the wiser, except myself -- with the Breath, comes wisdom.

I am going to describe the ideal way to do the Breath of Light and also give you a guided visualization to use with it. I strongly urge you to play the CD, "Breathe The Light – The Journey Home", which guides and teaches the Breath of Light and then leads you through a guided journey. The CD gives you safety and is a tremendous support as you learn how to breathe with the Breath of Light. Even for seasoned breathers, the CD makes it easy and helps remove the resistance to doing the meditation.

1. Lie down on your back (with your arms at your sides) so that your body is in the most comfortable position possible. Put a folded pillow under your knees and a small pillow under your neck or head. If you are not able to lie down, sit in a recliner or very comfortable chair. Comfort facilitates relaxation and safety for meditation.

2. Choose a time when you can Breathe/meditate for at least one hour.

3. Make it clear that you are not to be disturbed by phone calls, people or pets. Put a "Do Not Disturb" sign on door.

4. Put on the CD, "Breathe the Light, The Journey Home" which will guide you safely through the Breath of Light. I created it to be a healing journey and make it ever so easy to Breathe. While the Breath of Light is simple, it is profound and needs to be done correctly to get the exact results.

Play the CD or music rather on the loud side, as it helps to stop the mind from doing so much active thinking and analyzing. The CD is of the Theta frequency and will assist you in connecting in to the Breath of Light.

5. Use a meditation cover or eye cover, if you have one, to help you focus on your internal state. At any rate, always keep your eyes closed.

6. Say a prayer asking for healing in whatever area you need, whether it be physical, emotional, spiritual or of your critical, negative mind.

7. Start Breathing through either a slightly open mouth or your nose. Choose one and do not alternate. I suggest Breathing through the mouth for if you start crying, your nose tends to stop up. If you are Breathing through the mouth, you can cry and Breathe at the same time. However, with practice, you will find you are Breathing with both nose and mouth simultaneously. There is a powerful energy field that you can tap into by doing this. You may want to start off with only your mouth or nose, and move into the combination.

Bring the Breath from the base of the spine through the abdomen, allowing the abdomen to inhale and move inwards toward your spine, and your chest will expand and move out. Bring the Breath upwards through the diaphragm, into the chest and when you get to the heart area, give a powerful pull bringing the Breath up through the throat and feel it shoot upward through the top of the head. There is a very defined double Breath at the heart/throat, which is powerful and much like the sobbing action of a child. This action will move the shoulders, chest and head in a wave, upwards and back and also shoots the energy up to the top energy center which is about 12 inches above the head. Most people have a slightly claustrophobic feeling all the time and there is always that little space that they cannot get air into. It is a suffocating feeling and it stems from the heart space. By bringing the Breath all the way through the heart, you will start moving into the heart and opening up your emotions and feelings.

Immediately, allow the inhale to release and flow out. <u>Do Not Blow Out the Inhale!</u> Let it almost be a sigh. You can even allow a sighing sound to release with it. When you release the exhale, the energy drops to the heart and out. That is a beautiful thought – to see the energy going out from the heart of love.

The inhale should be stronger and more powerful than the exhale. In fact, you should make a powerful breathing sound when you are in the beginning stage of the breathing. If you do not have difficulty in doing so, put some power into the inhale for the first few minutes, and it really gets the energy going.

As you release the exhale, your head will flow forward, and down, as well as your shoulders. Your chest will contract and your abdomen will expand slightly. Don't push or force. It is to be more of a fluid wave type action and the inhale is to be connected to the exhale. This is the most important part of the Breathing. **It is not the force, but the connection that is the most important.** For people with asthma, emphysema, or other breathing difficulty, do the connected breathing gently.

Breathe powerfully for about 5 minutes and don't worry if you are doing it right. There is no right or wrong. You will get better with practice, and it will come more naturally and easily. I tell people to breathe until they feel as if they are bursting into a million points of Light. Then just relax. In about 5 minutes of Breathing, you will experience a mysterious phenomenon. The Breath will take over and become effortless. You will feel like the Breath is Breathing you. This is when your brain waves are slowing down, your metabolism is slowing down, your body is relaxing, and you start experiencing many physical sensations.

The reason for Breathing powerfully in the very beginning is to connect your circuitry, which, perhaps has been disconnected your whole life. Through a build-up of toxins and negative energy, which has caused blockages, your neurons have not fired and the neurotransmitters have not been able to function. You are a body electric, but have not been connected. You will feel the very powerful electrical energy moving through your body and especially in your hands, arms, legs, feet and face. You will feel tingly, numb, weightless, like you are floating and without a body.

This is your own life force moving through your body, maybe for the first time since you were a small child. It starts firing all your circuits with light. When this light force moves through the body, it starts releasing density, which is negativity polarized with toxins. This light will heat up the body, and serves to burn off toxins. You may find yourself perspiring and very hot. This is a good sign that you are healing yourself physically. It is also a way to cleanse and purify yourself spiritually so that you are not laden with heaviness caused by heavy emotions such as guilt, fear, shame, grief, and anger.

You may feel those emotions come up as they are released. Allow yourself to express them briefly, and then breathe deeply into them. You can breathe even when you are crying. You may find yourself resisting crying because of our culture's suppression of this healthy act. If you are in resistance, let yourself make a moaning sound with the exhale. The sound of grief enables the cells to resonate, releasing the corresponding emotion of sadness. If you haven't cried in a long time, you may have to almost make yourself start crying. In other words, fake it until you make it. Of course, you want to experience the "real thing." Don't let yourself get carried away with hysterics. Allow the Breathing to take the grief away and release it.

So feel the emotion, express it briefly and then breathe into it. **Note:** If you resist and do not allow your emotions to come up when they are demanding to be let free, you will experience a phenomenon we call "tetany." Your hands and feet will start to cramp up and you will tend to want to blow out the exhale. This is your sign that you need to let the emotions surface and express them. However, most people, especially men, are very controlling about emotions and it is very difficult. But if you start feeling tetany set in, you just might want to express a few tears, because tetany can feel very painful. If you find yourself in tetany, start taking bigger inhales than exhales, slow the Breath down to a more regular, gentle breathing pattern. You need to keep breathing through it, because stopping is not the answer. You will feel stuck with all those emotions just below the surface. So just keep Breathing and say a prayer asking for release from the powerful resistance and control that is hurting you.

A good way to get yourself out of resistance and into emotional release is to start Breathing into your heart. Feel the pink light of love warming your heart, and it will melt the resistance away.

You can probably see that you have had this pattern throughout your life and it only brings you misery. Would you rather be happy or right? Just breathe into your heart area and relax, knowing that you are safe. This is just showing you the inner self-destructive patterns, which run your outer life.

You will find that the Breathing will start slowing down as you move into Alpha. Your brainwaves will slow down as well. You will find that you are drifting and floating as you experience levels of this relaxed state. As you move down into the Theta state, you will feel yourself dreaming or you might even think you are asleep. While it is possible to fall asleep, most always, the person is just in deep states of Theta. The Breathing may stop altogether, and the person is unaware that it has stopped. The CD takes you to the very end of Breathing and you will be guided to relax and just allow. There is no need to try and figure out how many Breaths you should take.

If you find you are holding your breath purposely, you should immediately start Breathing again in order for whatever was processed to be integrated. Oftentimes, in this state the person does not realize their breath stopped until all of a sudden, they are aware they are no longer breathing. Usually, there is a gasp or a little jerk like you fell asleep and woke up. The process of integration has just taken place. Whatever emotional issue was brought forth was then integrated and released permanently. This is not a "quick fix," but a true healing of emotional traumas held in the cells.

The physical body is also healed in the Theta state. Studies have shown that all healing and change actually happens in the Theta state. So you can see how beneficial it is to be in Theta as much as possible - especially when you are ill.

You will have many cycles where you will move down from the original Beta (awake) stage into Alpha and Theta. Occasionally you will move over into the Delta (asleep) state in order to push you back up to Alpha and activate some other deep cellular pattern. When you feel yourself coming back from a "deep sleep" start Breathing the deep connected Breath in order to activate the next thing. You do not have to know what it is you are activating or even the event you just integrated and released.

Sometimes it will feel like shadows are passing and you can almost grasp and see them - but they are lightning quick and illusive. These are whole events you are processing and sometimes it is better that the mind is spared the details. The important thing is to release all negatively charged emotional patterns and allow yourself to be filled with light of the spirit.

Many people experience going into the Light and see it as Golden White Light, or a brilliant Violet, moving to vibrant Purples and sometimes to an iridescent light Blue. I perceive the Light as a Holy Presence brought by the Holy Spirit as the Great Comforter - a way to commune with God. Whenever "Breathers" go into the Light, they always feel as if they have received some sort of miraculous initiation and feel a transcendent experience of ecstasy or rapture.

Sometimes, I look into the eyes of the most embracing, enfolding, nurturing, loving and peaceful female angelic being that defies human description. I feel a love flow out from her eyes throughout my whole being that melts every care away. She feels like the mother of the world and I can only refer to her as Divine Mother of us all. Maybe she is the feminine, nurturing, unconditional love that is in all of us at our original core.

Many people have witnessed the appearance of Mary (the mother of Christ) as an illumined, angelic being. As they gaze upon her, they go into an ecstatic state of rapture. One of the most famous is her divine emanation to a group of children who would go into the rapture at her regular appearance. I, as well as others, have also been in the presence of Jesus, the Christ. His presence is always in a very bright light, and the great love is overpowering. St. Germaine often appears and brings the Violet Flame which envelops the whole being in purples, violet colors which is luminescent and very electric.

Some have visited with loved ones who have died, and settled unfinished affairs with them. Forgiveness is often experienced.

Whenever the Holy Spirit enters, I feel my whole being change. This visitation of Spirit is a true healing as you can actually feel endorphins being released into the body. Whenever one can feel love, it melts away the acid, critical thoughts, the turbulent, destructive anger, the consuming, terrible envy, and the heavy, disabling guilt. We do not take the time away from our strife-filled lives to commune with God and give over the burdens that we needlessly carry. That is what the Breath does. It releases us from burdens too heavy for any human being to carry. Instead, we are given reassurance that we are beloved, we are worthy, we are forgiven, and we do not need to suffer any more.

The Breath of Light is the greatest pain reliever I know. It can relieve pain permanently or temporarily, depending on how repetitive stress levels are in your life. Sometimes you will need to Breathe three or four times a day, every day.

I worked at the Contreras Hospital in Tijuana with cancer patients for over three years. We did a regular, weekly Breath Class with the patients -- as well as private Breath of Light Sessions with many of them. Again and again, the patients come into the session wracked with pain and at the end of just one session, the pain is almost or totally gone. Many report back to us months and years later that it is still gone. They are incredulous that something so simple as Breathing could be so powerful. Many people have experienced instantaneous healings during the Breath sessions. Some were at death's door or severely afflicted with cancer or other disease.

After you have Breathed for a few minutes, you will feel as if you could breathe forever. Indeed, you do not want to stop. This is when you know you are complete. Of course, you do not have to stop right away. After all, it is wonderful to experience peace and such great love. So just enjoy. If you feel you want to stop, and you are feeling fidgety, then you are not done.

Probably some very big issue is just right at the surface and resistance is coming up about dealing with it. You do not want to be stuck with that anxious feeling. Therefore, just go back into the original powerful Breathing for a few minutes, and guaranteed, whatever is lurking there below the surface will come up and be resolved. You can bet it is probably something pretty big. You will be able to end with peaceful thoughts and love in your heart if you move through it. So it is definitely worth going through it.

Your experience will be different from anyone else's. Every time you Breathe, you will have a different experience. Many times you will have feelings, you may see visuals or visions, you may feel physical sensations (such as pain) whenever a current or former symptom or disease is being released. It may intensify for a few minutes, and you have to keep Breathing into it until it finally releases, thus allowing a permanent benefit. You may have startling revelations about your life - sometimes about your past that you have suppressed. If a past emotional trauma comes up, you are able to view it as a detached observer, and see it all from a totally different perspective. Though you process and integrate the event, you do not have to relive it as you originally did. You are given a state of grace around events that would be too painful to accept. Just remember, you are safe and protected within the Breath. It is only when your ego puts up resistance and fear about what you might experience and you try to stop the process before it is finished that you will feel painful consequences (such as the tetany) mentioned earlier. Regardless, even tetany will wear off and you will just find that you have further work to do regarding this suppressed issue.

Do not try to do this work as a therapy with someone else unless you have Breathed many times yourself, and know how to deal with the intense effects it can have. Breathing by your self is fine because there is an inherent safety factor with the Breath. You will not be given more than you can handle. However, when you add your energy and direction to someone else's process of healing through the Breath, you bring a whole other dimension to the session.

Your own emotions had better be cleared and processed. When another person expresses emotions, your own resistance and fear of your personal unprocessed and charged emotions will surface. You then start sending vibratory signals of your own fears towards the person Breathing. This causes chaos and confusion for that person. It is not fair to lay your own "hang-ups" on someone else in their time of healing. To be a good healer, you have to be healed yourself.

In addition to clearing your own emotions, there is much to know about the effects of the Breath and how to assist the person to feel safe. The person Breathing must feel safe enough to go into his/her deepest hell, so as to then come to a heavenly awakening into spiritual union with God.

I would love to hear from you and the results that you receive from the Breath of Light in your life. I recommend that you make a commitment to do the Breath for one hour a day for two weeks. Then stop and see what happens. You will find that it is difficult to function without the support of the Breath in your daily life. Breathe everywhere - in the shower, in stressful meetings or situations (you can do a slower and less powerful breathing in public and they will never know what you are doing). Breathe when you go to sleep and you will sleep better. An hour of Breathing is worth 8 hours of sleep. It is very rejuvenating and certainly gives you a radiant glow of youthfulness.

I recommend that you use some visualization and imagery while you are breathing. Certainly use the Breath when you are getting any bodywork or massage. When cellular memories are being released, you will be able to integrate them easily. When you bring visualization into the process, you are consciously directing the Breath to go where you want it to, and focusing on certain things. The CD, Breathe the Light, is a full breathing meditation journey and has a wonderful visualization process that takes you to core and the cellular memory level.

The Breath of Light heals the physical first. Therefore, if you are dealing with disease or illness, the Breath will be working on that aspect first. Sometimes your body energy has to be restored before you can deal with deep emotional traumas. If you don't have the CD, you can use the following as a good visualization:

BREATHING VISUALIZATION

As you start your breathing, lay with your palms upturned at your side, or you can sit with your palms on your thighs. Breathe deeply connecting the inhale to the exhale and allowing your body to flow in the wave. Breathe in from the bottom of your abdomen bringing the Breath up and then a powerful defined double Breath at the heart and again the throat, shooting the Breath up through the head and on up to about 12 inches above your head where our connection with the Divine is. Breathe for a few minutes and then, as you Breathe, create two spheres of golden white light in your palms.

With every Breath you take, the spheres get larger and more powerful. Breathe into them and feel the electricity, feel the power, feel the love. They are growing heavy and magnificent with golden white light with every Breath.

Now bring your palms to your abdomen, your solar plexus area, and Breathe the golden white spheres of light into your center. Breathe the light throughout the cells of your whole body allowing it to flow from head to toe.

Now Breathe the Light into any area where there is disease, pain, stress, fatigue, or suppressed emotions. Allow the Light to fill that whole area and wherever there is any darkness, let the Light flow to that area. Allow the Light to go to your mind where resides your "board of directors" who are always yammering with critical, awful thoughts about yourself and others. Fill it with positive, illumined thoughts.

Allow yourself to receive wisdom and clarity about your life. Let the Light give you solutions to your problems. As you Breathe in, receive all goodness, healing, and peace. As you Breathe out, let the negativity, the critical thoughts, the illness, pain and stress flow out on the exhale. As the negativity and darkness flow out, they are transmuted into a great Light that is all around you. Now Breathe into your heart and let your heart be filled with this golden white Light which slowly turns to pink. Feel how warm it is in your heart. Feel that warmth spread throughout your body. Feel the love for yourself and everything and everyone. Just keep Breathing in that warm, pink love, and let it extend outward to anyone to whom you need to express that love.

And, allow the Breath to take the warm, pink love out to the whole world and envelop the planet and all the human race to be filled with that love, healing all mankind. Just Breathe in that wonderful Light and Peace and Sweetness. You can take this time to receive any answers, guidance or wisdom that you need for your life.

CHAPTER 6 TIME – HOW TO USE THE CONCEPT OF TIME FOR POWER, FREEDOM AND HAPPINESS

Time and our interpretation of time directly relates to our relationship with ourselves. Time can be our friend or our enemy--working for or against us. Time can cause us much anguish and pain or it can free us from our self-imposed prisons. Understanding time and how we use it can bring much enlightenment. We can also learn how to compact time or stretch it. We can make it work for us.

Time is always a choice. In the book, *Vivations,* by Jim Leonard and Phil Laut, they speak of momentary time and linear time.

Momentary time is being in direct experience -- there is no freedom in momentary time. Whatever exists is already here and is all that can exist in that moment -- including your desires for things to be different. In momentary time, motion is an inherent quality that is established by having the totality of past events be part of what we exist with in this moment. That is all. What happened in the past made you what you are and brought you to this moment which is an integration of experience. It can be said that when you are in momentary time, you are feeling, experiencing, and totally present. In momentary time, right now is the original "moment of creation," the only moment possible. It has been said, if you want to know the future, look at what you are thinking or doing right now. The future is made up of a series of momentary events.

Happiness is found in momentary time as you are in direct experience where there is no judgment or desire for things to be different. You are just happy and grateful for things just as they are. Being in the present moment brings acceptance.

Linear time is where we have freedom and movement. Linear time allows for the expression of motion - the change of position to something during an interval, which contains both past and future. Linear time is the context in which the past actually happened and the future will happen. In linear time, we evaluate the past, plan our future, set our goals and move toward the fulfillment of those goals. Power exists within linear time. You have the ability to create the results you envision and act on.

While some people may be powerful and live in linear time, if they do not integrate momentary time in their experience, they may not be very happy. Some people are only thinking of the past, and are stuck in that time frame.

That mode often brings regret, guilt and sadness. The "should have beens" come from the past. Often what we have come to think of ourselves - what we are in this world, our sense of failure or success - is not real. It is an interpretation based on the past - which is always filtered through our learned belief systems of the outer world.

When we find ourselves dwelling in the past, spiraling down in the judgment and guilt from the past, it is time to take some deep breaths, and Breathe ourselves into the present and back into our hearts. As we do, we can accept the dignity of our experience here on this earth. The truth is often veiled from us, but thankfully, it is a thin veil and readily lifted as we remember why we are here. Our appeal, as human beings, is that we may be allowed to have an experience of Grace in which we realize that Love does not condemn. Therefore there need be no despair about where we are or where we think we have been. When we can integrate the past into the present with compassion, it brings great wisdom of learning.

When we are in the future (where most people are), we find ourselves consumed with fear, worry and control. Often, we feel alone and perceive a changing world which seems to threaten us. We feel forced to carry on alone. When we feel fear in our loneliness, we might interpret this as weakness. However, this is just our longing for something that radiates love and never ceases to exist, something we can trust as safe. As we Breathe into this, an assurance comes that we can really trust beyond what we can see. There is a greater reality and truth within our hearts and souls. Wisdom is born of staying conscious and letting our attachments disappear. In this consciousness we are enabled to enter into a relationship with ourselves. This allows us to walk through the threshold between what is unseen and what is revealed. We enter the kingdom of mystery and spiritual reality, which brings the assurance that we are never alone and we will always be taken care of. With this faith in the great unending ocean of Love, we can truly celebrate life, live more in the moment and in our experience.

Remember, if you are not living in the moment, you are not here. You lose your will power, your ability to respond, and are unable to feel your feelings or your heart. If you are in the future, you can only be in the intellect. This brings disconnection with your heart and those around you. Do you have trouble with your memory? Could be that you are in the future too much and not present in your body or your life.

CHAPTER 7   BEAUTY

ESSENTIAL FOR HEALING

One of the most important healing elements in my life is beauty. Oftentimes, when you mention the word beauty, the mind immediately connects it to outward beauty especially of the female form. Our world has put so much emphasis on a sexual beauty that the essence of beauty has been lost and neglected.

They say beauty is in the eye of the beholder. Maybe that means that if you revere beauty you will be able to see it in all things. If you have beauty within you, it is translated into your surroundings. It is very important to surround yourself with beauty. What constitutes beauty?

In studying sacred geometry, we realize that the great masters of art understood the perfection of form. What Michaelangelo and Da Vinci painted and sculpted was not by happenchance. What made their work so beautiful was that it was composed of exact formulas of life forms originating from the very beginning of creation. Indeed, every angle, circle and line tell the story of creation. The power of evolution from the void to enlightenment is revealed as Life and unfolding that Life. Even the seed of a flower or tree contains the blueprint for the final life form -- which will share of its beauty and energy to heal man.

Everything in the universe is connected. Where there is a geometric shape, there is a musical note, and a color that corresponds and is the same vibration. All these variations connect to each other to create a highly organized form based on mathematical equations.

What makes beauty is perfection. The perfection contained in nature is what makes it so sensually appealing. Everything is ordered and repeats itself with guaranteed stability. As you gaze upon a flower, tree or the repetitive waves of the sea, it brings a sense of order to your being. In Nature everything is in constant renewal. It is like the outward flow of the heart. It is rejuvenating to experience that outward flow of energy - a high vibration of Life force. Of course, all of nature was created to heal man, to nurture, cleanse and restore his energy from the Life energy source - the sun.

No matter whether you are in an humble abode such as a grass hut or a palatial mansion, it is essential for your soul to create beauty. Part of beauty is cleanliness and order. When your home is dirty and in disarray, it sets up a discordant and confused vibration. The perfection of your form demands perfection in your surroundings. Not critical perfection, but rather, loving perfection. Everything is placed with love and reverence, creating a matrix of organized form, which emits a holographic model. The holographic models stimulate our own memories of order in each cell of our being.

There is an original memory in the organized fields of nature, which determines the form of everything. Structures of seeds, crystals - and including the form of embryos, which will develop into human beings. There is a resonance whereby all forms are influenced by the memory of similar forms that go all the way back to the original spark of life at creation.

Our human form organism is definitely affected by form and matter around us. These forms call forth ancient memories in our cells. These memories are our connection with all of life. By creating an environment with ocean and marine life, we evoke the life force of the oceans. I particularly relate to the ocean and have used ocean colors, forms and life of the sea. Being in that environment alone is enough to heal a person.

I always have fresh flowers and living plants in my home and all around me. When I was a child and in need of nurturing, I sat in my mother's flower beds and smelled the flowers. I would bury my face in them and put a petal in my mouth to savor the sweet nectar and essence of it. Now, I've learned of Bach Flower Remedies, essential oils from herbs and plants and Aromatherapy, which are potent for healing.

I had a wonderful experience, which gave me true understanding of the power of the essential oils for healing. I met Helen Stembridge, who has a company called Earth Angel Oils. She insisted on coming down and helping me create my own oils for the Breath of Light. I had known for some years that I would do this, but had not met the right person to do it with. I was in the middle of a building project with a deadline and I told Helen I could only give her a few hours. She said that would be fine. She knew all along how many hours it would actually take. But, I thank Helen for being so persistent, because after inhaling oils and doing the Breath of Light for 27 straight hours, we had birthed three oils: 1. *Lifting the Veil: Out of the Darkness – Into the Light*, 2. *Breath of Light, The Anointing and the Initiation*, and 3. *Dolphin Breath – The Integration*. I was in near exhaustion when we started, but after taking in those wonderful oils and doing the Breath, I was totally rejuvenated and healed. I became a believer. I also understood that the oils are a frequency just like the Breath of Light. I like to use an infusor to allow the air to be filled with a chosen oil.

Order is a very powerful force that will emanate throughout the whole building. If there is disorder in one area of the home or building, it will disturb the vibration of everything. There is an ancient science that is now being used by many. It is called Feng Shui. It is the art of placement to bring balance and harmony to your environment and can be used to neutralize negative influences. It can be used to transform your surroundings into a place of well being, positive energy and even prosperity.

Feng Shui has influenced me greatly in my attitudes of environment. I find that I work better, have better mental clarity and attract beauty to me when I surround myself with harmony and balance. Beautiful music, sweet incense, and candles all set up a peaceful vibration, keeping my physical body in a wellness state of balance. If you are working with healing, make sure you create beauty all around you.

The healing therapy room is a sacred space - a temple which is pristine, clean, inspiring, and should be decorated with soft colors. The room should be filled with the sounds of moving music and have low, gentle light - perhaps a candle. All of these elements, in addition to your prayer of protection, serve to set up a sacred vibration of safety.

"The thought that is beautiful is the thought to cherish. The word that is beautiful is worthy to endure. The act that is beautiful is eternally and always true and right. Only beware that your appreciation of beauty is just and true; and to that end, I urge you to live intimately with beauty of the highest type, until it has become a part of you, until you have within you that fineness, that order, that calm, which puts you in tune with the finest things of the universe, and which links you with that spirit that is the enduring life of the world." *Beautiful Thoughts, by Bertha Baile*

CHAPTER 8 THE LAST BREATH

What a dilemma we find ourselves in. We want out of this seemingly imprisoned life, but there are only two ways out. Death is one option. This may include creating a devastating, terminal illness, or a tragic accident, or suicide. Some people have such a strong death wish that they find themselves on a suicide course that is painful and creates destruction all around them. This death wish may not be conscious and, if you asked them if they want to die, they might reply, "Of course not!" As long as a person is alive, he or she does have a choice. If he/she is still alive, that is proof of a stronger desire to be alive than dead. He/she still has a chance to make a choice for life.

Those of us making a choice for life find it very tricky to keep ourselves in balance with all of the polarized energy around us. Here we are, "stuck" in this material, physical world trying to be spiritual. We are tempted every moment to embrace materialism. Materialism is one of the most powerful forces because it rules this world. Our values of success, achievement, and power are based on material gain and ownership. Seldom are soul virtues (such as love and peace) chosen over wealth and control.

Certainly we do not have to take a vow of poverty to choose a spirit directed life. However, it probably would be easier to do so. To have "things" but not be owned by them is the goal. As it states in the Scriptures, "to be in the world, but not of the world." I believe it is acceptable to own things if you can give them away in the next moment. Otherwise, they own you.

Many of us who are taking responsibility for bringing change in the world have to walk in two worlds at once. We are interfacing with corporate and world leaders, "languaging" ourselves in order to be heard by corporate management. In order to gain credibility and acceptance and, hopefully, have a profound effect on these leaders, we are dressing professionally, embracing accepted lifestyles and, generally, presenting ourselves as "normal." The only way to affect change is to be so impressive in who we are that others will be inspired to follow. We <u>do</u> have to gain entry to the mainstream in order to communicate our message.

There is the danger in walking in that world - we might get caught in the web of power and materialism. Integrity and commitment to our purpose have to be embraced and reinforced daily. We have to remind ourselves why we are here. It is not to own a Mercedes or a grand mansion. It is to bring about a world of peace and abundance for all.

My constant goal is "to marry heaven and earth." That is, to bring spiritual understanding and direction to all my earthly affairs. I know that any material possessions I might have or money accumulated are so that I can do my work. I subscribe to a law of abundance in the universe and gratefully accept all things that make my life more comfortable and free. I think the main reason to have money is the freedom to do what I want and to be able to keep the purity with all things. I do not subscribe to a law that says I can have an abundance of as much as I can accumulate and the rest of the world is starving to death. There is no joy or peace until all human beings have a home with enough food to eat. I am constantly grateful for my good life and pray that I give as much as I receive.

People are attracted to people who live from the heart. When you live from the heart, you have a magnetism that others desire. When they first start searching for this quality, they become like greedy, selfish, little children. They want what they want and now! They are still too much in the world, imbedded with the deep patterns of competition, scarcity and death urges. Part of the death urge is to kill off the next person before he you, or to pull others down and repress them, so that you can be more important or better than they are. Such people want a short cut to consciousness. They see consciousness as power. One of the first arenas most people enter in their quest is the psychic power area. To know something that no one else knows is very attractive to a power driven person.

The search for psychic power is very dangerous when you are seeking it for power. Yes, it is possible to reach into other dimensions (such as the astral) and obtain information. There is, however, a mixed bag of information in that realm. Just because a person died and is now an discarnate spirit without a body does not make that soul a wise, good being. Being dead does not automatically bring mastery. Think about it. There is probably someone in your family that is a real jerk. Do you think that when Uncle Fred dies, he automatically becomes some sort of saint? His spirit may be just as much of a dirty old man as he was in the flesh. Now, are you going to contact dear old Uncle Fred and ask him to get involved in your life? And, he is at an advantage, because you are attributing power to him because he is dead. Well, good luck! There is a lot of nonsense in the lower dimensions. It is no place to visit. You might get some good advice, if you are lucky, but you can't trust it.

So how do you get these intriguing psychic gifts? How are you able to tap into the power of manifesting what you want? How are you able to use your intuition to know the right way for yourself? How do you have this communion with God and heavenly forces? It is not something that comes overnight and it is not free. It has to be earned. You have to pay the price of admission to have these gifts. They come from right living. You are given gifts when you pass the tests.

While we observe that some have tapped into other realms of psychic powers and misuse them for their own benefit and against others, we might take this observation to a higher spiritual perspective. First, we know that all things, events and people are in our life to assist us in our learning. We have to look at our shadow side as well as our loving self. People who wield power are here to assist us in taking back our own power, to be vanquished by no other force than the Love that is God.

Sometimes, it is difficult to tell whether a person is an enlightened master or an evil-doer intent on abusing you. Sometimes the dark angels gather energy from around them - maybe even from your own light - and reflect that back to you.

First of all, you can trust that if you are giving out a constant flow of love, it is your life force field they will live off for awhile. But not for long, because darkness can't be in the light. Those of the dark will disappear as they are replaced with that Light.

It is difficult to sustain that loving energy from our being. It is in those interludes that we get into troublesome predicaments.

The only way to remain safe is to Breathe and say a constant prayer for protection. This prayer should not be uttered in a fearful expectancy of horrible events that *may* happen. Rather, utter a prayer of thankfulness, gratitude and love of your life.

When you Breathe, you are also able to ask for guidance and wisdom. You can ask if a person is from the light or from the dark. Breathing opens and heightens your intuitive powers. In the process, it heals, changes and purifies. I notice that people who are adverse to change are not able to breathe.

This means you have to do your homework. There are no shortcuts. It means choosing Life. It is a lifelong process. I don't think the learning ever stops. I do think the suffering can stop when you make a shift in your consciousness.

Suffering can only exist when you are attached to material things. Suffering exists when you perceive the loss of something you love and must have to be happy.

You cannot have one foot in one world and one foot in the other. You cannot have ulterior motives and exploit human suffering. I see many people posing as healers and teachers who are opportunists. They are not authentic and only want to profit from human suffering. They do not want to change it or change themselves. In the end, they will have sold their very souls and will be left with dust for profit.

When we have paid the price of admission (which is not about time, but about living in full commitment to life and restoring light within your own dark patterns), we can then start our evolution to a powerful and purposeful life. The cellular theta Breath of Light awakens us and quickens our process. When we Breathe, we have to change. As we start reaching into other higher dimensions, we are given power to effect change around us. With this comes the freedom, which we have longed for. Freedom is the only real power that exists.

As an enlightened human being who chooses life here in this very dense vibration, one pays a very high price. One would think that being enlightened when almost everything around is unenlightened, would be the ultimate.

However, once one becomes illumined in his soul and mind, he/she still has to deal with the density of the body. Many of the great spiritual leaders suffer physically. You would assume that if you are a Master, you could control your physical body to the extent you could heal anything.

The fact is the more you move into spirit, there is a rending of the thin veil, which separates the sixth and seventh level. This can cause the body to die - especially if the person goes too fast with extreme purification practices. If there is a disruption between the body we see and the spirit, which is not seen, living is impossible.

We have to harmonize and strike a balance between the body and spirit, matter and consciousness.

As Bringers of this New World, we are required to process immense energies which surge through our bodies. The more enlightened we are, the more these energies are attracted to us to find a mooring and a channel from which to issue.

There is a scientific explanation as to what this means. We think of life as being "solid matter," but life might be composed of something as insubstantial as light. David Bohn, a physicist, gives this description:

"As an object approaches the speed of light, according to relativity, its internal space and time change so that the clocks slow down relative to other speeds, and the distance is shortened. You would find that the two ends of the light ray would have no time between them and no distance, so they would represent immediate contact. You could also say that from the point of view of present field theory, the fundamental fields are those of very high energy in which mass can be neglected, which would be essentially moving at the speed of light. Mass is a phenomenon of connecting light rays which go back and forth, sort of freezing them into a pattern.

"So, matter, as it were, is condensed or frozen light. Light is not merely electromagnetic waves but in a sense other kinds

of waves going at that speed. Therefore all matter is seen as a condensation of light into patterns moving back and forth at average speeds which are less than the speed of light. Even Einstein had some hint of that idea. You could say that when we come to light we are coming to the fundamental activity in which existence has its ground, or at least coming close to it."

Surrendering to this task of purifying our dense vibration to finer vibrations of Light in order to bring this force field to a home on earth is part of our purpose for being here. It is a difficult job to refine our selves to that high place. Like attracts like, and we are setting up an electromagnetic field to attract this light. After we do, we have to be strong enough to bring it through. By bringing ourselves into the Theta state often, we are able to constantly let go of all negative forces that are all around us and which attach to us. Sick people, and those caught in the material, dense world, send out envious, hateful, critical thought forms. All are designed to kill off those of us striving for enlightenment. I find that Breathing allows the cleansing of those negative thought forms to purify my own energy and force field. I get in trouble if I am not Breathing constantly.

The whole current of vibratory force, which pervades the body-mind of an individual, has its source within the heart. Being in the heart, expressing love, being love is the only way to make it through the war of energies that is going on. An outpouring of love purifies everything in its path and nothing harmful can come back to the individual when he has that pure outpouring of love. Breathing into the heart helps to keep your center there.

The final awakening will happen only when there is radical explosion of the illusion of separate existence. This will be the final paradigm shift - when we see that we are truly body, mind, and spirit. We are not separate from any other living thing. Let us take that Last Breath into Theta, the state of breathlessness, and into the gateway to Light.

CHAPTER 9   THE ULTIMATE INVITATION

P robably the greatest quest of humankind today is that of eliminating disease from the physical body. Billions of dollars are spent on research trying to find cures for these devastating diseases. The more advanced man becomes with technology and progress, the more rampantly diseases are ravaging his life force energy. All of the money in the world and academic technology cannot free him from the bondage of disease. Yet, the simple and only permanent answer to this malady lies within his willingness to believe in his own inner wisdom and light of intelligence.

The cause of disease in the physical body is negative thinking - causing toxin accumulation in the membranes of the cellular structure. In order to cleanse the cells and keep them alive and functional, the immune response system must "boil" out the toxins. The result is disease. Disease has two purposes: one is for learning and the second for cleansing the cells. As the individual begins to change his thinking, cleanse the emotions and connect spiritually, he will no longer need disease. Disease will be completely eliminated from his physical life. The reversal of aging and rejuvenation is also part of the benefits of purification.

As a person attunes to a knowledge and intelligence of a higher vibratory frequency, and accepts this higher intelligence into the belief systems of the cells, his own vibratory frequency starts resonating higher and higher toward God. This, then, acts as a standard of qualification for his lower thoughts and automatically cleanses them to a purer level of vibration. The thoughts, then, do not contain the factor designated for disease and death. They do not "short-out" the electrical currents in the physical body. The necessity for learning from these thoughts has been eliminated. The person's higher source and Truth assesses and evaluates the thoughts automatically processing them without creating disease factors for his body. When a person reaches this level, he is thinking in the Light of his own wisdom/intelligence rather than false, negative thoughts.

This releases the immune system from its overworked condition of having to manufacture and maintain so many antibodies to keep the cells, molecules and blood clean enough to carry out their functions. At this point, the individual starts the reversing action in his aging process and starts the rebuilding action by daily manufacturing billions of perfect cells that are in complete harmony with the master form code of his etheric (spirit) and original cellular bodies. The blueprints for new cells are no longer scrambled and distorted by the disease factor.

Most people believe they are thinking for themselves, because the information is being received through their senses. It feels like truth because it feels like part of their experience. It is important to start observing how you receive information and thoughts. Is it because it satisfies some sensual need such as touch, vision, hearing, or taste? The addictions through the senses, while pleasant for the moment, are short lived and have to be repeated again and again for pleasure. Each person in his evolvement process, sooner or later, has to start sorting through the sensual addictions. One good practice is to "fast" from something you suspect to be an addiction and see what comes up when you give it up even temporarily.

The ego's responsibility includes processing sensory data. Since the emotions are directly connected to the senses, the ego is able to manipulate our reactions easily by this powerful combo.

The person must diligently focus his attention on what he wants and keep his thoughts attuned to a higher self-truth. If the individual commits to the willingness to hold information in the focus of his own conscious light of knowingness, he will have taken the greatest step forward that he has ever accomplished in his entire lifetime. When the individual begins to accumulate self-knowledge, he has set into motion the energy of love, which synergizes and increases in momentum ever upward each time it is utilized.

When the energy of Love is anchored within the person's consciousness and cellular structure, the physical structure begins a complete transformation process. This most powerful energy of the universe transmutes all of the unbalanced thoughts from the belief system. This removes the cause and core of all the diseases and unwanted problems that the person might be experiencing. With no negative thoughts to distort the blueprints for new cells, the DNA is able to return to original healthy pure cells.

For each person, the greatest secret of the universe is establishing his own Truth because his Truth will set him free. This is the ultimate fulfillment of "Know Thy-self." Each individual needs to know his own Truth on every facet of his own being - from the state of his health, right living in his life, right thinking about the lessons to learn, and finally the return or ascension into the Great Light from beyond - from whence he came. This is the purpose of our embodiment: to learn to qualify and direct the life force energy that constantly flows through our being.

That qualification and direction of energy determine everything about our life.

The first step in regaining sovereignty over our life again is the willingness to examine all our belief systems and new concepts that are contrary to what we have been taught. Some are unable to go past this and decide to go with the ego and hang onto their old, false, contradictory and confusing "facts of life." They feel secure with the old programming that everyone else embraces. They cannot be different and risk not being accepted.

If you find difficulty in this process - wanting to stop, you will feel resistance, as the ego cannot afford to be wrong. You will find a strong urge to be right. That is a sure sign that the ego is directing your thoughts. All you have to do is **direct your** energy of **attention to what you want.** Because it is the creative energy, **attention (*when applied to what the individual wants*)** will generate desire and feeling, which **motivates willingness** for the person. However, if the person holds his attention on the problem, it generates fear, which is the ego's strongest tool. Fear "shorts out" the energy of willingness.

The Breath of Light is a powerful tool to cancel the tools of the ego and get you into the higher planes of consciousness. It lets you quickly assume the "Observer of the Observer" viewpoint and you are taken out of the lower vibration of negative energy. The Breath being the Holy Spirit and the Bringer of all encompassing Love takes you to your own conscious Light of truth and intelligence. Once you begin the process with a commitment to come into your own Truth, the intelligence of your truth is merged into the involuntary nervous system. As the intelligent mind evaluates the information being brought to it and exposed to the Light, it is automatically given the force of Love vibration.

It is extremely difficult for the individual to love himself, because he is aware of all of his own faults, deficiencies and defects. He must establish his own Truth in order to get out from under the domination of the ego and all of the false teachings embedded in his belief system. You may have to create a meditation that embraces a new belief system such as: "I love myself and my new identity of consciousness because I AM perfect as the sovereign being that I AM created in the likeness of GOD. I approve of what I AM doing because I AM now the creator of my own reality. I AM now free to carry out the divine design of my life."

By focusing your own Truth on the energy of Love, you begin the transmutation of all unbalanced thoughts from your belief system. You cannot rid yourself of the many phobias, compulsions and negative patterns entrenched in the belief system just by talking them over, exposing them to the ego of others. The ego appeases you, but they will always emerge again and again until they are removed from the belief system. That is why talk therapy is not a complete answer for healing these patterns. The reason they won't just go away is that you are tied to the action of each one of these patterns by the emotional imbalance. You cannot be free until the purpose, the aim and balancing factor or learning has been fulfilled and been integrated cellularly. There is an electromagnetic current with a concurring vibration to the action of every thought. The creator of the thought is controlled by that action until the thought has been balanced and the current released. The balancing to take it to the higher transmuting realm is the perfect energy of pure Love. This redeems unbalanced thoughts, purifies the belief system and cleanses the emotions. This is healing.

The Breath of Light is the current of perfect energy of pure Love and heals the deep cellular patterns and belief systems. If you so accept to fulfill the purpose of your life, know your own Truth that sets you free and gives you back your remembrance of your true identity - you will be in the world, but not of the world. You will be set free of the addiction to suffering, which is the addiction to this world.

We have been taught that human nature cannot be changed. However, we are coming to the closing of this present consciousness and the cosmic hour is upon us. The bond of man-kind is being altered. The Breath is the gateway into this new consciousness. It is a conscious Breath into a higher vibratory frequency in the evolution of the human race. It is in the consciousness that evolution takes place. Physical matter is completely governed by consciousness. This change will affect the physical, chemical and mental aspect of the individual's being to the extent that our existence will be suddenly upgraded. It is time, it is overdue, to make preparation for our advancement on to the next level and open the door to the Light and enter the **I AM** Presence of an eternity of peace, joy, freedom and never-ending Love. Will you come with us?

Yes, this is the Ultimate Invitation!

Lift the Veil and gaze into the face of God.

Choose to Live, truly Live, forever and ever in God's Light of Perfect Love.

DECLARATION OF INTENTION

Writing your Declaration of Intention is very important because you are making a commitment to your purpose and when you write it down, the words are embedded in your cellular structure and create a new paradigm for you to live from. It is your new blueprint and magnetizes clarity, purity, events, people, and new energy which all synergize to close doors which need to close, and open new doors that resonate with your purpose. If something does not fit, it will be shown very quickly and very clearly. Don't fight it. Don't hold on to the old.

Fear may come up as you are envisioning your Declaration of Intention. Don't make it too lofty and high that you cannot fulfill it. You can always edit it later to set a higher level of your intention.

One of the greatest obstacles we face in our lives is that we do not trust ourselves and thus we cannot trust others. We have seldom done declarations of our intent and are like ships without a captain, just drifting in the ocean of life without any power or direction. We need to have accountability in our life and very seldom do we require it of ourselves, unless we consciously do Declarations of Intention. Then, we have to be accountable to ourselves and to the Divine. This action will keep us on course and bring more consciousness into our whole being. It is the I AM principle which declares our Truth.

I am giving you my own Declaration of Intention which you can personally tailor and design for your preference. There is no right or wrong way, and you may be surprised as to what surfaces. Just observe your fears, emotions, and thoughts as you write it. Now, here is my own that I have lived by for many years.

MY DECLARATION OF INTENTION

My intention is to be a powerful force in the world, aligned with others, empowered for the purpose of bringing the Breath of Light to the world. As we fulfill our mission, we will bring about a new world governed by a new energy, new laws, new rules, new behavior, and a freedom and love not experienced thus far on this planet. The Breath is the gateway, and the Universe is supplying the energy and support to get this work to the world. This is my reason for being and the fulfillment of my destiny.

I am showing up in the world as an observable definition of "ambition." The new definition within the paradigm shift of "ambition" is *Knowing who you are and Giving it.* My Intention is to establish a basis for trust -- which is accountability. In order to have trust, we have to act consistent with Intention. We are all accountable the minute we declare our Intention. I invite you to declare your intention as an act of empowerment. I invite you to stop indulging in survival mechanisms such as blaming, stories and excuses. I invite you to discipline yourself in order to take care of priorities. I invite you to join me as a world leader committed to bringing forth the paradigm shift.

DR. MARY C. MEADOWS

ABOUT THE AUTHOR

Mary C. Meadows has been active in the holistic health field since her own life experience led her to seek new ways of healing. In the early 70's, Mary was finally diagnosed as having Multiple Sclerosis, cancer and heart disease after years of despair and suffering. She experienced two near-deaths. Through holistic healing methods and her own inner work, Mary was miraculously healed. Dr. Meadows has synthesized many ancient as well as emerging rejuvenescence methodologies. Her continued commitment to her own self-healing has been in the area of the Breath of Light and her years of dedicated work has brought dramatic results for many people.

Dr. Meadows has studied internationally with many leading doctors, scientists, theorists and trainers in such fields as rainforest biology and medicine, therapeutic touch and massage, emotional and psychological processing, nutrition, cleansing, herbology, homeopathy, acupuncture, light and sound therapy, pH balance, Chelation IV therapy, colon hydrotherapy, kinesiology, and a host of other healing methodologies. She received her Doctorate of Natural Medicine degree while in Mexico. She served for four years on the staff of the Contreras Hospital, an alternative cancer treatment hospital in Playas de Tijuana, Baja de California, Mexico as Chief of Staff of the Body-Mind Program as well as Patient Services and Nutrition Protocols. Dr. Mary then did a European tour for several years in Greece, Holland and Germany training and teaching the Breath of Light and her Detoxing protocols to thousands of people. She held Detox Health Retreats at many of the major spas in Germany and Greece.

Feeling deeply the need for a true healing place, Dr. Mary built a Health Resort & Retreat Center in Rockport, Texas as well as an Environmental Medicine clinic in Corpus Christi, Texas where patients came from Europe, Canada, and the U.S.A. to receive the integrated medicine treatment protocols of the clinic and also participate in health, detoxification, spiritual retreats. The retreat was built using all of the elements given to us by the Divine for healing – Earth, Air, Water, Fire and Community. It was a Sacred Sanctuary. The clinic was very beautiful and sacred as well using those same elements. Instead of a cold, sterile clinic, it was a comforting, nurturing and healing place that felt like home.

Preventative care and education were uppermost in every treatment protocol and the patients were encouraged to participate in their everyday health program and empowered to become victors and not victims. The emerging reality for Dr. Mary is that the environment is a major concern for the health of humanity.

Dr. Meadows has been speaking at all major Expos in the US for the last 30 years and has made numerous television and radio appearances as an acknowledged leader in the healing field. Her goal is to take the Breath of Light to all the world. She led the earliest human/dolphin interactions for people of all ages in many countries and oceans. Her earliest Breath work was called *Dolphin Breath.* Dr. Meadows is also an ordained minister and her healing ministry through the Sacred Sanctuary has helped thousands of people.

Dr. Mary has authored two books, first published in 1993 with 3 reprints, as *Breath of Light*, and the second one just now being released, *Until I Breathe This Life.* She produced a CD in Amsterdam, *Breathe the Light, the Journey Home,* which is a guided Breathing Meditation with music by Jan deRoos.

Dr. Mary currently holds a Breath of Light meditation Healing Service, and a Feast every month in Phoenix to bring together other Bringers of Light for personal healing and to Be that Light for the world.

Health Protocols, Resources and Sources Recommended by Dr. Mary Meadows

I am sharing some of the more unusual health products and am choosing only a few of my favorites. I am picking some that are easy to do and not so well known. If I tried to cover all that I know and appreciate the health benefits, this would be a never ending book. Therefore, I had to narrow it down to some of the ones I especially like. I do not prescribe or promise any cures with these plants and supplements. I do know they can aid you in detoxing and nurturing your body. I have used all of them for myself and with patients around the world. Do your own research about them. Always meditate and ask your Higher self if this would be good for your health and healing. There are many Naturopaths who are knowledgeable. Muscle-testing is also a good idea. I do not accept patients or give consults, but I hope these ideas will be beneficial to you. Updated health protocols will be posted on my website: wwwdrmarymeadowsLLC.com. You are always welcome to email me with questions and information. Blessings and Breathe in the Light as you receive your Divine Healing.

ASPARAGUS contains a good supply of protein called histones, which are believed to be active in controlling cell growth. For that reason, I believe asparagus can be said to contain a substance that is called cell growth normalizer. That accounts for its action on cancer and can be used as a general body tonic for better health. In any event, regardless of theory, asparagus used as suggested, is a harmless substance. The FDA cannot prevent you from using it and it may do you much good. It has been reported by the US National Cancer Institute, that asparagus is the highest tested food containing glutathione, which is considered one of the body's most potent anti-carcinogens and antioxidants.

BERBERINE: Get your type 2 diabetes under control... without a single drug! Add Alpha Lipoic Acid with Bioperine (extract of black pepper for enhanced absorption) -

by Dr. Jonathan V. Wright, MD Excerpted from "Nutrition & Healing" newsletter, Vol. 17, Issue 9, November 2010

Best known for its natural antibiotic activity, Berberine deals a serious blow to common infectious organisms— organisms like "staph," "strep," Chlamydia, diphtheria, salmonella, cholera, diplococcus pneumoniae, pseudomonas, gonorrhea, candida, trichomonas, and many others. Berberine is a component (for the technically inclined, a "plant alkaloid") of the commonly used herbs goldenseal and Oregon grape, and of several other less well-known botanicals. A 0.2 percent solution of berberine has been found effective against trachoma—in "third world" countries, a major infectious cause of visual impairment and blindness, as well as many other types of conjunctivitis.

It's less well known that berberine has been found more effective than aspirin in relieving fever in experimental animals, and is able to stimulate some parts of the immune system. It's also a stimulant for bile secretion.

And it's not at all well known that research published in well-known, respected, "peer-reviewed" medical journals in 2008 found that berberine is just as effective— and of course much safer—than metformin, the formerly patent medicine most commonly now prescribed to help re-regulate blood sugar in type 2 diabetes!

Two studies were reported in one of the 2008 research reports.1 In the first study, 36 adults with newly diagnosed type 2 diabetes mellitus were randomly assigned to treatment with berberine or metformin (500 milligrams of either, three times a day) in a three-month (13-week) trial.

At the end of three months, average fasting blood sugars in the berberine group dropped from 191 to 124 milligrams per deciliter, average post-prandial blood sugar (blood sugar after eating) dropped from 356 to 199 milligrams per deciliter, average hemoglobin A1c (a measurement of longer-term blood sugar control) dropped from 9.5 percent to 7.5 percent, and fasting triglycerides dropped from an average 99 to 78 milligrams per deciliter.

The researchers wrote, "Compared with metformin, berberine exhibited an identical effect in the regulation of glucose metabolism, such as HbA1c, FBG [fasting blood glucose], PBG [blood sugar after eating], fasting insulin and postprandial insulin [insulin level after eating]. In the regulation of lipid metabolism, berberine activity is better than metformin. By week 13, triglycerides and total cholesterol in the berberine group had decreased and were significantly lower than in the metformin group."

Insulin resistance dropped by 45 percent!

The second study in this same publication involved 48 adults already under treatment for type 2 diabetes with diet and one or more patent medications and/or insulin. Despite these various treatments, their type 2 diabetes was still poorly controlled. Diet and all medications had been the same in each individual for two months before berberine treatment was added, and remained unchanged for the three months of this second study.

After just 7 days, the added berberine (500 milligrams thrice daily) led to an average reduction in fasting blood sugar from 172 to 140 milligrams per deciliter, and average postprandial blood sugar had declined from 266 to 210 milligrams per deciliter.

During the second week of added berberine, average fasting blood sugar dropped to 135 milligrams per deciliter, and postprandial glucose to 189 milligrams per deciliter. The researchers reported that these improvements were maintained for the rest of the three month study.

In addition, hemoglobin A1c decreased from 8.1 percent to 7.3 percent, fasting insulin decreased by 28 percent, insulin resistance was reduced by 45 percent, and total and low-density (LDL) cholesterol were both significantly reduced.

The researchers wrote that in their study of newly diagnosed diabetics who took berberine or placebo alone, "one of the patients suffered from severe gastrointestinal adverse events when berberine was used alone."

By contrast, the researchers wrote about the poorly controlled diabetics who added berberine to their on-going patent medication treatment: "Incidence of gastrointestinal adverse events was 34.5 percent during the 13 weeks of berberine…combination therapy."

These adverse events included diarrhea in 10 percent, constipation in 7 percent, flatulence in 19 percent, and abdominal pain in 3.4 percent. The side effects were observed only in the first four weeks in most patients. In 24 percent, berberine dosage was decreased from 500 to 300 milligrams thrice daily because of gastrointestinal adverse events, and all of these side effects disappeared within one week.

The researchers concluded, "In summary, berberine is a potent oral hypoglycemic [blood sugar lowering] agent with modest effect on lipid metabolism. It is safe and the cost of treatment by berberine is very low."

Better blood sugar control ...and a few pounds shed.

In a second publication, other researchers described results achieved by 116 individuals with type 2 diabetes and cholesterol and triglyceride abnormalities who participated in a randomized, double-blind trial that compared 500 milligrams of berberine taken twice daily with placebo, also taken twice daily. In the berberine group, average fasting blood sugar decreased from 126 to 101 milligrams/deciliter.

Two hours after a standardized glucose challenge, blood sugars decreased from an average 216 to an average 160 milligrams per deciliter. Average hemoglobin A1c decreased from 7.5 percent to 6.6 percent, average triglycerides decreased from 221 to 141 millgrams per deciliter, average total cholesterol decreased from 205 to 168 milligrams per deciliter, and average LDL-cholesterol ("bad" cholesterol) decreased from 125 to 97 milligrams per deciliter.

These researchers also reported "secondary outcomes." Body weight decreased from an average 151 pounds to an average 146 pounds with berberine, a significantly greater fall (five pounds) than in the placebo group, who went from an average 158 pounds to an average 155 pounds, a loss of three pounds. A greater reduction of body mass index (BMI) was also found at three months in the berberine group than in the placebo group. Systolic blood pressure decreased from an average of 124 to 117 and diastolic blood pressure decreased from an average of 81 to 77 in those treated with berberine, exceeding the fall from 126 to 123 systolic and from 83 to 80 diastolic in those who took the placebo. Side effects were few and mostly transient in the berberine group.

The recommended protocol is Berberine 500mg. twice daily, combined with Alpha Lipoic Acid 300mg, and Piperine 10mg.(increases absorbency) (Piperine is called Bioperine at Swanson Health Products) I personally take 800mg of Berberine twice daily with the above additives.

BLACK CUMIN: the secret miracle heal-all remedy
Black Seed and Black Seed Oil by Jonathan Benson

What if you were told there was a seed so densely packed with healing compounds that cancer, bacteria, viruses, ulcers, diabetes, chronic inflammation, and many other common health conditions hardly stand a chance in its presence? Not to be confused with black sesame seed which looks strikingly similar, black cumin, also known as "black seed," is the seed in question, and it is all these things and more, hence its historical reputation as "a remedy for all diseases except death."

If you have never heard of black cumin (*Nigella sativa*), it is probably because the seed is rarely talked about in modern Western society. Even though its use as both an herb and a folk remedy dates back many centuries, black cumin has long been shelved in favor of pharmaceutical remedies that are far less effective and elicit harmful side effects. But if you are tired of trying to overcome your ailments with patented drugs, you may want to consider adding black cumin to your diet.

Since 1964, there have been at least 458 published, peer-reviewed studies involving black cumin, according to *GreenMedInfo.com*, and these studies confirm what Middle Eastern and North African cultures have known for thousands of years -- black cumin is essentially a miracle heal-all remedy. According to the *GreenMedInfo.com* reference page for black cumin, the seed has been scientifically confirmed as being elements of the following:

- Analgesic(pain-killing)
- Antibacterial
- Anti-inflammatory
- Anti-ucler
- Anti-cholinergic
- Anti-fungal

- Anti-hypertensive
- Antioxidant
- Antispasmodic
- Antiviral
- Bronchodilator
- Gluconeogenesis-inhibitor-(anti-diabetic)
- Hepatoprotective-(liver-protecting)
- Hypotensive
- Insulin-sensitizing
- Interferon-inducer
- Renoprotective-(kidney-protecting)
- Tumor-necrosis-factor-alpha-inhibitor

Specifically, black cumin has been shown to provide pain relief for patients being treated for acute tonsillo-pharyngitis; prevent disease that would otherwise be caused by exposure to chemical weapons; aid in the long-term treatment of patients addicted to opioid drugs; alleviate the symptoms of allergic rhinitis; **fight *Helicobacter pylori* (*H. pylori*) infection;** treat type-2 diabetes; relieve asthma symptoms; lower blood pressure; prevent epileptic seizures; and eliminate fungi and candidiasis, among many other functions http://www.greenmedinfo.com/substance/nigella-sativa-aka-black-seed

Black cumin as powerful preventive, treatment for cancer
If all this is not enough, black cumin has long been regarded throughout the Middle East as one of the most powerful anti-carcinogenic herbs in existence. Studies have shown that

regularly taking black cumin or black cumin oil can help prevent the growth and spread of colon cancer cells, but the seed is also useful in preventing and treating cancer (http://science.naturalnews.com/pubmed/12881014.html).
In fact, researchers at the *Cancer Immuno-Biology Laboratory* in South Carolina found that black cumin helps stimulate the activity of neutrophil granulocytes, which are responsible for targeting cancer cells and eliminating them.

"Black Cumin Oil (Black Seed) generally helps stimulate the production of bone marrow and cells of the immune system," wrote the authors in their study. "It increases the production of interferon, protects normal cells from the damaging effects of viral disease, destroys tumor cells and increases the number of antibody producing B cells"

Because it has a spicy, nutty flavor, black cumin can be sprinkled whole or ground up on food, and the oil can also be used on salads and other dishes. The seeds can also be ground and added to water to create a mucilaginous gel similar to what develops when chia seeds are added to water. This gel can be drunk or used as an egg replacement.

Sources for this article and more information found at:
http://www.greenmedinfo.com/blog/black-seed-remedy-everything-death

P.S. I use Black Cumin Essential Oil from Earth Angel Oils Order at:
http://www.earthangeloils.com/148.php

BONE BROTH

I am excerpting an excellent article by Ryan Feeney: "The Power of the Almighty Bone Broth"

If I were to recommend one simple healing food that contributes to our overall health, it would be Traditional Bone Broth. This is one of the most healing, nutrient dense substances that we can add to our daily lives. Bone broth is a traditional healing food used by nearly every culture. Chinese Medicine believes that bone broth strengthens and nourishes our essence, qi, and wei qi, warms the yang and builds blood. The broth is said to enter and nourish our Kidneys, Liver, Lungs and Spleen.

So what makes bone broth so special? The exact nutrient profile of bone broth depends on the type of bones you use, how and with what it is cooked. We do know that it is rich in minerals that are found in bones and marrow, including Calcium, Magnesium, Iron, Silicon, Phosphorus, Sulphur and other trace minerals. The other unique and powerful substances found in bone broth are Marrow, Cartilage, Glycine, Proline, Collagen and Gelatin. The latter six substances are interrelated and in many cases either a part of one another or a different version of the same thing. For instance, cartilage, marrow and gelatin are merely forms of collagen. Proline and Glycine are amino acids that are foundational components found in collagen (or gelatin and cartilage). So broadly speaking it is the collagen that really provides the powerful health punch we experience from traditionally prepared bone broths.

To better understand the potential healing benefits of bone broth, I will discuss these six substances separately:

Marrow: Contains omega 3 fatty acids, minerals, vitamin A (maybe K) and stem cells. According to Cindy Micleu MTCM., L.Ac. "Red marrow is an important source of nutritional and immune support factors extracted in the cooking of bone soup. It contains myeloid stem cells, which are the precursors to red blood cells, and lymphoid stem cells, the precursors to white blood cells and platelets. The red marrow produces these immature precursor cells, which later convert to mature cell outside the marrow."

Highlights of the benefits of Marrow:

⊙ Contains AKG's (alkylglycerols) which increase RBC, WBC & Platelets.

⊙ Rebuilding after marrow suppression (chemo & radiation treatments).

⊙ Treats anemia.

⊙ Carries oxygen to other cells in the body via RBC.

Cartilage: Composed primarily of collagen and elastin proteins. It is rich in glycosaminoglycans (GAGs), hyaluronic acid, chondroitin sulfate, and keratin sulfate.

The cartilage in bone broth is found mostly in the joints.

Highlights of the benefits of Cartilage:

⊙ Greatly reduces joint deterioration & benefits joint and connective tissues.

⊙ Heals inflammatory bowel disease.

- Contains AAF's (antiangiogenesis factors) that starve blood supply to cancer cells.
- Stimulates B, T, and macrophage immune cells.

Glycine: Bone broth is rich in this "nonessential" amino acid that plays a wide variety of important roles in the body including glucose production & regulation. It is one of the three amino acids that make up Glutathione, a tripeptide that acts as our most prominent antioxidant. It is also crucial for protecting muscle, in muscle recovery, and in wound healing. According to scientist & nutritionist Dr. Ray Peat "Glycine is recognized as an "inhibitory" neurotransmitter, and promotes natural sleep. Used as a supplement, it has helped to promote recovery from strokes and seizures, and to improve learning and memory. But in every type of cell, it apparently has the same kind of quieting, protective anti-stress action." Another very important role of Glycine is its ability to increase gastric juices and thereby assisting in the prevention of ulcers and other digestive related conditions.

Highlights of the benefits of Glycine:

- Inhibitory neurotransmitter similar to GABA (gamma aminobutyric acid).
- Protects the brain.
- **Primary amino acid involved in gluconeogenesis.**
- Elevates gastric acid levels.
- Relaxes the mind and shows promise in treatment of insomnia and stress.
- Muscle recovery and wound healing.

○ Essential for Phase I & II liver detoxification.

Proline: Another nonessential amino acid, this is the primary amino acid required for Collagen formation, and therefore is essential healthy cartilage, tendons, bones, ligaments and skin. Proline is also helps keep the arteriesflexible and producing collagen, reducing arteriosclerosis and blood pressure.

Highlights of the benefits of Proline:

○ Collagen formation (best taken with Vitamin C).

○ Prevents arteriosclerosis and may reduce risk of developing heart disease.

○ Repairs damaged tissues.

Collagen: Referred to as **the "glue" that holds our cells together**, it is our main structural protein that makes up our connective tissues. There are several (15 or more), forms of collagen in the body and it comprises approximately 25% of the protein found in our bodies. It is part of all of our organs, arteries, veins, skin, ligaments, tendons, bones, and marrow. Collagen works together with elastin (another structural protein) to maintain connective tissue flexibility or elasticity. Collagen is destroyed by inflammatory processes. Essential to Collagen formation and health are antioxidant, particularly anthocyanidins (found in dark red/purple fruits) and vitamin C. Collagen and Gelatin are the same thing. Collagen is the term used to refer to what is found in the body tissues, whereas Gelatin is the term referring to extracted collagen used as food. Gelatin: The cooked form of collagen which is 35% glycine, 11% alanine, and 21% proline and hydroxyproline. Gelatin, as found in bone broth, is the ideal way to increase and feed the collagen in the body. In a warm liquid form it lends itself to easy digestion, and is generally well tolerated in people with gastrointestinal conditions and food sensitivities.

In traditional cultures, including in Chinese Medicine, bone broth makes an excellent base for feeding infants who cannot breast feed or are otherwise intolerant to cow or goat dairy. Gelatin is thought to heal mucus membranes and has been shown to heal inflammation and damage to intestinal walls. The regular consumption of gelatin helps replenish the secretory IgA (SIgA), mucosal barrier of the gut, which is the primary antibody of the intestinal system. It is now estimated that up to 70% of our immunity is found in our intestinal system. Gelatin has been shown to reduce inflammation and heal the small intestine in Leaky Gut Syndrome or intestinal hyper-permeability conditions.

Most current thinking in medicine sees intestinal permeability issues as being central in allergies, food intolerances, autoimmune conditions, and many other inflammatory chronic health conditions. Additionally Ray Peat makes the strong argument, "It is especially important to balance our diets with more gelatin because the amino acids found in muscle meats (methionine, cysteine, and tryptophan) should be balanced with a rich source of gelatin which counters their anti-metabolic effects and leads to a more efficient metabolism and healthy thyroid."

Highlights of the benefits of Gelatin:

o Anti-inflammatory.

- Helps heal damaged mucosal membranes of the GI tract and reduce permeability.
- Plays a strong role in immunity and the treatment of auto-immune conditions.
- Soft tissue and wound healing.
- Formation of healthy ligament, cartilage, and bone.
- Supports healthy thyroid and metabolism.
- Supports healthy sleep and neurotransmitter health.
- Treats anemia and enhances protein assimilation.

Adding traditionally prepared bone broths to you and your clients' diets is a simple yet powerful dietary recommendation. It's deeply nourishing, comforting and is tonifying to blood, qi and the essence. It is truly a superfood.

It is easy to make, freezes well, and can be used straight as a broth tea or as a base for soups, congees, stews, sauces, gravy, cooking grains, vegetables, savory baked goods, and added to beans. Bone Broth is simply made from cooking the bones of healthy animals or fish in water with vegetables, spices and herbs. The best broth is made slowly, 4 - 48 hours, steeping the nutrients from deep inside the bones and dissolving the marrow, cartilage and tendons into a silky rich fragrant broth.

To Make Bone Broth:

Broth can be cooked on the stovetop on low heat, or in a slow cooker (crockpot).

Ingredients:
• 2-3 pounds of organic bones (Include 2-4 chicken feet, or 1 sliced calf's foot for added gelatin; if using fish, use non-oily only. If using beef bones, you may want to roast them first for added flavor.)
• 4 quarts of cold filtered water
• 2 Tbsp to 1 cup vinegar (to taste)
• (optionally add 1 -3 onions, 2-3 carrots, 2-3 celery stalks, Spices as desired
• 1 bunch parsley

Directions:
1. Put bones, meat, vinegar, water, any spices and all vegetables (except parsley) in stainless steel pot or crock pot. Let stand for 30 minutes to 1 hour.
2. Bring to boil.
3. Skim the scum off of the surface of the water.
4. Reduce heat, cover and simmer. For fish, at least 2 hours; for poultry, at least 8 hours; for beef, at least 12 hours.
5. Add the parsley in the last 10 minutes.
6. Strain, let cool, and refrigerate. Observe amount of gelatin in broth, and make adjustments to cooking time, and vinegar amount, accordingly.
7. Remove congealed fat that rises to the top.
8. Freeze any broth that you won't be using within 7 days.

CABBAGE FOOT SOAK, This is absolutely miraculous and I have utilized it all over the world with amazing results. Cabbage has a powerful enzyme that pulls out of the body all manner of toxins and you want to do it in a foot soak bath as it pulls away from the heart and is safer. Use ¼ head of a fresh cabbage, slice very thin, put in pan large enough for both your feet, pour boiling water over the sliced cabbage and let it set for about 15 minutes in order to release the enzymes. When it is comfortable that you can put your feet in the water (still containing the cabbage) soak your feet for at least 20 minutes. You will not believe how much better you will feel. People have been relieved of pains in their bodies and sometimes even pus and other toxins come out discoloring the water. Throw out the water – do not reuse it. Do this several times a day for extreme cases, but definitely do once a day for at least 3 days. You can do it every day of your life if you want as it is not going to have any side-effects or ill effects. You can soak cabbage in boiling water and make a poultice over a part of your body especially for infection. Leave in place for several hours.

CALCIUM BENTONITE CLAY

It is important to use a clean, natural, pure, contaminant-free calcium bentonite clay internally to detoxify and cleanse the digestive system, liver and colon. It removes heavy metals and toxic chemical as well as internal parasites. It can neutralize stomach ailments from ulcers and Acid Reflux. It improves the immune system function and increases absorption of vitamins and nutrients. It alkalizes the acid pH of the body and fixes free oxygen in the blood stream. You can take it internally as a daily dosage in water or juice to increase your overall energy level and stimulate latent cell energy.

There are many uses externally and is used in most spas in the world. Foot baths are a wonderful way to pull out toxins and application on the skin for skin diseases and rashes is miraculous.

Be sure and use a clay with an 8.5 or higher pH and a Smectitie/Montmorillonite Clay which absorbs and adsorbs. You want a clay that is non-gritty, milled at least to a 325 screen mesh. Green swelling clays have long been known for their superior healing qualities.

Note: I have used Living Clay, personally, for some years with wonderful results.

See more benefits at www.aboutclay.com or contact Dr. Mary for more info.

CANDIDA: One of the products to use if you are dealing with low thyroid and also candida is coconut oil. You can get organic coconut oil at most health food stores. However, sites to order from are www.wildernessfamilynaturals.com and on www.luckyvitamins.com from Garden of Life. Another good product is the powdered coconut milk which is a highly nutritious product. I cook with it. I make smoothies with it and it helps with yeast/candida cleansing. People who cannot lose weight often times have yeast which swells up when you eat carbs, sugar, and you have to cleanse it from the body. It is a long process and you have to be pure with your food. **Coconut oil** is fabulous to detox Candida and it also helps to heal the thyroid. Be very careful not to take too much in the beginning as you will become very, very sick with flu-like symptoms with the Herxheimer syndrome which is a too rapid die-off of candida – releasing toxins which are very toxic. Believe me, you will regret it if you take too much. I would recommend ½ teaspoon of coconut oil daily for a couple of weeks and then start adding additional ½ teaspoons until you get up to about 2 tablespoons. You can cook with it, or just eat it with a spoon.

The ONLY oils that you should be cooking with are coconut and olive oils. There are other good oils that are good to ingest, but not so great to cook with such as Hemp Oil, Almond and other nut oils, and Sesame oil (which can be cooked with). Throw out all canola oil as it is made from rapeseed and that is a toxic industrial plant. Do not use soy of any kind. Soy is a huge culprit in destroying your thyroid.

Soy was grown in the beginning for industrial products, but since there was a massive amount of byproduct from the soy, a huge myth was perpetrated on the public calling soy a "health food" and then a marketing campaign followed to defraud everyone as to soy's health benefits. It is criminal that infants are being fed formula that is soy based. It will only be when the infants are in their teens that they will be diagnosed with hypothyroid disease. About 90% of the American people suffer from inactive or low thyroid disease. Peanut butter is the other culprit along with soy. Soy byproduct is in almost every processed packaged food. It is sometimes called protein powder or other terms but it is soy!!!! Read all the labels and try your best to sort them out. The best advice: don't use packaged foods.

And remember, just because you can find some fabulous products on the sites I have given you, they distribute a lot of products and not all of them are truly healthy and good for you

CASTOR OIL TREATMENT from Edgar Cayce. Another powerful poultice is to take castor oil – soak wool flannel with it and lay over the liver or other organs needing relief. Wrap with more clean flannel and sleep with it. It can go over areas of pain, inflammation or where you need to pull toxins out. Repeat until you get relief.

CHIA SEED is a true super food, one of nature's perfect foods. It provides a natural source for added energy and endurance, plus Chia Seed is the highest known plant source of omega-3 fatty acids which are important to your heart, joints and brain function. It has a very high protective antioxidant value and is rich in vitamins, fiber and protein. A member of the mint family, Chia is native to Central America and has been used traditionally for over 3000 years. Ancient Aztec warriors prized Chia as an endurance promoting Superfood, eating it just before battle, and drinking it in water before running long distance. Due to its high fiber content, Chia seed absorbs more than ten times its weight in water, making it an excellent source of hydration. Chia Seeds soluble fiber forms a gel that slows the absorption of sugar into the bloodstream, binds it to toxins in the digestive system and helps eliminate waste. Plus, Chia Seed is especially rich in essential fatty acids and high-ORAC antioxidants.

Now Chia has been rediscovered and you can benefit from Chia's unique and amazing nutritional powers! In fact, Chia is an ideal food for nearly everyone. The FDA has stated that Chia is a food, rather than a supplement and can be consumed without restrictions.

Chia, the World's First Grain Proven to Reduce Dangerous Inflammation by up to 21%

Recent groundbreaking evidence indicates the presence of "inflammation" in the body is a dangerous health concern, especially in the development of arterial disease, heart attack and stroke. Inflammation is easily measured with a simple test that determines your level of a chemical called C-reactive protein (CRP), which increases dramatically during inflammation.

In randomized clinical studies, Chia's extraordinary profile of antioxidants, vitamins, calcium, magnesium, other important minerals and its rich levels of omega-3 fatty acids **proved to be effective in reducing CRP levels by as much as 21%.**

Chia is unrivalled among all seeds and grains for providing **increased energy to both your mind and body**. Native people knew about Chia and made it their power food of choice. The energy and endurance of native athletes, runners and warriors is legendary, and now you can benefit from this affordable, rediscovered super food. Take Chia daily to feel energized, mentally sharp and alert.

One of Chia's greatest values as a super grain lies in its extremely high content of omega-3 fatty acids. Chia's natural oil contains the **highest-known percentage of omega-3 alpha-linolenic acid**, containing an incredible 63%! Since the 1970's, researchers have been noting the importance of omega-3's as a dietary factor in achieving optimum heart health.

Chia Seed Supports Improved Mental Focus, Mood and Concentration.

COLLOIDAL SILVER, a Natural Antibiotic: If I could have only one thing with me on an island, it would be colloidal silver. It is so potent and diverse as it kills all viruses, bacteria, fungi. It is non-toxic, non-addictive and is used both internally and externally. It can be purchased at health food stores or online at Lucky Vitamins – offers a really good product -ASAP Silver by American BioTech and they have it in the liquid and skin lotion. I have used it personally for years without any ill effects.

COLON CLEANSE

Some people may have parasites and need to do a parasite cleanse. Or a colon cleanse. These are good to do several times a year as we get re-infected with foods, water, etc. And, we all need to do a liver cleanse at least once a year. There are numerous products on the market. I am very fond of Rich Anderson's ARISE & SHINE cleanse. His products are very pure. Guidance by a health professional is a *good idea.*

DETOXIFICATION is a complex process and is essential to the healing process. It is simple in that for healing to occur, one must rid the body of toxins and then give it the nutrients to restore and rejuvenate. Nutrition is a huge part of the process and there are many protocols. It might be wise to find a Naturopath or Nutritional expert on Detoxing and follow their guidance. I am in favor of laboratory testing of blood and urine to see all your levels. Then you can address the problem areas.

Detox for Heavy Metals, especially Mercury

While I believe that Chelation IV therapy is the most effective way to detox, there are other ways to support your detox of heavy metals. Here are some that I have used. ACZ Nano by Results RNA is an Advanced Cellular Zeolite (Sub-Micronized Zeolite Clinoptilolite Nano Distilled Water) and has impressive power to chelate toxic molecules (chemicals and heavy metals) quickly and safely. They have lab results with pre and post 12 hour urine testing to show the amounts of all the many heavy metals removed – very significant results. This product came to my attention awhile back, but I was committed to IV Chelation and did not pursue this. However, I have to say that this nano spray that is an oral delivery is a good protocol along with the following methods to encourage the chelation process. And, luckily, Lucky Vitamins carries this product. Otherwise, you have to get this from a licensed health professional like a ND or MD. for a greater cost. Check it out on www.luckyvitamins.com. Chlorella is extremely helpful for detoxing chemicals and heavy metals. It can be purchased in tabs and it is important to choose a product which incorporates the process of breaking the indigestible chlorella cell walls. Another important product is chlorophyll and is often combined with mint which is also a healthy substance. NOW formulates both products and at a very affordable price on the www.luckyvitamins.com website NOW Foods - Liquid Chlorophyll Triple Strength Natural Mint Flavor – 16 oz. and Chlorella Green Superfood Certified Organic 500 mg.200 tabs. There are other brands which are excellent as well, such as SUN and their Chlorella tabs 300/200mg ea runs about $25. NOW has excellent quality and I can recommend their more affordable products. Lucky Vitamins offers most name brands at highly discounted pricing and even with the shipping it is much more economical. Swanson Vitamins www.swansonvitamins.com is also a great source with good pricing. They carry brand names as well as manufacture many products under their own name brand.

Another inexpensive but highly effective product for detoxing heavy metals, especially mercury, is **Oil of Cilantro** which can be bought at any health food store or order from Lucky Vitamins: North American Herb and Spice Essence of Cilantro for only about $12. You need to add folic acid to the regime as well.

DMSO (Dimethyl Sulfoxide) is unique in its almost unbelievable variety of applications to give pain relief in a hundred diseases and conditions. It has been used to control inflammation, swelling, reduce pain, slow the growth of bacteria, viruses, and fungi: relieve burns, sprains, strains, and arthritis. It has relieved the symptoms of shingles, herpes, tuberculosis, sinusitis, cancer, and is used in topical gels, liquids and in IV's. Can be purchased at health food stores and online. I especially love the gel form for easier application.

FIR SAUNAS

I believe that FIR (Far Infrared) Saunas are the most important and effective investment we can make in order to detox the body from chemicals and is believed to be the only way to detox phthalates or plasticizers from the body.

Why Sauna? Dr. Dietrich Klinghardt has written: "Peer reviewed literature shows that sweating during sauna therapy eliminates high levels of toxic metals, organic compounds, dioxin, and other toxins." Dr. Klinghardt recommends *Heavenly Heat* saunas exclusively. A majority of users: are chemically injured; parents of ASD children, or are fighting Lyme Disease. See their website: http://www.heavenlyheatsaunas.com/heavy-metal-detox

Another great FIR sauna website is www.sunlighten.com and read the founder's personal and very inspiring testimony at: http://www.sunlighten.com/founder.html This company has also incorporated some very awesome and enhancing modalities with the sauna. They also have an individual portable sauna which would be great for those who do not have the room for the larger cabinets.

Dr. Sherry Rogers, M.D. who I have personally studied with and I consider one of the experts in the world, in her book **"Detoxify or Die"** explains,

"Obviously not any old sauna will do, because high heat is contraindicated and poorly tolerated by heart failure patients and in fact is a cause of early death. But because far infrared sauna provides safe, low temperature depuration through sweat of the very heavy metals, pesticides, dioxins, PCBs, plasticizers, and other environmental chemicals that caused the heart damage in the first place, it is successful. And in contrast to drugs, it has no side effects.

The far infrared sauna pulls otherwise permanent toxins out of the body by causing a molecular dance with molecules of water and xenobiotics stored in the surface fat. In this way it does not drag chemicals out of safe storage and into the bloodstream where they could cause exacerbation of symptoms. Instead, it causes a resonance between the water and chemical molecules, enabling topical excretion via sweat where they can be wiped and showered away forever. This is the only known and proven mechanism for getting rid of the vast diverse array of disease-producing toxins and environmental chemicals. Medicine has no other option for lowering the body burden of chemicals that underlie all disease." Excerpt from Detoxify of Die by Dr. Sherry Rogers

Before the sauna, you should do about 10 to 30 minutes of exercise which will improve outflow of chemicals. If you cannot do exercise, use a loofa sponge or natural bristle body brush to stimulate skin circulation.

GO GLUTEN FREE – I recommend trying a gluten-free diet for at least 30 days in order to notice the benefits. I believe that most people actually have a wheat sensitivity and may even have a gluten intolerance called celiac disease. Gluten sensitivity manifests in many physical ways that one would not suspect.

Gluten Intolerance Symptoms – How Do You Know If Gluten Is Making You Sick?

What are gluten intolerance symptoms? Research shows that gluten sensitivity in some form, including celiac disease and mild gluten intolerance, affects approximately 15% of the US population. **These** statistics are likely to be similar in Western countries with similar health issues and dietary patterns. Are you one of these people? How do you recognize gluten intolerance symptoms?

First of all let's **identify the difference between celiac disease and gluten intolerance**. Celiac disease is an immune reaction, a severe sudden onset allergic reaction, to the protein called gluten. This is commonly found in grains such as wheat, rye, barley and oats. While celiac disease is initially an auto-immune disorder, it is also a disease of malabsorption, because essential nutrients are not absorbed. Therefore one of the most devastating symptoms of long-term undiagnosed celiac disease is malnutrition.

Gluten intolerance often has a slower onset than celiac disease, and may be hard to diagnose due to the broad range of symptoms and causes.

If you imagine a continuum of gluten intolerance symptoms, celiac disease is usually at the most extreme end with immediate autoimmune reactions. Some people with celiac disease may not have symptoms, but internally malabsorption and malnutrition can erode health over many years. Both celiac disease and gluten intolerance can be **exacerbated by emotional stress**, infection, surgery, pregnancy and childbirth. Every individual with some level of gluten intolerance or allergy may experience different shades of symptoms, hence the challenge for medical practitioners to diagnose.

So what are the specific symptoms of gluten intolerance and celiac disease?

    Weight loss or weight gain
    Nutritional deficiencies due to malabsorption e.g. low iron levels
    Gastro-intestinal problems (bloating, pain, gas, constipation, diarrhea)
    Fat in the stools (due to poor digestion)
    Aching joints
    Depression
    Eczema
    Headaches

Exhaustion
Irritability and behavioural changes
Infertility, irregular menstrual cycle and miscarriage
Cramps, tingling and numbness
Slow infant and child growth
Decline in dental health

Undiagnosed for long periods of time, food intolerances have been found to contribute to diabetes, bowel cancer, anemia and osteoporosis. There are many websites devoted to help in pursuing a gluten free diet. There are many wonderful foods, even breads like UDI Bread which is delicious and Gluten Free. Many supermarkets now clearly mark a food Gluten Free. It was not as difficult as I thought it would be and I am impressed at how profound the changes have been in my digestion and health.

HEMP OIL contains ingredients that help with lowering cholesterol, reducing heart attack risk, aiding the metabolic processing of fats and preventing cancer, according to Medical News Today. The beneficial ingredients in hemp oil are sterols, aliphatic alcohols and linolenic acids.

Sterols are steroid types of alcohol. Research shows that these drop cholesterol numbers and that daily consumption of sterols in the diet reduces the danger of a heart attack. Aliphatic alcohols also reduce cholesterol while fighting the gathering of platelets. Phytol, an aliphatic alcohol, offers benefits as an antioxidant, particularly in the prevention of cancer. It is also present in asparagus, beans, spinach and other raw vegetables, as explained by Medical News Today.

Tocopherol is another aliphatic alcohol that research has connected to improvement in patients suffering from Alzheimer's disease and atherosclerosis. Hemp oil has also boosted the processing of lipids, or fatty acids, in the body, and it has helped patients suffering from skin diseases.

Hemp oil is rich in beta-carotene and vitamins A, C and E, and it is also high in minerals, including calcium, sulfur, magnesium, potassium and phosphorus. It contains several polyunsaturated fatty acids, making it beneficial in cooking,

There are so many forms of Hemp available and the health benefits are endless.

HYPOTHYROID (LOW-FUNCTIONING THYROID)
Most everyone has a compromised thyroid and the tests they do at the labs are faulty. The thyroid controls every system of the body and is so essential to health. Synthetic thyroid is not good as the body does not know how to utilize synthetics. I use Armour Thyroid which requires a prescription and have had success with it. We should only use Desicated Natural Thyroid Formulations. A good one is "Raw Thyroid" by Natural Sources, which is a natural extract of Thyroid tissue, Adrenal Tissue, Pituitary, Thymus, and Spleen tissue. Raw tissue concentrated from bovine

sources specially processed (freeze-dried) at or below -5'C to preserve natural occurring vitamins, enzymes, nucleotides, lipoproteins and all other cellular components. Raw tissue concentrates imported from New Zealand are made from toxin-free lyophilized glands from animals grazed on rangeland free of pesticides, growth hormones, antibiotics or chemical additives. An excellent formulation to treat Thyroid deficiency because you have to also treat the adrenals at the same time. Guaranteed, the adrenals are compromised. Some thyroid products only contain iodine or kelp and that is good to support Thyroid balance, but not enough to correct hypothyroidism. Start off with 2 capsules per day for several weeks and try adding an additional capsule every few weeks – no more than 4. Back down if you feel any tightness in chest, chest pain, heart fibulations, and nervousness. And email me if you have questions. Order from www.luckyvitamin.com/itemKey/72802 .

INTERMITTENT FASTING: Aside from removing your cravings for sugar and snack foods, melting the pounds of excess fat away, and making it far easier to maintain a healthy body weight, modern science has also confirmed there are many other good reasons to fast intermittently, such as:

- Normalizing your insulin and leptin sensitivity, which is key for optimal health as insulin resistance (which is what you get when your insulin sensitivity plummets) is a primary

contributing factor to nearly all chronic disease, from diabetes to heart disease and even cancer
- Normalizing ghrelin levels, also known as "the hunger hormone"
- Promoting human growth hormone (HGH) production, which plays an important part in health, fitness and slowing the aging process
- Lowering triglyceride levels
- Reducing inflammation and lessening free radical damage

There's also plenty of research showing that fasting has a beneficial impact on longevity in animals. There are a number of mechanisms contributing to this effect. Normalizing insulin sensitivity is a major one, but fasting also inhibits the mTOR pathway, which plays an important part in driving the aging process. The fact that it improves a number of potent disease markers also contributes to fasting's overall beneficial effects on general health. In a new diet book, *The Fast Diet: Lose Weight, Stay Healthy, and Live Longer with the Simple Secret of Intermittent Fasting,* Dr. Michael Mosley[1] suggests the best way to lose weight is to eat normally for five days a week, and fast for two. On fasting days, he recommends cutting your food down to ¼ of your normal daily calories, or about 600 calories for men and about 500 for women, along with plenty of water and tea. This is another version of intermittent fasting, in which you simply restrict your *daily* eating to a *specific window of time*. Zinczenko and Moore recommend an eight hour window, which is doable and convenient for most people, but you can restrict it even further — down to six, four, or even two hours, if you want, but you can still reap many of these rewards by limiting your eating to a window of about 8 hours. This means eating only between the hours of 11am until 7pm, as an example. Essentially, this equates to simply skipping breakfast, and making lunch your first meal of the day instead.

IODINE: Taking a good quality Iodine is good for almost everybody as we are all deficient and our thyroid needs suffient iodine to make T3 and T4. If you don't have a functioning thyroid anymore, then you will have to take thyroid extract. www.magnesiumforlife.com has a good source. Dr. Marcus Sircus is expert regarding Iodine.

KRILL OIL You have to have the Omega 3's which are essential for the healing of the nervous system and heart. Krill oil is the highest and best form of Omega 3 as there are no heavy metals such as mercury which can be found in some salmon or other fish oils. If you use fish oil, make sure it is from the northern seas – cold deep water. Dr.Mercola has a good one and there are now several on the market.

LICORICE ROOT (Excerpted from WisdomHerbs.com)
As a herbal medicine it has an impressive list of well documented uses and is probably one of the most over-

looked of all herbal wonders. Licorice is useful for many ailments including asthma, athlete's foot, baldness, body odor, bursitis, canker sores, chronic fatigue, depression, colds and flu, coughs, dandruff, emphysema, gingivitis and tooth decay, gout, heartburn, HIV, viral infections, fungal infections, ulcers, liver problems, Lyme disease, menopause, psoriasis, shingles, sore throat, tendinitis, tuberculosis, ulcers, yeast infections, prostate enlargement and arthritis.

Hundreds of potentially healing substances have been identified in licorice as well, including compounds called flavonoids and various plant estrogens (phytoestrogens). The herb's key therapeutic compound, glycyrrhizin (which is 50 times sweeter than sugar) exerts numerous beneficial effects on the body, making licorice a valuable herb for treating a host of ailments. It seems to prevent the breakdown of adrenal hormones such as cortisol (the body's primary stress-fighting adrenal hormone), making these hormones more available to the body.

It has a well-documented reputation for healing ulcers. It can lower stomach acid levels, relieve heartburn and indigestion and acts as a mild laxative.

It can also be used for irritation, inflammation and spasm in the digestive tract. Through its beneficial action on the liver, it increases bile flow and lowers cholesterol levels.

Licorice also appears to enhance immunity by boosting levels of interferon, a key immune system chemical that fights off attacking viruses. It also contains powerful antioxidants as well as certain phytoestrogens that can perform some of the functions of the body's natural estrogens; very helpful during the menopause. Glycyrrhizinic acid also seems to stop the growth of many bacteria and of viruses such as influenza A.

In the respiratory system it has a similarly soothing and healing action, reducing irritation and inflammation and has an expectorant effect, useful in irritating coughs, asthma and chest infections.

It has an aspirin-like action and is helpful in relieving fevers and soothing pain such as headaches. Its anti-allergenic effect is very useful for hay fever, allergic rhinitis, conjunctivitis and bronchial asthma. Possibly by its action on the adrenal glands, licorice has the ability to improve resistance to stress. It should be thought of during times of both physical and emotional stress, after surgery or during convalescence, or when feeling tired and run down.

Recent studies have found that by limiting the damage from LDL ("bad") cholesterol, licorice may discourage artery-clogging plaque formation and contribute to the healthy functioning of the heart. Research indicates that modest doses of licorice (100 mg a day) have this effect.
Do not confuse with licorice confectionery which contains very little, if any, licorice and is in fact flavoured by anise.

Can cause water retention and raise blood pressure. Prolonged use should be avoided if you suffer from high blood pressure.

Indicated for

Addison's disease, allergic rhinitis, arthritis, athlete's foot, baldness, bronchitis, bursitis, canker sores, catarrh of the upper respiratory tract, chronic fatigue, colds, colitis and intestinal infections, conjunctivitis, constipation, coughs, dandruff, depression, duodenal-ulcers, emphysema, exhaustion, fibromyalgia, flu, fungal infections, gastritis, gingivitis and tooth decay, gout, hayfever, heartburn, hepatitis, inflamed gallbladder, liver disease, Lyme disease, menopause, prostate enlargement, psoriasis, shingles, sore throat, spleen disorders, tendinitis, throat problems, tuberculosis, ulcers, viral infections, yeast infections. Reducing stomach acid and relieving heartburn and indigestion. Increasing bile flow and lowering cholesterol. Improving resistance to physical and emotional stress.

LINSEED OIL AND LOW FAT COTTAGE CHEESE
A very effective **cancer treatment** was discovered by Dr. Joanna Budwig of Germany and has been used by thousands. Add 2 Tabl. Cold-processed, unrefined virgin linseed oil mixed with ½ to 1 cup cottage cheese. You can add herbs, raw vegetables such as cucumber, grated carrots, chopped tomatoes, basil or parsley, pineapple, raisins, tart apple, cinnamon or other fruits. Ground flaxseed added

makes it even more potent. You can eat this as many times a day as you can. Note: To start off, use only a scant teasp. of the linseed oil as your body may need to adjust to it. Dr. Budwig disovered that the right combination of essential fatty acids (potent and active in linseed oil) and sulphur-based proteins (present in abundance in low-fat cottage cheese) is the magic formula for conquering cancer and other diseases of fatty degeneration. Dr. Budwig while having medical training, also was trained in pharmaceutical science, physics, botany and biology. Linseed Oil is also beneficial for arteriosclerosis, strokes, cardiac Infarction, irregular heartbeat, fatty liver, Lung issues especially bronchial spasms, intestines to encourage activity, stomach ulcers (normalizes gastric juices), prostate (hypertrophic), arthritis, eczaema, old age, brain and Immune Deficiency syndromes ie: M.S., Fibromyalgia, Lupus, and other autoimmune illnesses.

MAGNESIUM/CALCIUM

It is recommended that you take about 1000-1500 units of Magnesium whenever you are taking the protocol. This is essential to your electrical system and keeps your circuitry connected. Magnesium oil from the Zechstein Sea which you spray on your body or can put in your bath is a good source. Sometimes when ingesting magnesium, it can cause diarrhea and digestive discomfort. By using the transdermal method, you avoid digestive issues. Magnesium is essential to take with calcium – equal to the amount of calcium, otherwise the calcium is not absorbed and you can develop bone spurs and also be deficient in calcium even though you are taking a goodly amount. Magnesium is a tremendous pain reliever and can contribute to healing from heart disease, cancer, neurological illnesses, mental disorders such as depression, and fatigue. You should also add Vitamin K-2 to this protocol to maximize the effectiveness. Swanson Vitamins has an inexpensive product by Dr. Barbara Hendell. For more information on Magnesium Oil go to www.magnesiumforlife.com and they have a great book and magnesium oil for sale on it as well. Dr. Mark Sircus is a valid authority on magnesium, as well as iodine, and sodium bicarbonate.

CALCIUM – Take about 1000-1500 units of plant based calcium – not coral calcium or oyster based. **POTASSIUM** – Take about 400 units and **FOLIC ACID** 400 units.

NUTRITIONAL YEAST   Benefit by eating nutritional yeast as it contains 18 amino acids, making it a complete protein, as well as 15 different minerals. For those on a low cholesterol diet, vegetarians or those looking to boost protein levels, nutritional yeast makes a great addition or substitution to meats, dairy and other high fat proteins.

Enjoy a reduction in stress and a boost in nutrition by supplementing your diet with nutritional yeast. Yeast is rich in B-complex vitamins, the most common vitamin deficiencies, which among other great benefits, help to regulate mood. For greatest nutritional value, select a non-GMO nutritional yeast that is fortified with vitamin B12.

Use nutritional yeast if you are diabetic or borderline, as nutritional yeast contains chromium, a trace mineral known as the Glucose Tolerance Factor, or (GTF). If you have fluctuating blood sugar levels or a tendency towards low blood pressure, regular intake of nutritional yeast may help.

PROBIOTICS AND ENZYMES – ABSOLUTELY ESSENTIAL TO TAKE BOTH.

Probiotics are "friendly" bacteria, thought to support our immune systems and enhance our health by keeping the numbers of "unfriendly" bacteria within our digestive systems in check.

Our large intestine is filled with thousands of strains of bacteria - all a part of our gut flora. Optimal health calls for a favorable balance among all of these various strains. When unfriendly bacteria predominate - a condition known as intestinal dysbiosis - we may experience an inflammatory state that results in physical symptoms.

When you lose "good" bacteria in your body (like after you take antibiotics, for example), probiotics can help replace them.

They can help balance your "good" and "bad" bacteria to keep your body working like it should.

Probiotics help move food through your gut. Researchers are still trying to figure out which are best for certain health problems. Some common conditions they treat are:

    Irritable bowel syndrome

    Inflammatory bowel disease

    (IBD)Infectious diarrhea (caused by viruses, bacteria, or parasites)
    Antibiotic-related diarrhea

There is also some research to show they help with problems in other parts of your body. For example, some people say they have helped with

    Skin conditions, like eczema

    Urinary and vaginal health

    Preventing allergies and colds
    Oral health
    Foggy thinking & Memory loss

    The best source of probiotics is good ole fashioned sauerkraut – make your own or buy it already prepared in a can or jar – it is all good. We should be consuming about ¼ cup at meals or at least twice a day. I make my own and it is quite easy. We know that yogurt and kefir have probiotics, but you cannot beat sauerkraut and it is very inexpensive compared to probiotics formulas.

You may need to supplement HSI Betaine if you are eating meat. Most of us do not have enough of the right acid to digest meat and proteins. Note: Apple Cider Vinegar (1 teaspoon in a glass of water works very well as a digestive enzyme.

A very powerful enzyme that we used at the Contreras Hospital in Tijuana as an essential part of our cancer treatment and detoxification protocol was **Wobenzyme** from Germany. For some years, the product was pulled from the market in the US, but it has been available again and being distributed by GARDEN OF LIFE under the name Wobenzym N. The exact formulation found in Wobenzym N has been featured in six human clinical studies with 2,489 patients studied. When you read that Wobenzym N provides temporary relief from everyday aches, pains and muscle soreness due to everyday activity, increased flexibility and mobility, and promotes a **normal inflammation response and** supports joint and tendon health, you know that these results have been clinically studied.

Wobenzym N is a unique blend of systemic enzymes that provides relief from aches, pain and muscle soreness due to everyday activity, supports the body's natural inflammation response, and leads to increased flexibility and mobility and supports overall joint and tendon health as well. Inflammation is a huge cause in all disease and has to be addressed. **Enzymes are fascinating essential biological catalysts that are involved in almost every single process in the body. They initiate millions of chemical reactions every second in the human body. It is easy to see why supplementing with systemic enzymes can have far-reaching benefits to the human body.**

The enzyme blend in Wobenzym N contains the following, clinically studied enzymes: pancreatin, papain, bromelain, trypsin, and chymotrypsin. Each one of these is a protease, which simply means that they break down proteins. There are certain proteins in the body that stimulate and others that repress inflammation. Under normal circumstances, your body balances the two. The systemic enzymes in Wobenzym N support that balancing process, assisting normal inflammation response that in turn, leads to relief from everyday activity-related aches and pains.

You can purchase Wobenzym N from both online websites, **Lucky Vitamins and Swanson Vitamins** at discounted pricing. While this product is a bit pricey, it is wonderful that we have it available. I went to Gemany and bought it there when it was not available in the U.S., and it was several hundred dollars for the large size. Expect to spend more on a good enzyme and in my opinion, this is the very best product that you can buy. You can buy the smaller bottles for a moderate price. In addition to the websites, you can find the product in most health food stores as Garden of Life is a recognized Brand for many products

SINUS AND VIRUS/FLU/BACTERIA PROTECTION: A great product by Super Good Stuff Nasal Spray at **www.supergoodstuff.com/nasalspray** is highly effective and I use it at the very first sign of sore throat and congestion/coughing. It is great for all those allergies in the springtime. It is highly pungent, but it really works. Try it!

XClear Nasal Spray with Xylitol is absolutely incredible. Xylitol kills all bacteria/viruses which enter the body through the mucosa tissues of the nose/throat. If you are concerned about catching a flu or the Swine Flu, use this nasal spray daily. It also destroys H Pylori Bacteria in the stomach which causes ulcers and cancer. This is very good for children

SLEEPING-AID: MELATONIN Melatonin, produced in the brain's pineal gland, is a hormone that plays a harmonic role in the body, modulating sleep patterns, circadian rhythms, and seasonal functions. Melatonin production is stimulated by darkness and inhibited by light. With all the gadgets, screens, and lights flashing in the eyes of people today, melatonin production can be restricted. Furthermore, the pineal gland is being calcified by environmental toxins like waste fluoride, which is intentionally added to many of today's water sources. Known as the third eye, the pineal gland is about the size of a grain of rice and is located in the epithalamus, tucked in a groove between the two hemispheres near the center of the brain. As an endocrine gland, the third eye is responsible for producing melatonin. This process is easily obstructed today, since the pineal gland is becoming more calcified and hardened by fluoride. Televisions, handheld devices, and computer screens keep a steady flow of artificial light going into many people's eyes, keeping melatonin production down. *Swanson Sleep Essentials* is an excellent formulation of many herbs including valerian and melatonin, chamomile, skullcap, L-taurine, GABA, hops flower, and passionflower. One capsule is a very good aide to sleep.

SODIUM BICARBONATE commonly known as baking soda, is one of the most inexpensive, potent substances to utilize for healing and restoring your body that I know. I take ½ teaspoon in a glass of water morning and night to keep my PH balance alkaline. By taking it internally, soaking in it, it is corrective for cancer, kidney disease, diabetes, treatment of flu, acid reflux, ulcers, colitis and other digestive problems, anti-fungal, tumors, asthma, detoxing heavy chemicals, ie: toxic poisoning from the Gulf disaster. It can be taken orally, nebulized transdermally, put in enemas, therapeutic baths, IV's. It can be mixed with Blackstrap Molasses for a cancer treatment.

UVA URSI BENEFIT The leaves of this small shrub have been used as an herbal folk medicine for centuries as a mild diuretic and astringent, and in the treatment of urinary tract infections such as cystitis, urethritis and nephritis, pyelitis and in pyelonephritis. Uva-ursi can help to reduce accumulations of uric acid and relieve the pain of bladder stones. Uva Ursi is also helpful for chronic diarrhea. As a nutritional supplement and muscle relaxant, Uva Ursi soothes, strengthens, and tightens irritated and inflamed tissues. Uva Ursi has a history of medicinal use dating back to the 2nd century. It has been widely used as a diuretic, astringent, and antiseptic. Folk medicine around the world has recommended Uva Ursi for nephritis, kidney stones, and chronic cystitis. The herb has also been used as a general tonic for weakened kidneys, liver or pancreas

EPILOGUE & UPDATE FROM DR. MARY: MY PERSONAL HEALING CONTINUES

I am currently healing from the effects of Cipro poisoning and the resulting breakdowns of other systems. The Cipro caused Diabetes, COPD, tendonitis, debilitating pain throughout my body and ongoing inflammation which has affected all organs. Thousands have been poisoned by the Fluoroquinole antibiotics, Cipro and Levaquin, and have suffered life devastating consequences. Please refuse these deadly drugs. Some, like me, suffer for years, and some never recover, even die. I can attest that there is hope.

I am very grateful to be blessed with so much information and I am committed to doing whatever I need to do in order to regain my health and energy completely. And, as I have written, healing is on all levels which have to be addressed. <u>I have used all of the products and methods</u> that I recommend in my Health Protocol, and can report wonderful results.

I am doing bone broth, with cabbage and sauerkraut, plus Probiotics for the inflammation. I make teas with the Licorice Root. I take the Berberine protocol and my diabetes is now "normal" and triglycerides are also normal. My breathing is much better which I attribute to the inflammation protocol. I have almost no pain now and I know that soon, I will have none. I take the supplements that I recommend and even more that I did not list. When our body has been so devastated, everything is out of balance and depleted. Much of my personal information has come to me out of the Breath and Silence where I have connected with Divine Intelligence. We do have the ability to know it all and receive the information if we but listen. I have a wonderful, loving physician who is willing to listen and learn, and order all of the diagnostic tests necessary to monitor my progress. I have had to bend as well and accept medical help when I needed life saving hospitalization and drugs. Then, the task is to balance out the damage and restore the body to a place that it can heal itself. Natural medicine is primarily preventative, but can be a huge assist to the healing process.

I do feel that I am being resurrected and being made anew. I have had several healings with Sara O'Meara at The Little Chapel, here in Phoenix. She holds healing services monthly, except in the summer, and she brings forth The Holy Spirit for each of us to receive our healing. Sometimes, we as healers, need other healers as our own energy is so depleted. I acknowledge that healing is of the Spirit, Mind, Emotions and Body! I know, personally, writing this book has been a catalyst and catharsis to heal. I pray that it will be an inspiration for the reader to be lifted up into the Light and Breathe into the remembrance of who you are and what your mission is here on this earth. We need each other's love, prayers, and support. I will love to hear from you and know about your journey.
In the Spirit of the Breath,
Dr. Mary

PRODUCTS AVAILABLE

Make checks payable to Sacred Sanctuary and mail to
17017 N. 12th St., #1125, Phoenix, AZ 85022

Or go to PayPal and order/pay with
drmarymeadows@hotmail.com

"Until I Breathe This Life" Book by Dr. Mary $18.99

Guided Breathing Meditation CD by Dr. Mary Meadows
Breathe the Light: The Journey Home,
Music by Jan de Roos $20.

Special Package of the Book, & the CD $35

For charge card orders, go to website. Shipping and Handling- Please add for orders (up to $50-): $6.00; ($50 - $150 up): $12.00 Out of the US, go to website to order.

Website: www.drmarymeadowsLLC.com

TESTIMONIALS

"It is my great honor to write a testimony for Dr. Mary and her work, "The Breath of Light." I feel privileged that I had the chance to have met Dr. Mary when she was touring Europe 16 years ago offering healing and training sessions with "The Breath of Light". After my first experience of her work, I committed to becoming a practitioner with her training and later became Dr. Mary's assistant and translator. My work and the practice of "The Breath of Light" has lead me deep into my spiritual searchings and findings, and has healed deep, old wounds. It helped me to embrace my life! In many ways, it was life changing and eye opening. The strong contact to my higher self through her work as not left me since. Having worked so close to Dr. Mary, showed me the highest dedication, integrity and compassionate love she has and that "The Breath of Light" has the potency to reach and heal on the deepest levels of physical, emotional, and spiritual woundedness. Even until today, the Breath is incorporated in my work as a Yoga teacher and therapist. Anyone who has the chance to read Dr. Mary's book on her very personal life story, is surely as blessed as I have been. My gratitude and love reaches out to Dr. Mary. Thank you" *Steven Barrett, Munich Germany*

"There are no words to express my amazement of what has happened. I have been in chronic back pain with a degenerated disc -- injured in an accident -- for over a year.

The pain has been so terrible I cannot even sit up, much less work. In only 10 minutes of the Breath, the pain was gone. With a couple of sessions, I am back to work, pain free and healing something I had given up on. I can only say, 'Thank you from the bottom of my heart!'" *Bill S., Key West, Florida*

"Today, I saw the Light. Today, I got in touch with my spiritual being. Today, I finally recognized that I was worthy. Today, I found love, peace and tranquillity. Today, I took my first Breath. With love and thanks for being my guardian angel." *Michelle B., San Diego, CA*

"Mary, I heard you speak at our Wednesday Metaphysical meeting in Surprise. I was quite taken by your message and bought your CD. Periodically I gazed at it but wanted the time to do your meditation to be just right. On a day when I was in my house alone, I put it in my CD player and layed down to listen. I asked that my meditation help me understand and accept my father's decision to leave my family when I was 14, and to forgive him. As often happens when I lie down to meditate, I eventually fell into a light sleep. When I awoke, I KNEW that my angst had been because I LOVED my father, and that is why I had felt such pain and loss. After years and years of being angry with him, your meditation led me to complete understanding and forgiveness. Thank you, thank you, thank you, for leading me to the answer to my prayers. Thirty five years later, I am at last at peace." *Jeanne Chasko, Phoenix, AZ*

"I was listening to your CD, *Breathe the Light,* just last night. The words, your voice, the music.....beautiful and clearly inspired, makes a powerful combination. I was deeply moved." *Gaynor Coller Suiter, Phoenix, AZ*

"For the first time I have experienced happiness. And I know it won't be the last. This has given me something I did not know possible. I have been in therapy and on anti-depressant drugs for over 12 years. Thanks to the *Breath of Light* and all the love I have experienced, I have reduced my medication by more than half and will continue to do so under my therapist's guidance. She is also astounded with my results. This has been highly effective in both the release of my negativity and my personal healing. I was a victim of ritual and sexual abuse and have not -- until now -- been able to heal it. This Breath is something I will use for the rest of my life." *Michael C., Boston, MA*

"No one would have been able to convince me that deep breathing could lead to such a spiritual and emotional cleansing. What happened today, in itself, is worth any price I could pay. You are one person that has impacted my life and my marriage forever. We are growing closer because of the Breath. We have breathed together every night since we've been home. And Collette is cancer free! We are implementing a major lifestyle change -- cooking healthy, juicing up a storm!" *Ed Q, Pittsburgh, PA*

"I have been doing the *Breath of Light* since November 2012. My experiences have been from complete clarity, peace and joy. In one of my experiences during a group Breathing Meditation with Dr. Mary, I felt I was embraced on my left and right side, there were physical presence on both sides. The thought of two angels came to mind. After the Breath Meditation, Dr. Mary said the Lady (Divine Mother) was present with her Angels. I knew the thought of those two Angels beside me was true. I did have two Angels on each side. I, also, use the Breath with my Mantra chanting meditation. I use the Breath first, then I chant a Mantra. Using the combination of both is a very powerful experience. The Breath takes me deep, quickly." *Louis Benabe, Surprise, AZ*

"For the last 25 years, I've been using the *Breath of Light* that I learned from Mary Meadows. It has been a powerful tool to use with teaching children to swim. It also helped the parents to calm themselves and the children, often using it at home later. I also use it with business associates to keep myself balanced. I have found the Breath to be a great tool for personal growth and for connecting with other people in my personal life as well as in my career. Thank you, Mary." *Janet McCabe, Swim Instructor and swim school owner for 50 years, Boulder, CO*

"Dear Dr. Mary, Here is what I experience when I play your CD, *Breathe the Light – The Journey Home*. Some nights I will wake up in the middle of the night and can't fall back to sleep because I'm thinking of what I have to do the next day or just worried about challenges I have to meet. So, I play my *Breathe the Light – The Journey Home* CD. Dr. Mary's angelic voice, the beautiful music and her words of comfort give me peace and make me feel safe. While listening, I start to relax, release any anxiety emotions and realize that everything is going to come into balance and harmony. I'll fall asleep resting until morning and wake up feeling peaceful and ready to start my day. Thank you for your gift. You have impacted my life in a very special way and I am grateful to know you". *Jan Vollinger, Phoenix, AZ*

"Congratulations & Best Wishes to Dr. Mary on the release of her new book – a timely, significant contribution to the uplifting of humanity in search of transformation and healing. I have witnessed the profound experiences and effects of her beautiful CD on those attending her Breath of Light meditations. The Time is Now! Breathe the Light – Experience the Love. Let your journey begin." *Diana Lang, Holistic Life Coach/Massage Therapist/Reiki Master, Phoenix, AZ*

"The work of Dr. Mary Meadows is mainly the reconnection of one with self, then the discovery of connection with the Divine invisible above. All you need is to understand self, therefore, love. Get ready to explore the Fifth Dimension in which you will find healing, happiness, and growth."   Dr. Meadows is the valuable KEY."
Si Djahedi, Architect, Phoenix, AZ

"Dr. Mary, I use your *Breath of Light* method frequently as I discover that this technique allows me more energy, decreased stress associated with fear, and a sense of general well-being." *Angie Seidel, Scottsdale, AZ*

"The Breath of Light work has been a personal life saver for me. It's a wonderful way to clear out energy and come into the day to day rejuvenated. It's been my go-to tool for many years and is something I can do for myself. Using the Breath is a way from pain to the path of love, self love and inner peace. I hope you choose to experience it for yourself."
Karen Burke-Stewart, owner of Kare Products, Boulder, CO

MY PERSONAL DECLARATION OF INTENTION

MY PERSONAL DECLARATION OF INTENTION

PERSONAL NOTES TO MYSELF FOR MY JOURNEY
Today, I am willing to Breathe and receive my guidance and direction from the Divine Intelligence....

PERSONAL NOTES TO MYSELF FOR MY JOURNEY
Today, I am willing to change....

PERSONAL NOTES TO MYSELF FOR MY JOURNEY
Today, I look at my addictions and attachments which I think I cannot be happy or even live without....

PERSONAL NOTES TO MYSELF FOR MY JOURNEY
Today, I release the need to blame anyone including myself.

PERSONAL NOTES TO MYSELF FOR MY JOURNEY
Today, I know that every person who has been a terrorist, bully, and tormentor has been a catalyst for my Initiation into the Light...

PERSONAL NOTES TO MYSELF FOR MY JOURNEY
Today is an excellent day to clear clutter – create beauty in my space and in my mind….
.

PERSONAL NOTES TO MYSELF FOR MY JOURNEY

Today, I know that yesterday is done and gone. Today is the first day of my future….

PERSONAL NOTES TO MYSELF FOR MY JOURNEY
Today, what I concentrate on is exactly what I attract. I take some deep Breaths and I Breathe in the Light....

PERSONAL NOTES TO MYSELF FOR MY JOURNEY
Today I leave the past..It's gone. I did what I had to do to learn….

PERSONAL NOTES TO MYSELF FOR MY JOURNEY
Today, I am willing to take the next step to change my life, my thinking and myself....

www.ingramcontent.com/pod-product-compliance
Lightning Source LLC
Chambersburg PA
CBHW060657100426
42735CB00040B/2876